JAPAN'S FUTURE

IN EAST ASIA AND

THE PACIFIC

Professor Peter Drysdale

JAPAN'S FUTURE

IN EAST ASIA AND

THE PACIFIC

IN HONOUR OF PROFESSOR PETER DRYSDALE

MARI PANGESTU AND LIGANG SONG (EDS)

ANU
THE AUSTRALIAN NATIONAL UNIVERSITY

E PRESS

ASIA PACIFIC PRESS
THE AUSTRALIAN NATIONAL UNIVERSITY

ANU
E PRESS

Copublished by ANU E Press and Asia Pacific Press
The Australian National University
Canberra ACT 0200 Australia
Email: anuepress@anu.edu.au
This title is available online at http://epress.anu.edu.au/jfeap_citation.html

Asia Pacific Press
Crawford School of Economics and Government
The Australian National University
Canberra ACT 0200
Ph: 61-2-6125 0178 Fax: 61-2-6125 0767
Email: books@asiapacificpress.com
Website: http://www.asiapacificpress.com

National Library of Australia Cataloguing-in-Publication entry

Title:	Japan's future in East Asia and the Pacific : in honour of Professor Peter Drysdale / editors, Mari Pangestu ; Ligang Song.
Publisher:	Canberra : Asia Pacific Press, 2007.
ISBN:	9780731538157 (pbk.)
	9781921313622 (online)
Notes:	Includes index.
	Bibliography.
Subjects:	Free trade—Japan.
	Japan—Economic conditions.
	Japan—Foreign economic relations—Australia.
	Japan—Foreign economic relations—East Asia.
Other Authors:	Pangestu, Mari.
	Song, Ligang.
Dewey Number:	337.52

Cover design: ANU E Press
The cover image is based on a woodblock print by Mototsugu Sugiyama
'Sumida River on the verge of Spring' (1997).

Contents

Figures

Tables

Symbols used in tables

n.a.   not available
..   not applicable
-      zero
.   insignificant

Contributors

Tina Chen graduated with a PhD in economics from the Australian National University and currently works with Vatyh International in Hong Kong.

Roger Farrell is senior adviser to the Japanese Embassy in Australia and a research associate of the Australian National University. He obtained his PhD economics from the Australian National University in 1997.

Christopher Findlay is Professor of Economics, Adelaide University. He has a PhD and Masters degree in Economics from the Australian National University and an Honours degree in economics from the University of Adelaide.

Yiping Huang is Chief Asia Economist for Citigroup, based in Hong Kong. He has a masters degree from Renmin University, Beijing and a PhD from the Australian National University where he studied under Professor Peter Drysdale between 1990 and 1993.

Adam Johns is a PhD candidate, Crawford School of Economics and Government. He has undergraduate degrees in Media Studies and International Business from the Queensland University of Technology, and a masters degree in Commerce from Waseda University.

Mari Pangestu is the Minister of Trade of Indonesia. She obtained her Bachelor's and Master's degrees from the Australian National University, supervised by Peter Drysdale and her PhD in economics from the University of California (Davis). She was formerly the Executive Director for the Centre for Strategic and International Studies, Jakarta.

David Parsons is Secretary to the APEC Business Advisory Committee, Indonesia.

Christopher Pokarier is Associate Professor of International Business at Waseda University, Tokyo. He has undergraduate and masters degrees from the University of Queensland and a PhD from the Australian National University.

Paul Sheard is Managing Director and Global Chief Economist for Lehman Brothers, based in New York. He has a masters degree and a PhD in Japanese Economy from the Australian National University.

Ligang Song is Director of the China Economy and Business Program, Crawford School of Economics and Government, Australian National University.

Takashi Terada is Associate Professor, Institute of Asian Studies, Waseda University. Before taking up the current position in June 2006, he was an Assistant Professor at Faculty of Arts and Social Sciences, National University of Singapore. He obtained his PhD from the Australian National University in 1999.

David Walton is a lecturer in the School of Humanities and Languages, University of Western Sydney. After his undergraduate degree at Griffith University, he obtained his masters and PhD degrees from Queensland University. As a student, and later, he was influenced by Peter Drysdale's writings.

Xinpeng Xu is Associate Professor of Economics at the Hong Kong Polytechnic University, Hong Kong. After completing undergraduate and masters degrees at Xiamen University, China, he obtained his PhD in economics from the Australian National University in 1999.

Hidetaka Yoshimatsu is Professor of International Relations at Ritsumeikan Asia Pacific University, Japan. He received his PhD from Australian National University with research on Japanese political economy supervised by Professor Peter Drysdale.

Dong Dong Zhang is an Analyst at Australia's Commonwealth Treasury and previously at Australian Agency for International Development. He has a PhD in East Asian economics from the Australian National University, supervised by Professor Peter Drysdale.

Shiji Zhao joined the Australian Bureau of Statistics after taking his PhD in economics from the Australian National University.

Preface

This book is in honour of Professor Peter Drysdale. It commemorates his academic and personal contributions after a lifetime of commitment to his vision for Australia and the Asia Pacific region and to his many students and friends throughout the world.

Peter Drysdale has been a powerful force for change for nearly four decades. With his mentors, Sir John Crawford of Australia and Dr Saburo Okita of Japan, he mapped out the vision and strategies needed to mobilise the diverse economies of the Asia Pacific region as an engine of growth.

With like-minded academics from the region, he established and nurtured the cooperation mechanisms that have given the region's governments, businesses and academic communities the confidence to pursue economic integration. With his colleagues in Australia, he has shaped the policy environment under successive governments, enabling Australia to build a comprehensive economic and political relationship with the Asia Pacific region.

Relatively unheralded among Peter's many valuable contributions is his mentoring role as a teacher and advisor to his many hundreds of students and friends in Australia and the region. They have become Prime Ministers and Ministers, captains of industry, prominent academics and fellow agents of change working in many walks of life. They are armed with his academic work and his practical insights and ensure that his vision is carried forward in the decades ahead.

Peter Drysdale has pursued his mission with a special intensity of purpose and focus that will remain one of his hallmarks. Whether dealing with senior government officials, diplomats, fellow academics or potential funders, everyone knows that Peter Drysdale will not lose an opportunity to engage them on a strategic piece of the jigsaw for his vision. He is tough with those who he believes are wasting energy or departing from his journey. And he commands respect and loyalty from those who have been co-opted, not letting them forget that they have entered a long-term contract. He keeps his band of former students and associates together through prodigious networking and a strong generosity of spirit, caring as much about their welfare as their achievements.

In his academic work, Peter Drysdale has always held a dynamic view of the world focused on growth and opportunity. This is his context of the Australia-Japan relationship that has been a central part of his research through the Australia-Japan Research Centre at the Australian National University. He saw how the emergence of Japan could provide vast opportunities for Australia if it could be a reliable supplier of raw materials. And he saw that Japanese growth depended on exports to the United States. This in turn cemented his view that engagement across the Pacific with the United States was paramount to economic prosperity as well as security for the whole region. He applied the same dynamic paradigm to the growing Northeast Asian and Southeast Asian tigers and expanded his research and networks to include them.

Ahead of the times, he has fostered engagement with an emerging China and saw how the economic might of such a large and resource and technology hungry economy could bring prosperity to Australia and the rest of the region.

But in these formative times, he knew that economic complementarity within the region was not enough to drive change. There were layers of long-standing political, cultural and historical diversity and vast differences in economic development that had to be bridged if the region was to integrate. These growing economies needed to shape and develop a shared vision and to exercise clear-headed political leadership to bring down the barriers to trade and investment. Peter's seminal 1989 work on international economic pluralism in the East Asia and the Pacific provided the insights and agenda for this.

In addressing this challenge, Peter Drysdale and his colleagues started with the region's thinkers and academics and formed the Pacific Trade and Development Conference to build a shared approach by encouraging an Asia Pacific research agenda.

In 1980, with the strong support of the Prime Ministers of Japan and Australia, he and his colleagues embarked on a bolder plan. They formed the Pacific Economic Cooperation Conference that informally brought representatives of governments together with their counterparts from business and academia to discuss how the region should be shaped. And later, he helped bring China, Chinese Taipei and Hong Kong into this group giving all the key players of the region a seat at one table for the first time. APEC acknowledges that it could not have been formed in 1989 without these foundations.[1]

Amid this broad picture, Peter Drysdale was very focused about his own research agenda and that of his students. His dynamic vision provided the backdrop for a specific view of industries, sectors and the economy as well as the political and economic linkages that brought them together.

This volume itself is testimony to the extraordinary breadth and scope of Peter Drysdale's career. It showcases the work of some of his former students who, with their own established expertise and in their own way, reflect the insights, context and forward-looking nature that Peter has always encouraged.

Typically, Peter Drysdale has not stopped his life's work despite retiring formally in 2002. He maintains an unflagging pace of public commentary, contributions to conferences, and strategic inputs to institution-building, always looking forward.

Finally, we acknowledge the support of the Crawford School of Economics and Government of the Australian National University, publishing assistance from Asia Pacific Press, and a grant from the Publications Subsidy Committee of the Australian National University, as well as the tireless editorial efforts of Peter's longtime friend Trevor Wilson. Without such assistance and support, this publication would not have been possible.

Christopher Findlay and David Parsons

---

1 See Chairman's Summary statement from the first APEC Ministerial Meeting, Canberra, November 1989. Text available at http://www.apec.org/apec/ministerial_statements/ annual_ministerial/1989_1st_apec_ministerial/chair_summary.html.

Abbreviations

ADSL	Asymmetric Digital Subscriber Line
AFTA-CER	ASEAN Free Trade Area-Closer Economic Relations (between Australia and New Zealand)
APEC	Asia Pacific Economic Cooperation
ASEAN	Association of Southeast Asian Nations
ASEM	Asia Europe Meeting
BIMP-EAGA	Brunei, Indonesia, Malaysia and Philippines East
BOJ	Bank of Japan
BSE	Bovine spongiform encephalopathy
cHTML	compact Hypertext Markup Language
CIS	of Independent States (of the former Soviet Union)
CPI	Consumer Price Index
CSI	Container Security Initiative
C-TPAT	Customs-Trade Partnership Against Terrorism
DFAT	Department of Foreign Affairs and Trade
EAU	Economic Analysis Unit
EAEC	East Asia Economic Caucus
EPAs	Economic Partnership Agreements
EU	European Union
EVSL	Early Voluntary Sectoral Liberalisation
FTA	Free Trade Agreement
FTA–CER	Free Trade Area - Closer Economic Relations (between Australia and New Zealand)
FTTH	Fibre to the Home
GATT	General Agreement on Tariffs and Trade
GDP	Gross Domestic Product
GMS	Greater Mekong Sub-region or Scheme?
HTML	Hypertext Markup Language
ICTs	information and communications technologies
IMF	International Monetary Fund
IMO	International Maritime Organisation
INTERFET	UN Intervention Force in East Timor
IP	Intellectual Property
IPPH	Intellectual Property Policy Headquarters

ISPS	International Ship and Port Facility Security Code
JBIC	Japan Bank for International Cooperation,
JETRO	Japan External Trade Organisation
JICA	Japan International Cooperation Agency
JKFTA	Japan-South Korea FTA
JMFTA	Japan-Mexico FTA
JSEPA	Japan-Singapore Economic Partnership Agreement
KDDI	Kokusai Denshin Denwa International
KOF	Swiss Institute of Business Cycle Research
KPN	Koninklijke PTT Nederland
LDP	Liberal Democratic Party
m-commerce	mobile commerce
MAFF	Ministry of Agriculture, Forestry, and Fisheries
METI	Ministry of Economy, Trade and Industry
MFN	most-favoured nation
MITI	Ministry of International Trade and Industry
MOF	Ministry of Finance
MOFA	Ministry of Foreign Affairs
NAFTA	North American Free Trade Agreement
NTBs	Non-tariff barriers
NTT	Nihon Telegraph and Telecommunications
NIE	Newly industrialising economy
ODA	Official Development Assistance
OECD	Organisation for Economic Cooperation and Development
OIE	UN World Organisation for Animal Health
PAFTAD	Pacific Trade and Development Forum
PBEC	Pacific Basin Economic Council
PC	Personal Computer
PECC	Pacific Economic Cooperation Council
PPP	Purchasing power parity
PRRI	Revolutionary Government of the Republic of Indonesia (*Pemerintah Revolusioner Republik Indonesia*)
RFID	radio frequency identity
RFIDS	radio frequency identity systems
RIETI	Research Institute for the Economy, Trade and Industry, Japan
SARS	severe acute respiratory syndrome
SDF	Self-Defence Forces
SITC	Standard International Trade Classification
SMEs	Small to medium enterprises
TAC	Treaty of Amity and Cooperation
TFP	Total Factor Productivity

TNCs	Transnational corporations
UNCTAD	United Nations Conference on Trade and Development
UNTEA	UN Temporary Executive Authority (in West New Guinea)
WCO	World Customs Organisation
WIPO	World Intellectual Property Organisation
WNG	West New Guinea
WTO	World Trade Organization

1 THE JAPANESE ECONOMY: WHERE IS IT LEADING IN THE ASIA PACIFIC?

ANATOMY OF AN ABNORMAL ECONOMY AND POLICY FAILURE

Paul Sheard

The fifteen years until 2005—the post-bubble period—was a challenging one for the Japanese economy. It is almost as if history had played a trick on Japan. At the end of the 1980s, Japan had been riding on the crest of a bubble economy. The stock market and land prices had soared, real GDP had averaged close to 5 per cent year-on-year for the previous five years (and nominal growth more than 6 per cent), and the coming 'Pacific century' appeared to be Japan's for the taking. By 2005, the stock market was less than 40 per cent of its end 1989 peak and official land prices were still falling, trailing five-year average real GDP growth was less than 2 per cent (and nominal growth slightly negative), and Japan had ceded the economic limelight—if not future economic leadership in Asia—to China.

How did this happen? I believe that Japan's prolonged deflation in the post-bubble period was largely a 'policy story' and that the answer to that question lies in understanding the policy challenges and how, in my view, they were largely mishandled. Understanding this is also the key to formulating an informed view of what may lie ahead for the Japanese economy. Will the economy remain in a prolonged quasi-deflationary state or will it fully normalise and resume vigorous non-deflationary growth?

Lurking below the policy story there may well be a more fundamental political story, but I will leave that to others to tell.

Japan's abnormal economy

As of 2005, the Japanese economy was in an abnormal state of affairs. There are three related ways in which Japan was not a 'normal economy', and these abnormalities all can be traced to the bubble economy and how its unwinding was mishandled.

The first abnormality is that deflation reigned in Japan. The second is that the government continued to prop up the banking system. The third is that the central bank operated monetary policy at the zero interest rate, bound under a policy of 'quantitative easing'. In a normal economy, there is moderate inflation, banks stand on their own feet, and the central bank targets interest rates. Japan enjoyed none of these features.

The three abnormalities were closely inter-related. To boil down the story of how they came about, the bursting of the asset bubble of the 1980s wreaked havoc on financial and corporate balance sheets and rendered inoperable the bank credit transmission mechanism. Monetary policy was slow to react and poorly coordinated with fiscal policy (and other policies) and the economy slipped into deflation, undermining the potency of monetary policy. To stave off a run on the banking system, the government guaranteed all bank deposits and this slowed down the necessary balance sheet adjustment process, which in turn further stymied the effectiveness of monetary policy. The Bank of Japan kept easing monetary policy, but eventually cut interest rates as far as they could go—that is, to zero—after which it adopted a policy of quantitative easing, supplying progressively more reserves to the banking system than was needed for a zero interest rate. This is how Japan ended up with deflation, a protected banking system, and quantitative easing.

There is an irony here, because the 'abnormal' conditions had been in existence for so long that they had become 'normal' features of the contemporary Japanese economic landscape. Take deflation. The GDP had been falling in year-on-year terms since the second half of 1994 (adjusting for the impact of the 2 per cent increase in the consumption tax in fiscal 1997). By the second quarter of 2004, it was −1.6 per cent year-on-year. The Bank of Japan focused on the core CPI as the important measure of inflation in conducting its monetary policy: the year-on-year rate of change in the core CPI had been below 1 per cent since May 1994 and had been below zero for most of the period.

The government had been using extraordinary guarantees to prop up the banking system since June 1995. Under the legal framework at the time, only small-lot deposits were automatically guaranteed by deposit insurance, but as an emergency measure the government announced that all bank deposits would be guaranteed until the end of March 2001. In the event, the government decided in December 1999 to extend the blanket guarantee on large-lot demand deposits until the end of March 2003 and then decided again in October 2002 to extend the guarantee until the end of March 2005. Even then, zero-interest-bearing large-lot demand deposits continued to be fully guaranteed permanently, and a framework existed that automatically guaranteed all deposits whenever the government judged that there was a threat to the maintenance of financial stability. In other words, the abnormal situation of the government guaranteeing the claims of large creditors on the banking system, rather than the banks using their own capital to do so, appeared to be a permanent feature of the regulatory landscape in Japan.

As for abnormal monetary policy, this was also virtually a decade-long phenomenon. The Bank of Japan operated quantitative easing regime for five years from March 2001 to March 2006. However, except for a short period (August 2000–March 2001) when a clear policy error was committed, the Bank of Japan operated monetary policy at the zero interest rate bound for the seven years (since February 1999). And for the three and a half years before then, the Bank of Japan targeted the extraordinary low rate of 50 basis points or less.

The three abnormalities are also closely related in terms of the logic of why the conditions persisted in this way. Again I will boil down the story. Because deflation continued, monetary policy was tighter than the Bank of Japan would like it to be, given that real policy rates were positive and could not be pushed into negative territory (unlike what the Fed has been able to do in the United States twice in the past decade or so). Because banks have been given years to work through their balance sheet problems slowly, the credit transmission mechanism remains impaired and the banking system did not create credit, undermining the effectiveness of monetary policy. And because deflation continued, the asset values in the banking system continued to erode. Meanwhile, to strengthen its policy stance, the Bank of Japan committed to maintain quantitative easing for as long as deflation (as measured by the core CPI) continued. Deflation, impaired banks needing government support, and zero interest rates/ quantitative easing all formed a mutually reinforcing set of equilibrium conditions.

Anatomy of the policy response to the bursting of the bubble

Let us delve a little more into how the Japanese economy got to this state by focusing on how policymakers responded to the unwinding of the bubble of the 1980s. That can be summarised in one word: forbearance.

Japan's asset price bubble of the 1980s, weighted by the size of the Japanese economy, may have been the biggest bubble in recorded financial history (Figure 1.1). The broadest index of land prices in Japan more than doubled from the start of the 1980s to when it peaked, and

---

Figure 1.1   **Japan's real estate price bubble, 1956–2006** (index, Q1 1956=1)

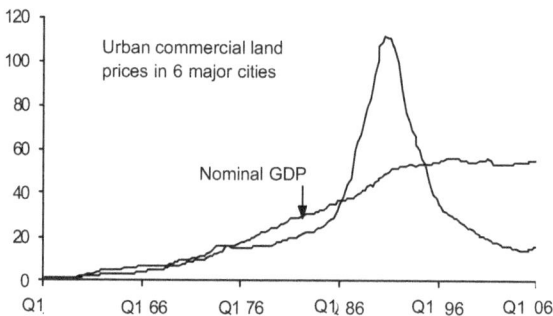

Urban commercial land prices in 6 major cities

Nominal GDP

Sources: Bloomberg; Japan Real Estate Institute; Cabinet Office.

Table 1.1	Japanese land prices: measuring the size of the bubble					
	Q1 04 (% change h-o-h)	Q1 04 (% change y-o-y)	Increase from 1980 to peak (x)	Q1 04 as % of peak	Q1 04 level lowest since	
Nationwide						
All land	−4.1	−8.4	2.09	50.3	Q3	80
Commercial	−5.0	−10.2	2.28	33.7	Q1	73
Residential	−3.2	−6.4	2.07	64.8	Q1	84
Industrial	−4.4	−8.7	1.88	62.7	Q1	82
Six urban areas						
All land	−3.4	−7.4	4.29	24.5	Q3	80
Commercial	−2.3	−6.0	6.26	12.9	Q1	73
Residential	−2.6	−5.9	3.72	34.5	Q1	84
Industrial	−5.5	−10.9	3.32	32.3	Q1	81
Tokyo (23 wards)	−0.8	−2.7	n.a.	17.5	n.a.	
Osaka (13 cities)	−5.0	−10.2	n.a.	23.5	n.a.	
Nagoya (11 cities)	−3.4	−6.7	n.a.	53.3	n.a.	
Non-big-6 urban	−4.2	−8.5	n.a.	51.2	n.a.	

Sources: Japan Real Estate Institute; Bloomberg.

subsequently has almost halved (Table 1.1). The real estate price bubble was most acute for commercial property in the major urban areas: the index of commercial land prices in the six major urban areas increased more than six-fold in the 1980s and has fallen by 87 per cent since the peak. Notwithstanding some signs of bottoming in parts of Tokyo, all major land price indexes in Japan are still falling in year-on-year terms. Even after fourteen years, real estate prices in Japan continued to deflate.

The bursting of the stock market and real estate price bubble had the predictable effect of throwing the economy into recession in the early 1990s. Industrial production—to quote one statistic—fell by 14.4 per cent from its peak in mid–1991 to its trough at the beginning of 1994. Thus began a period of prolonged low growth, deflation, and financial system problems, which continued for more than a decade (Figures 1.2 and 1.3). In the ten years to 2005, real GDP growth in Japan averaged 1.2 per cent year-on-year while nominal GDP growth has averaged just 0.2 per cent (the GDP deflator fell by 1.0 per cent on average). In the

Figure 1.2   **Japan's real GDP growth, 1982–2006** (per cent year-on-year, four-quarter moving average)

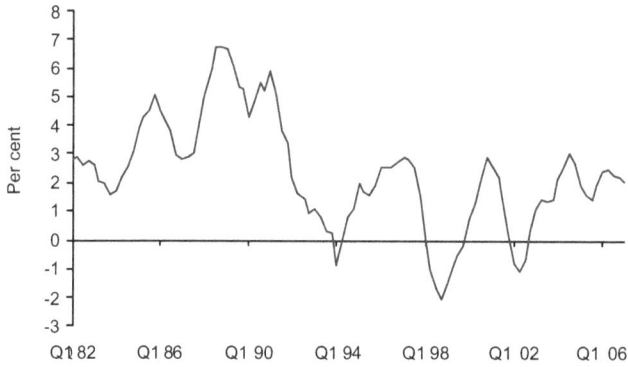

Sources: Cabinet Office; Consensus Economics.

Figure 1.3   **Japan's nominal GDP growth and GDP deflator, 1982–2006** (per cent year-on-year, four-quarter moving average)

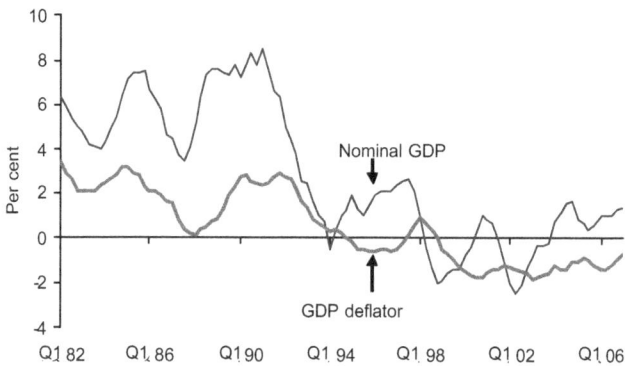

Source: Cabinet Office.

prior five years, economic performance had been particularly dismal: real GDP in Japan grew on average by 1.3 per cent year-on-year, but nominal GDP actually fell by 0.1 per cent (the GDP deflator fell by 1.3 per cent on average). This is a far cry from the second half of the 1980s (let alone the earlier 'high growth period') when real GDP growth averaged 4.8 per cent year-on-year while nominal GDP growth averaged 6.3 per cent (the GDP deflator rose by 1.7 per cent on average).

A more serious consequence of the unwinding of the bubble than an initial nasty recession was the impact that the loss of asset values had on the banking system: thus began the non-performing loan (NPL) problem (Figure 1.4) and the ongoing process of debt de-leveraging in the corporate sector (Figure 1.5). Bank lending growth decelerated sharply and bank lending began to fall in 1996, and the stock of outstanding bank lending was down 150 trillion yen (28 per cent, or equivalent to 30 per cent of GDP) since that time. The Bank of Japan started cutting the official discount rate in 1991, after it had raised it progressively to 6 per cent from June 1989 to August 1990 in order to 'prick' the bubble, taking it to 0.5 per cent by September 1995. However, with the banking system sitting on a dramatically escalating, but as yet undisclosed, asset impairment problem, despite the Bank of Japan's monetary policy actions, the economy slipped into deflation: the domestic corporate goods price (then the domestic wholesale price index) started falling in year-on-year terms at the end of 1991, the GDP deflator in the third quarter of 1994, and, on a sustained basis, the core CPI in the second half of 1998 (Figure 1.6).

By the end of the 1990s, deflation was entrenched (and real estate prices were continuing to fall), the banking system was propped up by the government but was dysfunctional in creating credit, monetary policy was stretched to its conventional limits, and the fiscal finances were deteriorating steadily; to boot, periodic bouts of a strong yen threatened to make matters worse, the export sector being the strongest pillar in the economy.

How did Japanese policymakers respond to the bursting of the bubble and the collateral damage that this caused to the financial system and to the economy? With a mixture of reactive crisis management and policies

Figure 1.4   **Official non-performing loans of all banks, 1992–2005**
                    (yen trillion)

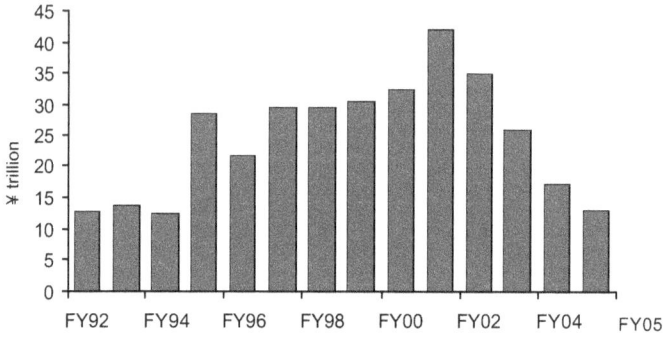

Source: Financial Services Agency.

Figure 1.5   **Corporate debt to nominal GDP, 1970–2000** (per cent)

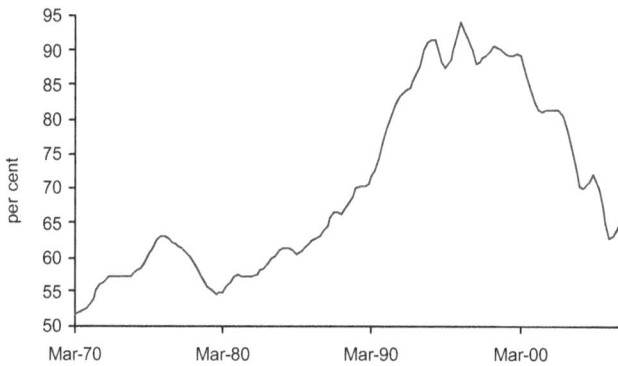

Sources: Ministry of Finance; Cabinet Office.

Figure 1.6   **Measures of deflation, 1990–2006** (index; levels)

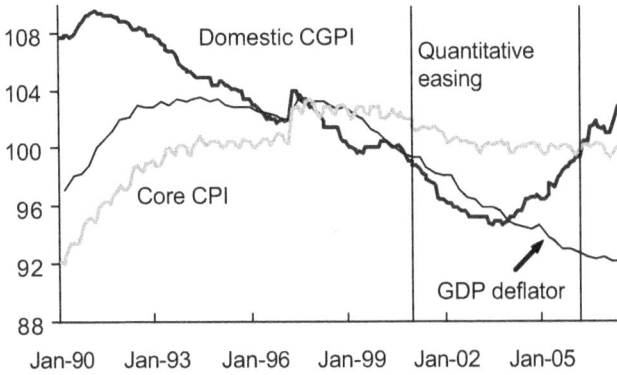

Sources: Bank of Japan; Cabinet Office.

aimed at helping the economy to grow slowly out of the problems, taking as much time as necessary. The two key planks of post-bubble policy were blanket government guarantees of bank deposits and easy monetary policy, which was later implemented as 'quantitative easing'. Having put in the necessary policy planks to buy time, the government did implement some proactive policies aimed at promoting growth: as discussed further below, monetary policy was used as the growth-stimulating policy of choice; fiscal policy was used intermittently to try to spur growth (but in a flawed way); and there was ongoing deregulation both in the private sector and the public sector, which supported growth over time.

The single most important policy, in my view, for understanding the course of Japan's economy in the post-bubble period, is the government guarantee of bank deposits, as innocuous a policy as this may sound to many observers. Real estate prices began falling in 1990, as policymakers successfully 'pricked' the bubble, and small banks and credit unions began to fail shortly after. However, it was not until the fallout from the failure of two Tokyo credit unions at the end of 1994 (and the dramatic rise in the yen and collapsing stock market in early 1995) focused the minds of policymakers on the fallout of the bursting of the bubble that the issue came to be addressed as a systemic one. On 8 June 1995, the Ministry of Finance made a momentous announcement: all bank deposits, not just those covered by the existing deposit insurance system, would be guaranteed by the government, and a five-year plan (later set to end at the end of March 2001) would be implemented to 'cope with the non-performing loan problem' (Ministry of Finance 1995). Forbearance policy had moved from implicit to official policy.

The decision by the government to stand behind all bank deposits was by no means inevitable. The deposit insurance system guaranteed 'small-lot deposits', that is, deposits up to 10 million yen per depositor per bank, which comprised about half of all bank deposits in total (Figure 1.7). The blanket guarantee extended this guarantee to large-lot depositors, who in legal terms at that point were unsecured creditors on the banking system, or creditors who relied on the strength of bank capital to secure their claims. No bank depositor had lost money in the postwar period,

Figure 1.7   **Evolution of the government guarantee on bank deposits, 1992–2007** (per cent of total deposits)

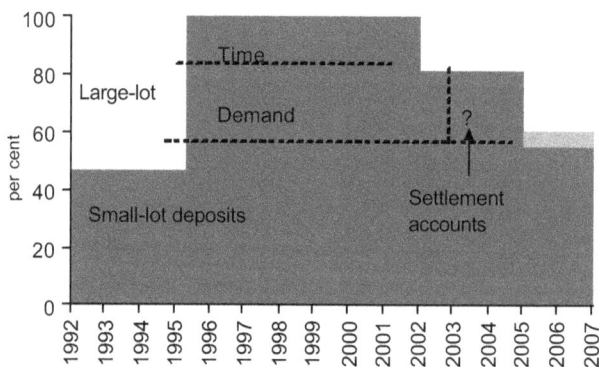

Source: Compiled on basis of Bank of Japan data.

notably in the first half of the 1990s during which period seven institutions had already failed: the government always engineered a rescue merger, and since 1991 these deals were sweetened by the Deposit Insurance Corporation providing financial assistance to the rescuing bank.

The situation was so bad by 1995, however, that, had the government not announced that all bank deposits, not just small-lot deposits, would be fully guaranteed, a run on the banking system and a financial crisis would have surely ensued sooner or later. Policymakers never seem to have contemplated the option of not extending a blanket guarantee to all bank deposits. Some sort of banking system 'crisis' would have ensued in that case, as non-secured investors in the banking system realised that the asset backing for their deposits had gone up in smoke with the collapse in asset values and that the government was not going to step in kindly to make them whole. Policymakers would have needed to have been on their toes to prevent a full-fledged melt-down of the financial system (Table 1.2).

But a 'financial crisis' can be one way of bringing balance sheets into line with economic realities and of confronting and dealing with underlying financial system problems. A decision not to guarantee all deposits would have been a decision to allow the losses from the bursting of the bubble to have fallen where they lay—on the direct and indirect owners of the assets. It would have been a decision to confront, rather than delay, the recognition and resolution of the underlying asset market and balance sheet problems. It would have been the financial system equivalent of letting water flow downhill.

The June 1995 decision was crisis management, but little else. The decision obviated the need for depositors to withdraw deposits from the banking system, but the assets that had been lost were not going to come back. No government wants a financial crisis on its hands, so one can have some sympathy with the government's decision to guarantee all bank deposits. But all this did was to buy time to deal with the underlying problems, and it did so by transferring any contingent losses of bank depositors to the government, that is, to taxpayers. The government's decision meant that taxpayers were bailing out bank depositors in order to secure financial stability in the face of a massive impairment of assets in the banking system. This was a legitimate (and, most observers argued,

Table 1.2   Current cyclical upswing compared with previous two
                 post-bubble recoveries, 1993, 1999 and 2002

(a) Contribution of components to real GDP growth (ppp) purchasing power parity

| | Through of recovery cycle | | | Last three |
	Q3 93	Q1 99*	Q1 02	quarters
GDP	4.6	5.3	8.2	3.9
Final private domestic demand	3.6	4.0	5.4	2.0
Consumption	3.3	1.6	2.5	1.5
Business investment	0.2	2.1	3.0	1.5
Residential investment	0.1	0.2	0.0	0.0
Inventory investment	0.3	0.9	1.6	0.3
Public demand	1.9	0.3	–1.0	–0.3
Net exports	–1.2	0.2	2.2	1.0
Reference: GDP deflator	–0.7	–3.6	–6.0	–2.4

(b) Contribution of components to nominal GDP growth (ppp) purchasing power parity

| | Through of recovery cycle | | | Last three |
	Q3 93	Q1 99*	Q1 02	quarters
GDP	4.0	1.5	1.7	1.4"
Final private domestic demand	2.9	1.7	1.8	1.6
Consumption	3.2	0.2	0.7	0.9
Business investment	–0.3	1.2	1.1	0.8
Residential investment	0.1	0.2	0.0	0.0
Inventory investment	0.3	0.8	1.2	0.0
Public demand	1.9	0.0	–2.0	–.05
Net exports	–1.2	–1.0	0.7	0.3
Reference: Worker compensation	3.2	0.1	–2.8	0.0

* This recovery lasted for just eight quarters
Source: Cabinet Office.

compelling) policy decision, but the ramifications—that the lost assets
were unlikely to come back and that somebody, presumably the
government, would have to foot the bill—should have been better
understood and acted upon. The government should have followed up its
momentous decision to guarantee deposits with a commensurate injection
of public funds into the banking system to make bank balance sheets
whole. This could have been done through a carve-out of NPLs at or close

to face value to a 'resolution and trust corporation'-style entity, or by injecting a large amount of common equity, that is, equity not required to be re-paid: the government did neither (although much later pale versions of these policies were implemented).

A major flaw in banking system policy in Japan in this period is that policymakers have never accepted, or even acted as if they realised, that guaranteeing bank deposits to head off a financial crisis and injecting fiscal funds are two sides of the same policy coin. Moreover, in a classic circular argument, because the blanket guarantees succeeded in preventing financial instability (particularly a run on bank deposits), policymakers were consistently able to deny the need to inject public funds, on the grounds that were was no crisis.

The government did not want a financial crisis—that is, a market-based resolution to the fact that market values of assets were way below their book values—but it did not want to foot the bill for a bailout either, although this would have allowed the whole episode of the bubble and its aftermath to have been assigned to the history books relatively quickly. That just left forbearance as their underlying policy: playing for time and banking on growth to eventually heal balance sheet wounds. Notwithstanding some stop-start attempts to use fiscal policy to stimulate growth, policymakers clearly looked to monetary policy to be the mainstay of macro stimulus. The Bank of Japan dropped policy interest rates from 1.75 per cent at the start of the year to 50 basis points by September of 1995, a level of rates seen at the time as 'extraordinary'. However, by the time that the 'financial stabilisation five-year plan' had been put in place, the economy had already slipped into deflation, meaning that the Bank of Japan had lost the opportunity to give the economy a shot in the arm by experiencing negative real rates, and land prices were continuing to plummet. In fact, exemplifying another inconsistent cross-current in policy, the official policy goal of bringing down land prices—adopted at the start of the decade—continued to be in place until the Cabinet announced a new land policy in February 1997. This meant that for a period of about twenty months, one arm of policy was operating to impose more losses on banks while another arm sought to transfer these (contingent) losses to the government's balance sheet.

More to the point, it made little sense to rely on monetary policy to deliver growth if the main transmission mechanism of monetary policy—credit transmission through the banking system—was inoperable, and likely to remain so for a number of years as the government gave the banks time to repair their balance sheet wounds slowly. This was a policy contradiction in terms. In effect, the implicit policy in Japan for a decade was to rely on a 'broken' banking system as the primary transmission channel (of monetary policy) for fixing itself. No wonder the economy floundered!

What could, and should, the government have done instead? In short, the government should have implemented a coordinated and strategic package of macro and micro policies, centring on three elements. At the macro level, the authorities should have announced that macro-level deflation would not be tolerated and implemented a sustained and coordinated fiscal and monetary expansion to be continued until the economy emerged from deflation. Bridging the macro and micro levels, the authorities should have fixed the banking system by injecting enough fiscal funds into the banking system to enable banks expeditiously to clear away bubble-era excess corporate debt and recapitalise themselves. Conceptually, this capital injection could be thought of as the government 'marking to market' its guarantee of deposits since by fully guaranteeing bank deposits the government became the contingent owner of any residual losses in the banking system associated with the balance sheet cleanup after bank equity was wiped out. At the micro level, the government should have pursued an aggressive program of deregulation and public sector reform (rather than a slow and piecemeal one) so to open up new consumption and investment opportunities and raise the potential growth rate.

The policy framework in existence in 2005 rested on the same principles and embodied the same flaws. Under the policy framework as re-defined by the Koizumi administration, the economy was envisaged as being in the final year of a 3–4 year 'intensive adjustment period'. The aim during this time was to 'complete the resolution of the non-performing loan problem' and establish the conditions for the economy to exit from deflation. The Bank of Japan was committed to maintaining its extraordinary quantitative easing regime until it was 'convinced' that the economy would not slip back into deflation (as measured by the core CPI). The government continued to fully guarantee large-lot demand deposits (some 31 per cent of total bank deposits) and, in effect (via the financial crisis response framework in the deposit insurance system) to fully guarantee all bank deposits. In short, the economy had not yet emerged from its post-bubble deflationary path and policy was still in post-bubble deflation-fighting, financial system-stabilising mode.

The authorities continued to use two central planks of policy—financial stabilisation policy centring on guarantees of bank deposits, and monetary policy—to 'play for time' and 'bank on growth'. The problem is that, as in the past, these policies were unlikely to deliver an end to deflation and a transition to sustainable growth. Japan is by no means out of the post-bubble deflationary woods, notwithstanding the recent impressive-looking real growth rates (Table 1.3).

First, take bank guarantees. The government continued, in effect, to fully guarantee all bank deposits. Initially the blanket government guarantee on bank deposits was supposed to expire at the end of March 2001, after which time only small-lot deposits would be automatically guaranteed by the deposit insurance system (what the Japanese refer to as 'the pay-off' system). However, the government extended the guarantee on large-lot time deposits to the end of March 2002, and the guarantee on large-lot demand deposits ('large-lot' being deposits above 10 million yen per depositor per bank) first to the end of March 2003 but then later to the end of March 2005. On paper, the government allowed the blanket guarantee on large-lot time deposits to expire at the end of March 2002. This change in formal guarantee status had the predictable effect: it triggered a huge shift in deposits from time deposits to demand deposits, since under quantitative easing (zero interest policy) these deposits were almost perfect substitutes, other than in their guarantee status, which clearly favoured demand deposits (Figure 1.8).

A key choreography of policy in Japan was that the remaining government guarantee on large-lot bank deposits would expire at the end of March 2005, ushering in the era of the 'full pay-off regime'. If only that were the case! This portrayal is, at best, wishful thinking, at worst

Table 1.3   Japan's banking system workout framework, 2004

Deposit Insurance Corporation (DIC) and Industrial Revitalisation Corporation (IRC) loan guarantees (yen tr)	Maximum amount	Amount used	Amount available
Depositor protection	19.00	5.01	13.99
NPL purchases by RCC	14.00	4.56	9.44
RCC losses/recapitalisation	6.00	0.81	5.19
Financial crisis response	17.00	1.96	15.04
'Old' bank recapitalisation	1.00	0.01	0.99
'New' bank recapitalisation (planned from FY04)	2.00	0.00	2.00
DIC investment in IRC	0.15	0.15	0.00
DIC sub-total	59.15	12.49	46.66
IRC funds	10.00	0.51	9.49
Total	69.15	13.00	56.15

Sources: Deposit Insurance Corporation of Japan; Industrial Revitalisation Corporation of Japan; Nikkei newspaper.

Figure 1.8   Shift in large-lot time deposits, triggered by removal of guarantee, 1995–2007 (per cent year-on-year)

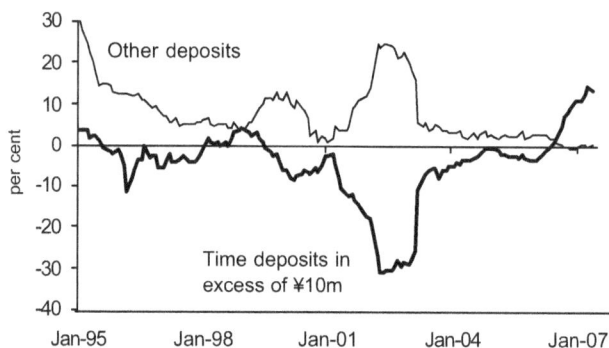

Source: Bank of Japan.

disingenuous. True, under sunset legislation, the blanket guarantee on large-lot demand deposits expired at the end of March 2005, and the authorities did not extend this guarantee for a third time. This deadline coincided (purposely) with the target date for the completion of the government's 'financial revival program' (the so-called 'Takenaka plan') unveiled at the end of October 2002 (Japan, Financial Services Agency 2002).

However, there were two loopholes relating to this change in the status of the government guarantee of bank deposits. One is that, under legislation passed in December 2002, deposits earning a zero interest rate (so-called 'settlement deposits') continued to be fully guaranteed. There was no 'pay-off' for these deposits, which at the time represented about 21.1 per cent of large-lot demand deposits and 6.5 per cent of total deposits. This created a loophole in the removal of the government guarantee, as interest rates at the time were so close to zero that it hardly mattered (0.001 per cent): accepting a zero interest rate would mean giving up just 100 yen of interest income on a minimum-size large-lot deposit (10 million yen). This meant that, should there be lingering concerns about the strength of bank balance sheets or should such concerns re-surface, there could well have been a shift from non-zero large-lot demand deposits to zero demand deposits, analogous to (although likely not on the same scale as) the shift from time to demand deposits triggered by the removal of the automatic guarantee on the former (Figure 1.8).

A second loophole was more systemic: even when the blanket guarantee expired, a state of affairs that was tantamount to a full government guarantee on bank deposits continued to exist. The 'financial crisis response' framework, which came into existence in April 2001, can be used whenever 'it is feared that, should measures not be implemented, very severe obstacles would arise in the maintenance of orderly credit [conditions] in the country or in the region where the financial institution in question operates' (Deposit Insurance Law, Article 102). This framework has been invoked on two occasions, to provide a capital injection to Resona Bank and to nationalise Ashikaga Bank. It is designed in such a way that, whenever it is invoked, the deposits of the financial institution concerned are fully guaranteed.[1] The blanket guarantee was introduced in 1995 in order to head off a financial crisis; the thrust of the framework that replaces it is that deposits will continue to be fully guaranteed after the event if that is necessary in order to maintain financial stability. Put another way, the blanket guarantee is to be removed, but only in those cases in which is not needed.

A policy critique of forbearance

Japanese policymakers appear to take it as self-evident that it is sound policy for the government to fully guarantee bank deposits. After all, as long as the market retains confidence in the sovereign credit, it is a sure-fire way to prevent a run on bank deposits and to maintain financial stability. And it is cheap—as long as the guarantees are not called in, there is no overt fiscal cost.

However, as a policy tool, government guarantees of bank deposits have a serious drawback: they serve to slow down the whole bank resolution process and impose a high cost on the economy in terms of lost growth and the ultimate fiscal costs incurred. In fact, the very thing that makes government bank deposit guarantees so potent in putting out financial system fires—the removal of the balance sheet pressure on banks and of the need for depositors to worry about the safety of the principal they have invested in the banking system—creates a bias in this direction. This can be counter-productive in the long run, however, as by virtue of the success of the deposit guarantees, the underlying problems are prevented from surfacing, and hence are slow to be addressed.

Disclosure, and credibility of the regulatory framework, also suffer under a policy of forbearance, the more so the bigger the scale of the underlying problem. The decision to take what on any official reckoning would be almost ten years from the official recognition of the problem (which I date to June 1995) to its aimed-for resolution (March 2005) to restore balance sheets to sufficient health for banks to operate without being propped up by the government implies that full information about the 'true' (such as that can be ascertained at all) underlying state of bank balance sheets can only be revealed gradually over time. This is because, had the 'true' state of bank balance sheets been revealed at the start of the process, the market, political, regulatory, and popular pressures for dealing more quickly with the problems would have forced immediate policy action, contradicting the underlying assumption of forbearance. Incremental and minimalist action goes hand-in-hand with incremental disclosure. However, enormous damage is inflicted on the credibility of the regulatory framework, as each incremental bank failure puts the spotlight on how much has been covered up in the past and for how long.

More generally, the use of extraordinary deposit guarantees, after the event, to deal with a banking crisis involves a trade-off. By converting increasingly risky claims on bank assets into safe claims on the government, such guarantees prevent a damaging financial crisis from erupting, but at the same time they serve to impede the recognition of losses and the necessary balance sheet adjustment process. This suggests that *ex post* guarantees and forbearance work best when the damage to bank assets is small and/or temporary. The extraordinary guarantee then serves to bridge the inherent asset/liability mismatch in a banking system's balance sheet. But if the assets have permanently disappeared, as in Japan's case (see Figure 1.1), there is little to be gained in 'playing for time' in the hope that asset values will be restored, whereas the long-term costs of not recognising and reacting to such a fundamental change in balance sheet circumstances are high. Given Japan's situation, where the banking problem clearly involved a one-off monumental loss of asset value rather than a temporary one which could be expected to reverse itself with time, forbearance has offered a particularly poor benefit-cost trade-off.

The second plank of policy, complementing the use of government bank deposits guarantees, was the easing of monetary policy. Three years after the Bank of Japan cut official interest rates to 50 basis points in September 1995, the Bank had to start to cut rates even further, culminating in an unprecedented policy of zero interest rates in February 1999. Following an abortive and controversial attempt to raise rates in August 2000, the Bank of Japan abandoned interest rate targeting in March 2001 and moved to 'quantitative targeting' (or 'quantitative easing'), implying zero overnight interest rates but going well beyond that in terms of the provision of reserves to the banking system (Figure 1.9). According to the Bank of Japan, it 'decided to implement these policy measures with firm determination with a view to preventing prices from declining continuously as well as preparing a basis for sustainable economic growth'.[2]

Figure 1.9   Bank of Japan quantitative easing: current account
balances targets, 2001–2006 (yen trillion)

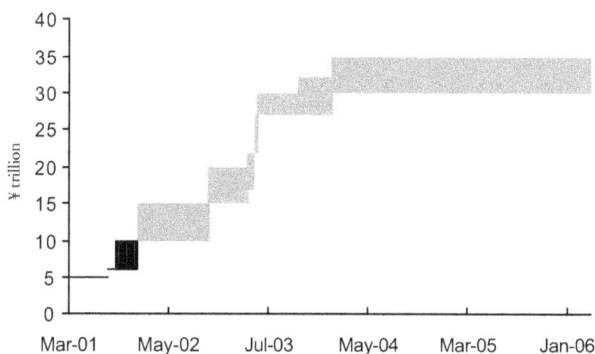

Source: Bank of Japan.

According to economic theory, easing monetary policy when the economy is on the verge of, or actually in, deflation is definitely the right policy. However, there has to be a transmission mechanism. The credit transmission mechanism, through the banking system, is the natural candidate, particularly in an economy such as Japan's with its dominant banking system. However, if the corporate sector has a huge overhang of excess debt on its balance sheets due to the bursting of a massive real-estate price bubble, and if the banking system does not have the capital to take quick action to clean up both its and the corporate sector's balance sheets, then monetary policy may not be effective in getting the economy out of deflation and onto a sustainable growth path. This has been the case in Japan.

As Figure 1.10 shows, bank lending had been falling since about 1996, and particularly sharply since 1998. In terms of stimulating the economy, banking system policy had been working at cross-purposes to monetary policy. Monetary policy had been relied upon, rather than a more sensible coordinated fiscal-monetary policy, as the principal anti-deflation tool in the forbearance policy framework. Yet there has been a glaring contradiction in the policy approach: monetary policy has been expected to work through

Figure 1.10   Bank lending growth: headline, adjusted for special
                factors, 1995–2007 (per cent year-on-year change)

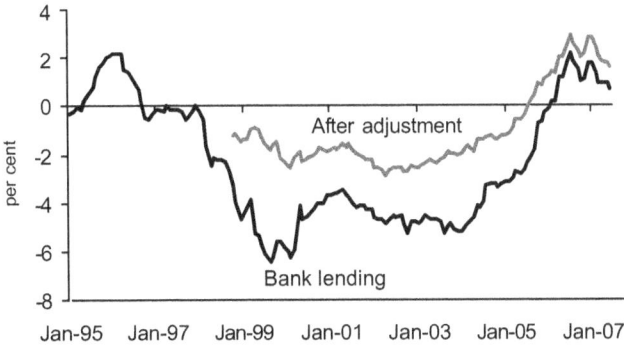

Note: 'Special factors' include NPLs and so on.
Source: Bank of Japan.

the credit transmission process of a banking system to help rescue a banking system that had been deflating. A damaging policy circularity is thus created: the banking system is given time to help it 'grow out of' its problem, but without a sound banking system, strong and sustained growth is difficult.

Figure 1.11 shows the conundrum at work. After quantitative easing began, base money increased by a cumulative 64 per cent, driven by the policy-induced increase in current account balances (mainly bank reserves), but bank lending fell by a cumulative 16 per cent during this period (March 2000–March 2004). Monetary policy was unable to gain traction through the banking system, and nominal GDP fell by 2 per cent over the period before finally rising after March 2006.

There are other transmission channels. Monetary economists focus particularly on the expectations channel.[3] By communicating a strong message that deflation will not be tolerated and by taking aggressive monetary policy action aimed at achieving that goal, a central bank may be able to change private sector expectations, and hence consumption and investment behaviour, in a way that makes an exit from deflation a self-

Figure 1.11   Monetary aggregates and nominal GDP, 2000–2007
(index, March 2001=100)

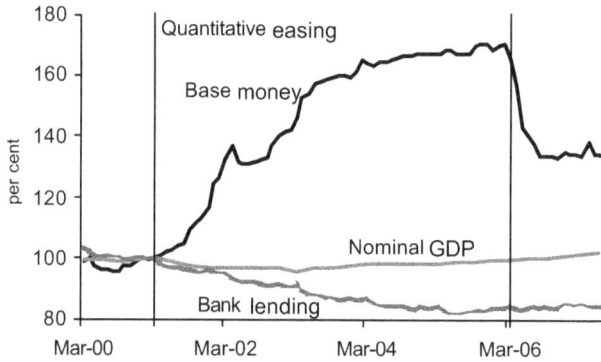

Sources: Bank of Japan; Cabinet Office.

fulfilling prophesy.[4] However, the Bank of Japan consistently eschewed reliance on, or belief in the potential efficacy of, the expectations channel, on the grounds that the transmission mechanism of monetary policy was impaired and therefore the means by which monetary policy could operate upon expectations was lacking.

There are two responses to this kind of claim. One is that it is wrong, accepting that 'one can argue that monetary policy works mostly (entirely?) through its effects on expectations' (Blanchard 2000:191).[5] In that case, however, the damage is done because the denial by the Bank of Japan that it could influence expectations is tantamount to a declaration not to rely on this channel. Ironically, such beliefs by a central bank will be self-reinforcing. Another is to accept the logic, but to argue the obvious point that, if the transmission mechanism of monetary policy is 'broken', then it should be 'fixed' as a matter of the highest policy priority. Policymakers, time and time again in Japan, have appeared to accept this logic, and have appeared to be in the process of developing plans to fix the banking system, only to disappoint by failing to execute policy.

One could point in particular to: the 1996 'financial stabilisation five-year plan', which purported to have the aim of 'bringing the non-performing loan problem under control by the end of FY00'; the 1998 'finance Diet' which produced the 60 trillion yen bank work-out plan (whose successor is outlined in Table 1.4) (Financial System Council 1995); the April 2001 'emergency economic package' that pointed to 'the existence of excessive corporate debt', the 'delay in balance sheet adjustments [imposing] a heavy burden on economic growth', and the fact that 'without a quick resolution of this issue, [firm] progress towards economic recovery cannot be expected', thus (to paraphrase) 'the critical importance of solving such structural issues still present in the asset markets for the Japanese economy to achieve dynamic growth' (Ministerial conference 2001); the June 2001 blueprint document laying out the Koizumi structural reform agenda, whose starting point aim was to 'resolve the non-performing loans problem within two or three years' (Council on Economic Fiscal Policy 2001); and the October 2002 'financial revival program' (the so-called 'Takenaka plan'), which took as its starting point the 'need to solve the non-performing loan problems of the major banks' by focusing on 'making asset evaluations stricter, bolstering capital levels, and strengthening governance'. Notwithstanding the no doubt well-intentioned policy rhetoric and the numerous associated schemes introduced, official non-performing loan levels, fell from March 2002 peak levels, but remained almost as high as they were at the start of the official work-out in 1996 (Figure 1.4), and there were no signs of the banking system becoming an effective transmitter of monetary policy (Figures 1.10 and 1.11).

Table 1.4   **Foreign exchange intervention, 1999–2003** (yen trillion)

	FY99	FY00	FY01	FY02	FY03
1Q	3.039	1.385	0.000	4.016	4.612
2Q	2.388	0.000	0.000	0.000	5.876
3Q	1.634	0.000	0.000	2.387	7.551
4Q	1.558	0.144	3.211	0.000	14.832
Total	8.628	1.529	3.211	6.403	32.870
Per cent yen/ dollar appreciation*	12.4	−12.4	−7.4	10.5	9.3

* using March averages
Source: Ministry of Finance.

It is a similar story with the Bank of Japan, when it comes to fixing the banks. When the Bank of Japan implemented 'zero interest rate policy' in February 1999 it stated that: 'In order to bring [the] Japanese economy back to a solid recovery path, it is important not only to provide support from monetary and fiscal sides but also to steadily promote financial system revitalisation and structural reforms. The Bank of Japan strongly hopes that the decision to make money market operations more accommodative will, combined with various efforts made by the parties concerned, contribute to surmounting the economic difficulties we face' (Bank of Japan 1999). When the Bank introduced quantitative targeting in March 2001, it similarly stated

> In order to make this monetary easing fully effective in restoring Japan's economy on a sustainable growth path, progress in structural reforms with respect to the financial system, for example, resolution of the non-performing asset problem, as well as in the area of economy and industry is essential. Structural reform may be accompanied by painful adjustments. Without such adjustments, however, neither improvement in productivity nor sustainable economic growth can be obtained. The Bank of Japan strongly hopes that decisive actions be taken to address fundamental problems both with a clear support of the nation for structural reform and under a strong leadership of the government of Japan (Bank of Japan 2001, point 5).

In September 2002, the Bank of Japan announced a 'new initiative towards financial system stability', unveiling a 'course of action to facilitate resolution of the non-performing loan problem and to secure financial system stability'. The Bank argued that 'in order to resolve the overall problem, a comprehensive and is needed, centring on a more appropriate evaluation of non-performing loans, the promotion of their early disposal, and efforts toward higher profitability on the part of both firms and financial institutions'. The Bank pledged to 'conduct a comprehensive review of the non-performing loan problem and publish the result' (Bank of Japan 2002) and the next month announced that it would take the extraordinary step of buying up to 2 trillion yen of equities held by banks (increased to 3 trillion yen in March 2003) (Bank of Japan 2002). At the time, this was widely regarded as a case of the Bank of Japan having thrown the central bank equivalent of a hand grenade at the banking authorities. However, judged by ultimate results, which is what counts, the results were disappointing.

Things appeared to have taken a serious turn for the good in March 2003, when, virtually immediately upon assuming office, the new governor of the Bank of Japan, Toshihiko Fukui, called an extraordinary monetary policy meeting, at which he 'instructed Bank staff to examine a wide range of issues related to the enhancement of monetary policy transparency and the strengthening of the monetary policy transmission mechanism based on the experience of quantitative easing so far' and 'with respect to specific measures, …particularly instructed Bank staff to explore possible measures to strengthen the transmission mechanism of monetary easing in the areas of corporate finance and money market operations' (Bank of Japan 2003). However, what came out of this initiative in terms of measures aimed at strengthening the transmission mechanism was an anticlimax: a scheme to purchase by March 2006 up to 1 trillion yen of asset-backed securities (mainly) of small and medium-sized enterprises. But 1 trillion yen is equivalent to only 0.2 per cent of Japan's GDP or 1 per cent of monetary base, and is only a drop in the macro bucket when it comes to getting the credit transmission mechanism working in Japan. Actual implementation of the scheme has been even more modest, with the Bank currently holding only 192 billion yen of asset-backed securities under this scheme an amount equivalent to less than 0.2 per cent of monetary base (Figure 1.12).

The government had a well-articulated (albeit flawed) framework for carrying out a banking system work-out (Table 1.3). Aggressive use of this framework, to give the banks directly or indirectly enough capital to remove the corporate debt overhang, would have helped to establish the pre-conditions for the credit contraction process to be brought to an early end, and for monetary policy to start to gain traction through the banking system. It still could have. However, notwithstanding the recapitalisation of the fifth largest banking group and the nationalisation of the tenth largest regional bank in 2003, the Bank of Japan persisted with its deep-seated reluctance to use the framework to expedite a work-out rather than as a tool of forbearance.

Figure 1.12   Purchases of asset-backed securities by the Bank of
               Japan, 2003–2006

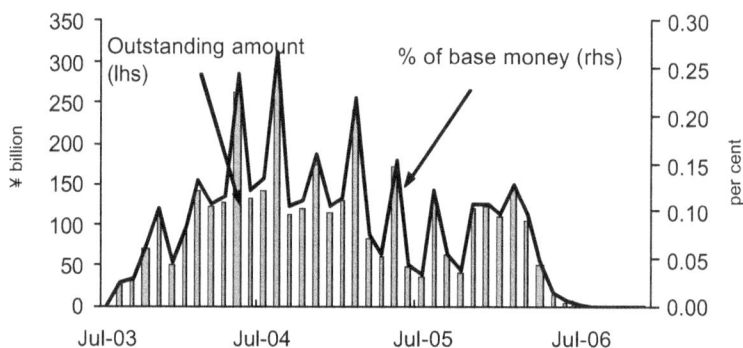

Source: Bank of Japan.

If actions speak louder than words, the transmission channel that the authorities are really prepared to use is the exchange rate. Japan conducted unprecedented foreign exchange intervention in the FY 2003, selling 32.87 trillion yen of domestic currency to buy (overwhelmingly in US dollars) an amount equivalent to about twice Japan's annual current account surplus (Table 1.4). As a result, Japan's foreign exchange reserves increased to US$806 billion at the end of March, an increase of 69 per cent year-on-year (Figure 1.13). In the course of accumulating so many foreign reserves, the Ministry of Finance literally ran out of money, running up against its Diet-authorised borrowing limit by the end of 2003. Not to be deterred, the Ministry of Finance temporarily 'borrowed' the central bank's balance sheet, by entering an agreement with the Bank of Japan on 26 December to purchase up to 10 trillion yen of the Ministry's foreign exchange reserves (which it did in the first two months of 2004). Moreover, the authorities signaled to the market that they would be prepared to continue with this policy on even a larger scale if necessary. The Ministry increased the total budget available to raise intervention funds from 79 trillion yen in FY2003 to 140 trillion yen in FY2004 (in two stages, 21 trillion yen in the FY2003 supplementary budget and 40 trillion yen in the FY2004 Budget).

Figure 1.13   Foreign exchange intervention and official reserves,
               1994–2004

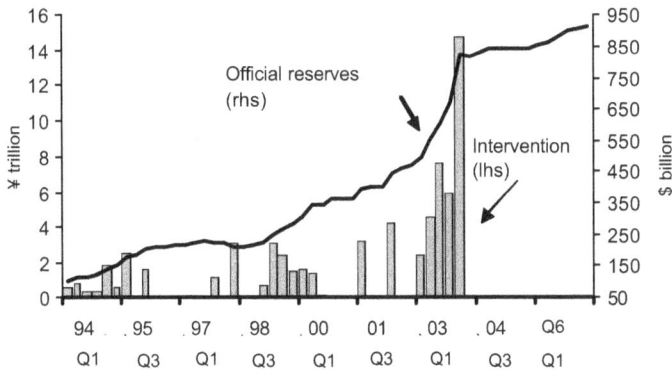

Source: Ministry of Finance.

While massive foreign exchange intervention backed up by monetary easing has its merits as a policy to overcome deflation, there are a number of problems. One, the idea seems to be at odds with policymakers' own diagnosis and prescription for countering deflation, as laid out in numerous policy documents. Two, and related, the policy stimulus would appear to be poorly directed, because the export sector arguably is already strong and the transmission mechanism from an export-led recovery to domestic demand appears to be weak. Three, policy implementation has been poor, in that the authorities have not communicated a strong and coordinated anti-deflation message between the Ministry of Finance and the Bank of Japan, such as could have had a significant impact on expectations.

Conclusion: what may lie ahead

Despite the recently improved sentiment towards Japan, surveying the economic landscape in 2005 it appeared that neither the government nor the market was expecting the economy to resume robust growth any time soon. One of the casualties of the post-bubble period has been bullish growth expectations about the future. According to the government's own medium-term fiscal and economic plan, under the scenario in which the government successfully discharges its reform plans during the 'intensive adjustment phase' after which the economy achieves sustainable growth, real growth would average 2 per cent over the next five years (and only 2.1 per cent in FY2008) and nominal GDP growth 1.9 per cent. According to the Consensus Economics numbers of major market forecasters at the time, the market consensus was that growth would be 4.2 per cent in 2004, but would decelerate to 1.8 per cent in 2005. Thus the consensus appeared to be forecasting that this third post-bubble recovery would stay within the post-bubble trend of low-growth, deflationary cyclical ups-and-downs.

While Japanese policymakers talked about the need to put an end to deflation and get the economy on a sustainable (domestic demand-led) growth path again, they did not appear to have a credible policy framework in place to bring that about, and it was unlikely to happen autonomously. The most likely scenario was that policy 'muddling-through' would continue, based on defensive and open-ended deflation-fighting policies, with intermittent periods of more aggressive policy responses triggered by market (crisis) events, and this is what occurred.

As of mid 2007, Japan is on the road to becoming a 'normal', albeit lower growth, economy again. The listed banking sector, adequately capitalised by a more than trebling of its market capitalisation since its April 2003 trough, is largely able to stand on its own feet again, and the Bank of Japan has started to move policy rates into positive territory for the first time in seven years. However, deflation is not fully vanquished in Japan, as evidenced by both the GDP deflator and the core CPI being in slight negative territory in year-on-year rate of change terms (–0.3 per cent and –0.1 per cent respectively).

As long as Japan remains trapped in a quasi-deflationary twilight zone, and assuming that China can keep on its current high-growth course— reminiscent in many ways of Japan's own high-growth period—the relentless slide in Japan's relative standing as an economic powerhouse in Asia looks set to continue. This prospect does not augur well for Japan to exercise an economic leadership role in Asia commensurate with its economic responsibilities and potential.

Notes

1   Even if a bank is nationalised, and even when there is no *ex ante* guarantee on large-lot deposits (that is, the 'pay-off' is in effect), there is no way within the framework to impose a 'haircut' on depositors. Thus, when Ashikaga Bank was nationalised, it was immediately announced that all depositors would be guaranteed. Few observers seemed to comment on the apparent inconsistency of this automatic *ex post* guarantee with the 'partial pay-off', in effect from 1 April 2002.

2   Bank of Japan, 'New Procedures for Money Market Operations and Monetary Easing', 19 March 2001.

3   To quote Michael Woodford on the general topic: 'Not only do expectations about policy matter, but, at least under current conditions, very little *else* matters' *(Interest and Prices: Foundations of a Theory of Monetary Policy*, Princeton University Press, Princeton, 2003:15).

4   This was clearly the strategy employed by the Federal Reserve in 2003 when Chairman Alan Greenspan and Governor Ben Bernanke, particularly the latter, pointed in public speeches or comments to the implausibility of a central bank with a fiat currency and a 'printing press' not being able to counter deflation.

5   See Olivier Blanchard, 2000: 'Bubbles, liquidity traps, and monetary policy', in Ryoichi Mikitani and Adam S. Posen (eds), *Japan's Financial Crisis and its Parallels to US Experience*, Washington, DC:185–93.

References

Bank of Japan, 1999. Change of the Guideline for Money Market Operations.

——, 2001. "New Procedures for Money Market Operations and Monetary Easing' point 5, 19 March.

——, 2002. 'New Initiative toward Financial System Stability' [English statement on Bank of Japan website], 18 September.

——, 2002. 'The Outline of the Stock Purchasing Plan', (English statement on Bank of Japan website), 11 October.

——, 2003. Bank of Japan Monetary Policy Meeting, (taken from English statement on Bank of Japan website), March.

Council on Economic Fiscal Policy, 2001. Council on Economic Fiscal Policy (Basic principles for structural reform of economic and fiscal management and structural reform of economic society), 26 June 33:1.

Financial System Council, 1995. Financial System Council ['Kin'yu shisutemu anteika no tame no shisaku'], (various measures for the stabilisation of the financial system), 22 December.

Japan, Deposit Insurance Law 2001. Deposit Insurance Corporation of Japan, website www.dic.go.jp.

Japan, Ministry of Finance, 1995. 'Kinyu shisutemu no kino kaifuku ni tsuite (On restoring the functioning of the financial system)' (mimeo document).

Japan, Financial Services Agency, 2002. Kin'yu saisei puroguramu (Financial revival program), 30 October:1.

Ministerial statement at ministerial conference for economic measures, 2001. (B11pp (quotes are from p.1, 6 April).

2 AUSTRALIA, JAPAN AND THE REGION

THE WEST NEW GUINEA DISPUTE, 1952–1962

David Walton

Indonesian and Dutch claims over West New Guinea in the period 1949 to 1962 presented one of the first opportunities for regional dialogue in post-war Australia-Japan relations. The aims of this chapter are to chart changes in the Australian attitude towards Japan's role in regional affairs and to examine how dialogue on West New Guinea assisted in laying the foundations for further regional cooperation and consultation between the two countries. The chapter examines the beginnings of post-war consultation between Australia and Japan. It is argued that the diplomatic intrigues involving the West New Guinea dispute (1952 to 1962) led to a substantial effort by Australian officials to bring Japan into closer alignment with Australian foreign policy objectives. As part of this initiative, regular meetings between Australia and Japan resulted in the relatively rapid development in the quality and scope of discussions and exchange of information on regional issues. Accordingly this chapter provides evidence of the formative processes towards institutionalising regular bilateral consultation and exchange of sensitive political information on regional issues. Regular diplomatic consultation on regional issues was important as it provided a basis for broadening the structure of the bilateral relationship and improved both countries' understanding of contemporary bilateral relations.

Overview of the West New Guinea dispute

The political landscape of early post-war Asia was dominated by the notions of nationalism and demands for independence from European colonial powers. In the case of Indonesia, Indonesian nationalists proclaimed independence in August 1945 prior to the return of the Dutch colonial administration. The desire for independence led to a protracted and armed struggle against the Dutch in the ensuing four years. After intervention by the United Nations and considerable negotiation, a resolution was reached through The Hague Round Table discussions, which took place in October and November 1949. The result was the transfer of power to Indonesian nationalists led by Sukarno in late December 1949. Dutch withdrawal and international recognition of the Indonesian Republic took place early in the following year. Importantly, the fate of West New Guinea (hereafter WNG)[1] was not decided at the 1949 Round Table conferences. Instead, the WNG question was deferred for 12 months while negotiations took place and the territory of WNG was excluded from the transfer of sovereignty.[2] This led to over thirteen years of episodic discussions between the Netherlands and Indonesia, which served only to inflame passions on both sides.

The WNG dispute went through three essential phases before its resolution in August 1962: 1949–1954, 1954–1957 and 1958–62. From 1949 to 1957 the WNG dispute was negotiated through bilateral discussions and appeals to the United Nations General Assembly. Four attempts were made by the Indonesians through the General Assembly of the United Nations to resolve the dispute.[3] By late 1957, however, Indonesian strategy had changed. This was mainly due to the failure to gain sufficient support within the United Nations and a hard-line Dutch position that rejected Indonesian claims. A more forceful approach was subsequently adopted by Indonesia, involving a 'Contest of Power' with the Dutch. In 1960 Indonesia formerly severed diplomatic ties with the Netherlands and several small-scale clashes occurred in WNG. India's use of military force to reclaim Goa from the Portuguese in December 1961 offered a precedent for the Indonesian Government to engage in direct military conflict. At this stage the Dutch Government, due to domestic pressure and the paucity of international support, became more willing to negotiate. On 15 August 1962, Dutch representatives reluctantly agreed to an international trusteeship for WNG.

The resolution to the dispute came after negotiations in early 1962. Ellsworth Bunker (a retired United States diplomat) acted as a mediator during these proceedings at the request of acting UN Secretary General U Thant. Known as the Bunker Plan, the resolution involved: the transfer of the administration of WNG to a United Nations Temporary Executive Authority (UNTEA) established by and under the jurisdiction of the Secretary General; a United Nations appointed administrator who would have the discretion to transfer all or part of the administration to Indonesia at any time after 1 May 1963; and exercising their right of self determination by the inhabitants of WNG before the end of 1969.[4]

Early Australia-Japan dialogue on regional issues: differences on West New Guinea

Australia-Japan dialogue on regional issues in the early post war years was on an *ad hoc* and infrequent basis. The process towards more regular discussions began in 1957 as Australian officials applied considerable pressure on the Japanese Government to support the Dutch position on the WNG dispute. The Japanese had supported Indonesian claims until late 1957 and then pursued a policy of neutrality. It is not clear what impact, if any, Australian pressure had on the policy shift in Tokyo. The burgeoning trade relationship may have had some influence on the outcome. Nonetheless, Japanese negotiations with Indonesia on reparations and the United States position on neutrality were of far greater significance to overall Japanese foreign policy. The change in Japanese policy, however, allowed for smoother relations between Australian and Japanese officials. From this period the focus of discussions became broader due, in part, to shared interests as staunch US allies and regular consultation on regional matters.

In an assessment of Australian discussion with Japan on WNG and broader regional issues, three distinct periods are evident: 1952 to 1957, the year 1957 and 1958 to 1962.

1952–57: blundering through

The first few years after diplomatic relations were restored were awkward. From an Australian perspective there was a considerable amount of tension in public perceptions of Japan. Diplomatic activities were taken up with establishing embassies and receiving the credentials of diplomats in Canberra and Tokyo. It was not until August 1954 that the Menzies Cabinet made a serious effort to develop the bilateral relationship. The change in policy was also reflected in the decision to support Japan's involvement in international forums such as the United Nations.

The softening of Australian attitudes toward Japan was a pragmatic decision. It fitted into the regional objectives of the United States and the United Kingdom and suited Australian interests as a potentially lucrative bilateral trade relationship was starting to emerge. Normalising relations and the co-sponsorship of Japan into several international organisations also began the process of regional dialogue. Most pressing from an Australian perspective was the need to thwart attempts by Indonesia to gain United Nations support on the question of sovereignty of WNG. Consultation with Japan on WNG, which was part of the overall strategy to offset Indonesian plans, began in December 1954. Arthur Tange (the Secretary of the External Affairs Department) invited the Japanese Ambassador Haruhiko Nishi to discuss a number of issues of which WNG was the first on the agenda. Tange took a soft line in discussions with Ambassador Nishi but nonetheless made it clear that the Department had been concerned over WNG. As a means to influence the Japanese approach, Tange discussed the Indonesia election. The Secretary expressed the hope that as a result of the election, the Indonesians would not bring the WNG issue up again in the United Nations.[5] The meeting ended on a cordial note and although no direct pressure was applied on Japan, Tange's intentions were made abundantly clear: Australia expected Japan to support the Dutch in international forums either now or in the near future. In many respects the Tange-Nishi discussion marked the beginning of a campaign within the External Affairs Department to influence Japan on this issue through an ongoing process of consultation. Australia had provided considerable support for Japan at international forums and External Affairs officials intended to use this as leverage to pressure Japan to support the Dutch position.

In April 1955 Masayoshi Kakitsubo (Embassy Counsellor) called into the Department of External Affairs upon his return to Australia from a Japanese diplomatic representatives meeting in Karachi. In his discussion with James Plimsoll (a senior official and later Secretary of External Affairs), Kakitsubo discussed the forthcoming Bandung Conference and the issue of Japan's stance on WNG as a foreign policy dilemma. He noted that the final recommendation at the Japanese diplomatic meeting was that Japan would remain neutral and try to avoid any specific issue such as WNG ever coming on the Bandung agenda.[6] Kakitsubo's information was corroborated by a cablegram sent by Ronald Walker (Australian Ambassador to Japan, June 1953–December 1955) in early April 1955. In a discussion with Mr Tani from the Japanese Foreign Office, Walker reported that based on procedure, which had already been submitted to the conference on the first day, the Japanese representatives felt it was unlikely that specific controversial issues such as Formosa or WNG would be raised.[7]

However Indonesia raised WNG at the Bandung Conference. According to Ambassador Saburo Ohta (then Japanese Ambassador to Burma and later to Australia) the Arab delegation raised the issue of Palestine and this gave the Indonesians the opportunity to discuss WNG. Ohta spoke disparagingly about Indonesia as hosts and said several countries including Japan had been rather embarrassed by the discussion of WNG.[8]

The decision by Japan to support Indonesian claims at Bandung caused some consternation in Canberra. There was concern about the reliability of information being received from the Japanese Government and the level of influence that Canberra could exert on the Ministry of Foreign Affairs. Annoyed that Japan chose Iran and Peru rather than Australia to sponsor her into the United Nations General Assembly, Australia's Ambassador to Japan Alan Watt expressed concern that Japan was 'fobbing off' Australia. In a memo to Arthur Tange in December 1956, Watt stated 'If however, they [Japan] learn in some polite but firm way that their words are not deceiving us, it would help them to understand that international friendship depends upon acts rather than words'.[9] Watt's concerns about Japanese foreign policy and approach to WNG were highlighted in a letter to External Affairs Minister Casey the following day. Watt commented on Japan's entry into the United Nations and how this was a turning point in Japanese foreign policy. He noted that Japanese policy was most likely to be cautious, restrained and opportunistic with care being taken not to antagonise the Afro-Asian bloc. In short, Australia could expect little or no support on colonial issues.[10]

Despite these concerns, consultation between Australian and Japanese officials continued to develop and was further refined in 1957. Frequent discussions on WNG took place throughout the year. Japan's support for Indonesia at the eleventh and twelfth sessions of the General Assembly in 1957 led to pro-active effort by Australia to change thinking in Tokyo. Voting at the General Assembly was very tight and Australian activities formed part of an overall strategy to thwart Indonesian efforts to gain a two-third majority support for a Good Offices Commission to examine the dispute. Given the signing of the Agreement of Commerce between Australia and Japan in July, the WNG offensive by External Affairs signalled the beginnings of the practice of frequent consultations on regional issues between the two countries.

1957: Australia intensifies pressure on Japan to support its WNG policy

1957 was a landmark year in bilateral relations. Events during the year included the signing of the Agreement on Commerce Treaty; the first exchange of prime ministerial visits by Robert Menzies and Nobusuke Kishi; ministerial meetings; and dialogue among senior bureaucrats. Notably, nine major consultations were held on WNG in Canberra and Tokyo. During the year substantial pressure was placed upon Japan by Australia to support the Dutch position or to abstain. Australian pressure was based on the strong support that had been given to Japan to enter international bodies and on the goodwill that now existed between the two countries. Expressions of gratitude came from a wide range of Japanese diplomats and the new Foreign Minister and soon-to-be Prime Minister Nobusuke Kishi.

The Australian lobbying on WNG took a number of forms, but central to all efforts was the request that Japan carefully reconsider its position. In January 1957 James Plimsoll began the year with renewed pressure on Japan to revise its WNG policy. In a meeting with Japanese Counsellor Uyama, Plimsoll restated the Australian position and emphasised that Australia had a defence interest in the security of WNG. He made it very clear to Uyama that Australia hoped Japan would not support Indonesian claims at the forthcoming session at the General Assembly.[11]

The tempo of Australian pressure began to intensify in February 1957 as Indonesia planned to invite the Assembly President to exercise 'good offices' either personally or through a committee on WNG for the March session. Watt actively sought to ensure that Japan was aware that this was the first step to strengthening the legal claim that sovereignty already belonged to Indonesia. The Australian position, as Watt reminded Japanese officials, was that a political assembly should not settle legal issues.[12] As a follow-up, Watt also attempted to check Japan's policy for the upcoming session of the General Assembly. Domestic affairs (Prime Minister Ishibashi was about to resign due to ill health) had preoccupied Foreign Minister Kishi so that no firm or positive Japanese line on the issue had been taken in Tokyo.[13] Four days later (27 February) Kishi became Prime Minister. Despite support for abstention at the Foreign Office level, Kishi personally intervened to ensure that Japan voted in support of Indonesia at the United Nations. Watt expressed his surprise at this decision, as this was contrary to informal advice he had received and the Department expressed its disappointment. The official reason given by Mr Ohno (Vice Minister of Foreign Affairs) was that 'Japan must give special consideration to political and economic cooperation with neighbouring Asian countries'.[14] No doubt a contributing factor in Kishi's decision was his personal business interests. The new Prime Minister had close ties with Kinoshita Trading Company, which had the largest share of reparation contracts with Indonesia.[15]

Watt was annoyed by Japan's vote, which he saw as part of a growing pattern of empty UN resolutions urging members of the UN engaged in disputes to resolve the problem. In this context Watt argued that Australia must be more forceful with Japan. In particular, Watt wrote

> [i]t is unwise to let pass without registering polite disapproval Japanese actions which we feel are open to criticism.... So far as I am aware however, the only comment made to Mr Suzuki in Canberra on this issue was a statement that Australia had been glad to help in any way Japan desired. I fear that such an attitude will merely encourage Japan to ignore Australian interest or Japanese obligations to Australia whenever she finds this convenient.[16]

Watt's memo appeared to have triggered a major offensive by External Affairs in April. Plimsoll, in registering Australian displeasure at Japanese voting in the UN and countering the response that questions of sovereignty were best solved in the United Nations, made the point to Ministry of Foreign Affairs official Nara that

> ...surely he would not maintain that any country, by simply raising a claim to somebody else's territory, could have it considered by the General Assembly? What would Japan say if the representative of Korea suddenly laid claim to Tsushima?[17]

This was followed up by an attempt to develop a strong line within the department on this issue. Indicative of this was the departmental brief for Prime Minister Menzies' historic visit to Japan in April 1957. The brief stated that it was essential that Prime Minister Kishi be made aware of the value of the relationship with Australia and that Australian interests and reactions were of importance to Japan. In part, according to the brief, this lack of awareness by Kishi explained why Japan voted against Australia on WNG, which was contrary to the advice given on the likely Japanese policy.[18] The paper argued that there were three reasons why Japan should support the Australian position on WNG: the first was the unjustified nature of the Indonesian claim; the second was the danger of submerging its identity in the Afro-Asian bloc regardless of the merits of the issue; and third that Japan had a more friendly reception from Australia than from most countries in South and Southeast Asia.[19]

Menzies, no doubt due to the importance of overall bilateral relations and the upcoming trade agreement in particular, did not pursue the

External Affairs recommendation while in Japan. He did, however, raise the issue with Kishi on the last day of the visit. In a rather oblique message Menzies said that 'Australia had played a big part in getting Japan into the UN and it was up to Japan to do something for Australia'.[20]

After some lobbying by Australian officials in the first few months of 1957, WNG did not figure prominently in discussions until after the Agreement on Commerce was signed in July. From available evidence it is not clear whether this was a policy decision or was affected by the ebb and flow of the WNG debate in international forums. However the debate and Australian pressure re-emerged in July after the trade issues had been sorted out. Clearly this suggested that there was a co-ordinated policy orchestrated from Canberra to ensure a start to the new trade relationship that was as smooth as possible. Within the political sphere, however, the WNG issue remained a key area of disagreement. In July Arthur Tange invited Tadakatsu Suzuki (the newly appointed Japanese Ambassador) to the Department for discussion. Tange first raised the issue of strong Australian support for Japan's candidature at the Security Council of the United Nations. The next topic was WNG. Without directly linking the two issues, Tange made it clear that he hoped that the Japanese delegation to the next session of the General Assembly would take into account the Australian position when formulating its approach on WNG.[21]

In late July Watt reported on a discussion with Foreign Minister Fujiyama and Miyazaki (Director, International Cooperation Bureau) on WNG. Fujiyama made clear to Watt that Japan had its hands tied by the Bandung communiqué. Watt commented that it was

> ...unlikely Japanese will in the foreseeable future modify their attitude... [the] Japanese Government is preoccupied with economic questions and a major effort will be made to secure agreement with Indonesia on reparations before Kishi's visit in November.[22]

This did not deter further attempts at lobbying. In August Australian Foreign Minister Richard Casey began increasing pressure on the WNG issue. Casey put forward to Ambassador Suzuki that the WNG issue was causing difficulties in the relationship. To emphasise this point, Casey told Suzuki that Japanese support for Indonesia was seen as opposition to

Australia and that this could affect the bilateral relationship. In an uncompromising statement Casey warned that a vote for Indonesia

> …could have a bad effect on Australian public opinion and the campaign amongst Australian manufacturers against the trade agreement might well be intensified if Japan should cast a vote unfavourable to Australia.[23]

Interestingly, the lure of trade and investment in a Dutch-controlled WNG was also considered by some Australian officials as a means of influencing the Japanese Government. The notion was rejected within the Department however, on the basis that it would not guarantee a change in Japan's position.[24]

In the following month (September), a departmental paper reviewing the bilateral relationship was the first indicator of a more sanguine approach. The report stated that by adopting its 1954 position Australia had developed a cooperative approach to Japan and as such had assisted in keeping Japan in the 'Free World' and had encouraged the forces of moderation within Japan. In doing so Australia accepted some disadvantages for a greater good. Japan's policy of voting in support of the Indonesian position on WNG was seen in the report as a source of embarrassment for Australia. In its conclusion the report stated that Japan would continue to make demands on Australia as the country would 'suffer the attraction of Asian policies promoted through the Afro-Asian bloc'.[25]

In November, as part of the continuing campaign, Casey again presented Suzuki with the issue of voting on WNG in the UN. Casey pointed out that the resolution went further than last year and that Japan might find it easier to abstain. He also pointed out that a number of Asian and other countries had already indicated their intention to abstain on the Indonesian proposals. Moreover, Casey added that Kishi's visit to Australia scheduled for December would be spoiled by this issue.[26] However, by this stage it was clear to Watt (based on numerous discussions with Japanese officials and in swapping notes with Dutch officials in Tokyo) that pressure on Japan was not effective. According to Watt, the Japanese position was not based on the soundness of the Indonesian claim but rather on their recent membership of the Afro-Asian bloc and by reparation negotiations with Indonesia. Indeed, Watt wrote to the Secretary to inform him that too much pressure and insistence could weaken rather than strengthen the Australian WNG cause.[27]

Despite sustained Australian efforts Japan did vote for the Afro-Asian resolution in the UN. The change in Japan's position on the territorial claims to one of neutrality in November 1957, though, did have an impact on the process of consultation. In November, reparation agreements with Indonesia were completed and this offered the Japanese Government a greater degree of flexibility on regional matters. Indonesia, for strategic and economic reasons, was a critical factor in Japanese post-war planning. As well, the importance of resolving the reparation negotiation with Indonesia should not be underestimated. Negotiations had been bogged down for several years and in the end the Japanese Government made major concessions. As a result of the agreement Kishi was able to stabilise the Indonesian economy, enhance his own prestige and also Japan's image in Asia.[28]

The extent to which Australian pressure affected Japanese policy towards WNG is difficult to gauge. Lobbying by Australians was influential, but the issue should also be seen in the context of American neutrality and the completion of reparations agreements with Indonesia. The sustained actions by Australian officials nonetheless allowed for regular contact through frequent and increasingly familiar discussions that offered opportunity for closer relations. Dr Ronald Walker (Australian representative at the United Nations and former Ambassador to Japan), for example, reported that the Japanese delegation to the United Nations attempted to take a moderate role and was possibly toning down the expression of anti-colonialist and related prejudices on WNG.[29] Another example was the decision by Ambassador Suzuki to inform Tange of the Japanese decision to support Indonesia prior to the commencement of the 12th Session of the General Assembly. Suzuki told Tange that the Japanese delegation had made a commitment and would find it difficult to abstain this time.[30] The information gave the Australian Government advance warning of Japan's voting on the proposed resolution in the General Assembly and an indicator of possible change in Japan's position. Prime Minister Nobusuke Kishi's visit to Australia in December 1957 marked the end of an aggressive Australian campaign. During the visit a noticeable lowering of intensity on WNG was evident in Australian policy and in discussions with senior Japanese representatives.[31]

Throughout 1957 Australian officials monitored the UN General Assembly votes on WNG. In this context Japan was viewed by the Australians as a nation that was supporting Indonesia, but susceptible to pressure to change its stance (to abstention or even a pro-Dutch position). The decision in Tokyo to abstain from voting removed an important barrier to the improvement of bilateral relations with Australia. During the year both External Affairs and Foreign Affairs officials used bilateral consultations to maintain dialogue on WNG. The information passed on by both sides served to highlight the importance of the relationship and the growing awareness of the usefulness of maintaining regular *ad hoc* discussions on regional issues. In many respects these developments represent an important turning point. Trade discussions were supplemented by political dialogue on regional matters and as such the bilateral relationship was becoming, albeit slowly, multidimensional. Clearly this marked the beginning of a new framework for consultations and established an environment in which External Affairs officials and Japanese counterparts would consult and share information on a wider range of political matters over the next few years.

Towards closer consultation 1958–1962

Indonesian policy of direct action on the WNG dispute from late 1957 to 1962 and the PRRI–Permesta rebellion (1958) was the next set of issues discussed. Officials from Australia and Japan, who were concerned by the security implication of these developments, conveyed interest in discussing Indonesia and regional issues on a more regular basis. Foreign Minister Casey met with Ambassador Suzuki on several occasions in early 1958 to discuss the Sumatran rebellion and domestic developments in Indonesia. Moreover the habit of consultations became more entrenched during this period. For example, while in Jakarta on a short visit in March 1958, Suzuki also liaised with Laurence McIntyre (Australian Ambassador to Indonesia 1956–59) about the domestic development in Indonesia.[32]

Evidence of closer relations was the sending of parliamentary delegations by Australia and Japan in 1958. The general upgrading of political relations and the importance of bilateral relations in general can also be seen in increased contact at the highest levels. Ambassador Watt, in a Ministerial dispatch to Casey, noted that Kishi made the point of attending the farewell dinner for the Australian delegation despite the budget session in the Diet, problems within his own faction and President Sukarno's recent arrival.[33]

Within External Affairs a marked increase in the importance of Japan as a regional actor was also noticeable. One example was the debate generated by the exclusion of the Tokyo Mission from the 1958 Heads of Mission meeting. Gordon Jockel (Head of Pacific and Americas Branch) wrote to Plimsoll (now Assistant Secretary) and documented reasons why the Tokyo Mission should attend. His argument included the following

> Japan represents a non-communist influence in competition with communist China in Southeast Asia in many fields
>
> Japan has made Southeast Asia an area of major Japanese interest for vital political and economic reasons, and
>
> Japanese reparations are an important element in the economy of certain Southeast Asian countries.[34]

The importance of Japan within the Department was emphasised by the decision to broaden relations through enhanced political dialogue. By 1959 Japan was increasingly important to Australia as a trading partner and as an emerging regional power. Walter Crocker's comments on Japan and its growing importance were indicative of Australian thinking. He wrote: 'a regional conference which omits an expert assessment of a Japan perspective is seriously incomplete'.[35] There was, however, residual annoyance at Japan's tendency to support the Afro-Asian stance on WNG. It was clear that senior officials saw US neutrality as a decisive factor in Japan's relative freedom in policy. Alan Watt reported on domestic developments in Japan and made the following suggestion for discussion at the next ANZUS Council meeting (September 1958).

> Since the last elections Japan has seemed to stress her position as an Asian nation disproportionately to her association with the free world countries and even her support for the United Nations. The strongest evidence of

this is her attitude towards the Middle East crisis. The United States is more likely to be sensitive when Japan acts as an Asian nation in the Middle East, than when she acts as an Asian nation in regard to the WNG question. Australia is entitled to relate the two problems and to claim that the United States indifference towards WNG question has an unintended effect of encouraging Japan to apply the Asian approach to other questions, including the Middle East.[36]

Although the issue received limited attention at the ANZUS Council, the use of United States influence was still central to plans to change Japanese views. In February 1959 there was a flurry of press reports in Japan that the Prime Minister had expressed Japan's readiness to take up the question of WNG in the United Nations at some stage. These developments led Watt to discuss the matter with United States Ambassador MacArthur on the basis that MacArthur could, due to his regular contact with Kishi and Foreign Minister Fujiyama, influence their way of thinking.[37]

Richard Casey's visit to Japan in March 1959 and discussion with Foreign Affairs Minister Fujiyama, was an important development in the exchange of political information. Notably, WNG and Indonesia's stance were key issues on the agenda. Both Foreign Ministers expressed concern about United States policy on Indonesia. Casey was of the opinion that United States policy was now more sensible after private pressure from Australia. On WNG Casey discussed Dr Subandrio's recent visit to Canberra that had relieved some tension in bilateral relations with Indonesia but had not resolved the problem of WNG. He noted that Japan, as a member of the Afro-Asian group, did not automatically support the Afro-Asian position and hoped that Japan would exercise a calming influence and continue to look at problems in the United Nations on their merits.[38]

The exchange of information on WNG and on regional issues more generally was becoming a feature of bilateral relations. The original objective was part of a strategy between the United States and the allies to bring Japan closer to 'Free World' countries. However there was already a sharp distinction between Australian and British views of Japan. Australian officials noted with interest a British Foreign Office report on Kishi's visit to London in July 1959. Branch Head Herbert Marshall commented for example, '[o]ne can't escape a sense of distance in the UK approach to Japan. I would think there is evidence that the UK does not see Japan-free world relations with the sharpness that we and the US do'.[39]

The tempo of exchange of information increased after Casey's visit. The Australians were able to monitor President Sukarno's activities while in Tokyo through contacts in the Japanese Foreign Office. Watt was able to ascertain the extent, if any, of Indonesian pressure on Japan. Watt reported on the Sukarno visit to Tokyo (6–19 June) which included an entourage of 29, that there was no reference to WNG at all or the wider dispute with the Netherlands. Japanese contacts stated that from 11 June the purpose of Sukarno's visit was for unofficial relaxation and, interestingly, expressed concern about Sukarno embarrassing himself and hosts.[40]

The *Karel Doorman* affair 1960

The *Karel Doorman* affair was the first real test of Japanese neutrality on WNG. The *Karel Doorman* was a Dutch aircraft carrier on a 'friendly visit' in the Pacific with planned visits to Australia, New Zealand and Japan before returning to the Netherlands. The proposed visit to WNG waters in August 1960 led to Indonesia severing diplomatic ties with the Dutch Government.[41] The reaction in Jakarta was a reflection of the highly charged atmosphere by now openly evident between the Indonesia and the Dutch Governments over WNG. For Indonesians this was a particularly emotional period as sustained efforts in the United Nations General Assembly had not been successful. Another source of Indonesian concern was the Dutch Government decision to pursue a policy of granting independence to the people of WNG within ten years. Combined, the two issues ignited Indonesian passions.

The planned visit by the *Karel Doorman* to Yokohama Port between 8 and 12 September severely tested Japanese relations with Indonesia. Eventually, fierce pressure from Jakarta forced the Japanese Government into the embarrassing position of cancelling the visit. The diplomatic back-down by the Ikeda Cabinet came at a particularly sensitive time given the forced cancellation of President Eisenhower's visit to Japan in June.[42] Moreover, the visit of the *Karel Doorman* to Japan was originally intended as part of commemoration of the 350th anniversary of Dutch-Japanese relations.

From an Australian perspective the *Karel Doorman* affair demonstrated an improved understanding of domestic constraints on Japanese foreign policy. Although there was a mixture of empathy and annoyance with the manner in which Japanese officials dealt with the problem, the final decision to cancel did not come as a surprise. External Affairs Departmental coverage of the *Karel Doorman* affair was extensive and was assisted by an improvement in understanding of domestic politics in Japan. In this sense, reporting from relevant posts such as The Hague, Washington and Jakarta clearly supplemented Tokyo reports on Japanese difficulties with appropriate policy. Indeed McIntyre's coverage of Japanese domestic constraints and departmental concerns over domestic issues such as the Security Treaty issue, led to considerable attention being placed on the *Karel Doorman* affair.

There were, from an External Affairs perspective, a number of positive outcomes from the incident. In particular, the lines of diplomatic contact and communication with Japan, enhanced since 1957, were used during this period. The familiarity between Australian and Japanese counterparts allowed for fairly extensive and frank discussions to take place and importantly this ensured that External Affairs was aware of the difficulties being faced in Japan and prepared for the reversal in policy. Nonetheless there was disappointment and annoyance within the department that Japan's decision was a blow to the success of the *Karel Doorman* as a Dutch public relations exercise.

Towards resolution 1961–62

The *Karel Doorman* affair raised concerns in Canberra about the seeming irrationality of Indonesian policy. The Indonesians appeared willing to risk important trade and investment with Japan over this issue and there was concern that such perceived 'erratic behaviour' might lead to a major conflict. Such fears began to escalate after 1961, as Indonesia pursued a policy of small-scale conflict with the Netherlands. India's use of military force to reclaim Goa from the Portuguese in December 1961, moreover, was an important landmark. The Indian decision to resort to military conflict after negotiations had failed created an international precedent. The Goa precedent also ensured that any solution on WNG would favour Indonesian claims. The Bunker Plan, which was agreed upon in August

1962, with ongoing small-scale Indonesian infiltration of WNG and preparations for a large-scale invasion of Biak, essentially recognised Indonesian claims to WNG.

During this period the level of contact between Australian and Japanese officials specifically on WNG diminished. WNG was raised in bilateral discussions but not with the intensity of earlier meetings. To a certain extent this was understandable as Japan consistently maintained a policy of neutrality on this issue in international forums. The *Karel Doorman* affair, moreover, had been an embarrassment to the Japanese Government and there was a sense of caution in policy making and a tendency to keep a low profile on regional issues.

From an Australian viewpoint, Japan was not central to resolving the WNG dispute, but became increasingly useful as a source of information on developments in Indonesia. Through the close connections Japanese officials and businessmen had established in Jakarta, Australians received a variety of information on Sukarno and domestic issues in Indonesia.

By 1962, with the end of Dutch control of WNG in sight, the issue of establishing trust with Japanese officials and tapping into their information on regional issues became an important objective for Canberra. By February 1962 there was considerable debate within the Department of External Affairs about developing a regular exchange of information with Japan. By the middle of the year broad agreement appears to have emerged about implementing this process within the Department, subject to security checks. Indicative of this view was the information provided for the preparation of Garfield Barwick's visit to Japan in June 1962. Barwick received two briefs from the department. The first, in late May, was a special brief written by W. D. Forsyth (Assistant Secretary Division 2) on developing closer political ties with Japan. Forsyth advocated the need to build an atmosphere of trust that included passing selected political information gathered by Australians in order to receive information from the Japanese on areas of special interest to Australia.[43] In the departmental brief written in June, Barwick was provided with the key issues affecting bilateral relations such as Article 35 of GATT. He was also advised to gather Japanese views on Chinese representation in the UN, developments in Korea and the situation in Laos and Vietnam.[44]

Barwick met with Japanese Foreign Minister Zentaro Kosaka a few days later. The Tokyo leg of the Foreign Minister's visit (9–15 June, 1962) appears to have had a profound impact on Barwick. He cabled Canberra on his last day in Japan to urge the amendment of article 35 of GATT and to raise the idea of a regular Japan-Australia ministerial conference.[45] Neither issue was new but the Barwick's cable suggested that he was impressed with the level of interaction with Japanese officials and the overall importance of Japan to Australian national interests.

Events in Indonesia turned Australian and Japanese attention back to WNG. In July and August of 1962 as negotiations were being finalised, Indonesian troops were involved in infiltration of WNG and there still existed considerable tension due to the possibility of outright conflict. In late July this concern was sufficient for Japanese Ambassador Ohta to call in to the Department and suggest closer consultation and cooperation on Indonesia. Ohta was reported as saying

> ...in the long term there was likely to be need for particularly close consultation and cooperation between Australia and Japan, for both of whom relations with Indonesia were of a very great importance, in their policies towards that country.[46]

The development of closer consultation on Indonesia took several forms and continued throughout 1962. In mid August, as an agreement on WNG was finally reached between Indonesia and the Netherlands, the Japanese were relieved and publicly expressed satisfaction with the result. Yet there were serious concerns within the Foreign Ministry. In discussions with Deputy Vice Minister Shigenobu Shima in late August, McIntyre reported on Japanese unease with the nature of the agreement and the way the settlement was reached.[47] It was a clear indication of Japanese unease with Indonesian policy. Undoubtedly this was welcomed in Canberra where such Japanese sentiment had been noticeable in discussions since the *Karel Doorman* incident two years previously. In order to encourage closer alignment in regional policies, officers were instructed that they could draw on, with discretion, material such as fortnightly summaries from the Australian Embassy in Jakarta in discussing Indonesia with the Japanese Ministry.[48]

Conclusion

The WNG dispute signified the beginning of regular close consultation between Australia and Japan on regional matters and the process of exchange of political information. Discussion moved from the narrow issue of voting in the UN to a broader set of concerns about regional security and a pooling of political information.

The dispute, moreover, was a catalyst for the development of Australia-Japan political relations. From an Australian perspective, the Japanese sympathetic position towards Indonesia would have been perplexing and frustrating. At this stage there was only limited first-hand knowledge of Japanese foreign policy objectives. Moreover there was limited appreciation in Canberra of the bonds forged between Japanese and Indonesians during the Japanese occupation of Java. Indeed the pro-active style adopted by External Affairs officers on the dispute would also suggest a degree of annoyance at Japan's unwillingness to comply with Australian pressure to support the Dutch position.

Despite this low-level tension, there were compelling reasons for political consultation; both countries were firmly anchored in the US strategic alliance, were beginning to enjoy a highly profitable trade relationship, and shared the view that Indonesia was of critical importance to regional stability. In essence these shared interests were the basis for regular consultations on other regional matters. Notably the frequency of dialogue and the gradual increase in the range of issues discussed continued despite the change in personnel on both sides. Clearly senior officials in Canberra and Tokyo supported the new engagement and were looking at new initiatives to further develop bilateral relations.

A notable feature of regular consultation on WNG was a sense of familiarity not readily evident in earlier meetings. A useful working relationship developed between key senior officials. Casey and his Departmental Head Arthur Tange encouraged this process and offered strong leadership. Watt and McIntyre in Tokyo and their Japanese counterparts in Canberra (Ambassadors Suzuki, Narita and Ohta) actively strove to pursue these goals and were entrepreneurial in their efforts. Within External Affairs, moreover, senior officers such as Plimsoll, Shaw, Forsyth and McNichol had prior personal and professional experience of Japan: Shaw and McNicol had both been posted to the Tokyo Embassy in the 1940s; Plimsoll was at one time Australia's representative on the Far East Commission. As such, officers in the Department were searching for ways to expand regional dialogue. An example was Departmental support for the reciprocal exchange of political information in 1962. The regular exchange of information offered increasingly valuable information on developments in Indonesia.

Clearly the WNG dispute and political issues in Indonesia had a longer-term effect on bilateral relations. Regular dialogue on Indonesia offered the opportunity and the disposition for policymakers to exchange views and work towards a more collaborative environment on regional matters. This was a mutually beneficial process and led to a heightened understanding of foreign policy objectives in both countries. However Australia was not ultimately successful in influencing Japanese policy on WNG as this regular dialogue had only minimal impact on Japanese policy. What is significant was the increased appreciation and awareness within Canberra of Japanese policies and Japan's potential as an emerging regional economic power.

An examination of Australia-Japan dialogue on WNG also adds to an understanding of how Australia dealt with the WNG issue. Understandably research on WNG has concentrated on the major players: Indonesia, the Dutch, the United States and Australia. From an Australian perspective the impact of the dispute on regional diplomacy and overall Australian foreign policy has also been examined. However, the case study adds a new dimension to the existing literature. The dialogue between Australia and Japan highlights the proactive style of diplomacy pursued by Australians, particularly from 1950 to 1959, and offers insight into Australian efforts to monitor closely voting patterns in the United Nations General Assembly. Japan was not a key player in the dispute; nonetheless the Australian initiatives to influence Japanese policy reveals how determined the Australian Government was during the period. Although the chapter focuses on the development of dialogue on political issues between Australia and Japan, the case study underlines the importance of Indonesia in Australian policy and how this served to foster closer bilateral relations between Australia and Japan.

Notes

1 West New Guinea is also referred to as Netherlands New Guinea, Dutch New Guinea, West Irian and by its Indonesian names Irian Jaya and Papua Barat (West Papua) during this period.

2 See T.B. Millar, *Australia in War and Peace*, ANU Press, Canberra, 1991, 2nd edition, p.185 and Alan Watt, *Australian Foreign Policy, 1935–66*, OUP, Melbourne, 1968, p. 251.

3 The four failed attempts, between 1954 and 1957 were in the form of resolutions in the 9th, 10th, 11th and 12th sessions of the General Assembly.

4 *Yearbook of the United Nations*, Columbia University Press in Cooperation with the United Nations (New York, 1962: 124–25). The plebiscite was held in 1969 under dubious conditions and resulted in an overwhelming majority in favour of being part of the Republic of Indonesia.

5 National Archives of Australia (NAA): Department of External Affairs (DEA) files on Japan A1838/278 file 3103/10/1 pt 3, record of conversation between Japanese Ambassador Haruhiko Nishi and Secretary DEA, 12 October 1954.

6 NAA: A 1838/278, file 3103/10/1 pt 4, record of discussion between Japanese Consul Masayoshi Kakitsubo and James Plimsoll, 1 April 1955.

7 NAA: 956/2, 4 April 1955, file 221/4/4, record of discussion between Australian Ambassador Ronald Walker and Mr Tani in Tokyo, 4 April 1955.

8 NAA: A 9564/2, file 221/4/4 part 1, record of discussion between Australian Ambassador T. Moodie and Ambassador Ohta in Rangoon, 7 May 1955.

9 NAA: A 5105/3 file 223/1 pt 2, Alan Watt to Arthur Tange, memo 1006, 12 December 1956.

10 NAA: A 1838/278, letter, Alan Watt to Richard Casey, 13 December 1956.

11 NAA: A423, file 3103/10/1 pt 4, record of conversation between Atsushi Uyama, Counsellor, and James Plimsoll, 4 January 1957.

12 NAA: A5105/3, file 227/18/2 pt11, Alan Watt to DEA, Canberra, 16 February 1957.

13 NAA: A5105/3, file 227/18/2 pt11, Watt to DEA, Canberra, Cable no 62, 21 February 1957.

14 NAA: A5105/3, file 227/18/2 pt11, Watt to External Affairs, Canberra, Cable no 78, 8 March 1957.

15 For a detailed account of Kishi's involvement with the Kinoshita Trading Company and the associated ships scandal see Masashi Nishihara, *The Japanese and Sukarno's Indonesia: Tokyo-Jakarta Relations, 1951–1966* University Press of Hawaii, Honolulu 1975:102–12.

16 NAA: A5105/3, file 227/18/2 pt 11, Watt to External Affairs, memo no 239, 11 March 1957.

17 NAA: A 1838/278, file 3103/10/11/2/1 pt, record of discussion between Plimsoll and Nara, 15 April 1957.

18 NAA: A1838/278, file 3103/10/11/2/1, Prime Minister's brief on Japan for 1957 Visit, March 1957.

19 NAA: A1838/278, file no 3103/10/11/2/1, Prime Minister's brief on Japan for 1957 Visit, March 1957.

20   NAA: A1838/278, File 3103/10/11/2/1 pt 1, cablegram from Australian Trade Commission in Hong Kong, 18 April 1957.

21   NAA: A1838/278, file 3103/10/1 pt 5, record of conversation between Arthur Tange and Tadakatsu Suzuki (Japanese Ambassador), Canberra, 19 July 1957.

22   NAA: A5105/3, file no 227/18/2 pt1, Watt to External Affairs, 22 August 1957.

23   NAA: A1838/278, file 3103/10/1 pt 5, record of conversation between Tadakatsu Suzuki, Atsushi Uyama, Foreign Minister Richard Casey and Allan Loomes, 27 August 1957.

24   NAA: A1838/277, file 3036/11/89, report by officer Blakeney, ' Confidential view of Japanese interest in economic development of West New Guinea', 2 December 1959.

25   NAA: A1838/280, , file 3103/10/11/1 pt1, Australia-Japan Relations—A Balance Sheet, Departmental Report, 27 September 1957.

26   NAA: A1838/278, file 3103/10/1 pt 5, record of conversation between Suzuki, Casey and Loomes, 13 November 1957.

27   NAA: A5105/3, file no 227/18/2 pt1, Watt to Tange, Memo no. 1066, 8 November 1957.

28   Despite concessions, the final reparations agreement was more favourable to Japan than to Indonesia. For a detailed examination see Masashi Nishihara *The Japanese and Sukarno's Indonesia*, Chapters 2–5.

29   NAA: A1838/280, file no 3103/10/1 pt 6, Ronald Walker (Head of Australian Mission, UN) to External Affairs, Cable no 1867, 26 November 1957.

30   NAA: A1838/280, , file 3103/10/1, record of conversation between Japanese Ambassador Suzuki and Secretary DEA recorded by Officer Marshall, 19 November 1957.

31   NAA: A1838/280, file 3103/10/1 pt 6, Kishi's visit, Record of discussion, 4 December 1957. The WNG issue was deliberately set aside during Prime Ministerial and other formal discussions.

32   NAA: A 1838/280, file 3103/10/1 part 6, record of discussion between Minister of External Affairs and Ambassador Suzuki, 31 March 1958. The main point discussed was the possibility of rapprochement between Sukarno and Hatta.

33   NAA: A1838/283, file 3103/10/10/2/1 pt 1, letter from Ambassador Watt to Foreign Minister Casey, 30 January 1958.

34   NAA: A 1838/280, file 3103/10/6 pt 2, letter from Plimsoll to Jockel on Tokyo representation at Heads of Mission meeting, 10 February 1959.

35   NAA: A1838/280, file 3103/10/6 pt 2, Australian High Commissioner William Crocker to External Affairs cable no 51, 24 January 1959.

36   NAA: A9564/2, file 221/4/2 pt 4, Alan Watt to The Secretary, memo no 803, 31 July 1958.

37   NAA: A1838/283, file 3036/6/1 pt 35, record of conversation between Watt and Douglas MacArthur, 17 February 1957.

38   NAA: A 1838/1, file no 3103/10/11/1 pt, record of conversation between Foreign Ministers Richard Casey and Mr Fujiyama, 25 March 1959

39   NAA: A1838/283, file 3103/10/1/pt 8, file note from H. Marshall to Gordon Jockel, 25 June 1959.

40   NAA: A1505/3, file no 227/11/12/ pt 3, memo no 614, Alan Watt to the Secretary, 25 June 1959.

41   K.V. Kesavan, *Japan's Relations with Southeast Asia: 1952–60*, Somiya Publications 1972 Bombay:170.

42   The Eisenhower visit to Japan was cancelled due to unprecedented protests in Tokyo and other major cities over the signing of the 1960 Security Treaty.

43   NAA: A 1838/280, file no 3103/10/1 pt 9, 'Australian Policy towards Japan', Secret information brief for Minister, 21 May 1962 (McIntyre had replaced Watt as Ambassador in Tokyo in May 1960).

44   NAA: A1838, file no 3101/10/11/2 pt 5, 'Brief for Minister's visit to Japan', June 1962.

45   NAA: A1838, file no 3101/10/11/2 pt 5, Barwick to EA, 15 June 1962.

46   NAA: A1838/2, file 915/9 pt 49, record of conversation between Ohta and H. Anderson, 20 July 1962.

47   NAA: A1838/280, file 3103/7/1 pt 3, conversation with Deputy Vice-Minister for Foreign Affairs, 30 August 1962.

48   NAA: A 5105/3, file 227/1/2 pt 6, memo no 551, W. D. Forsyth (Assistant Secretary) to Tokyo Embassy, 2 October 1962.

References

Australia, National Archives, 1954–62. Department of External Affairs, files on Japan.

Kesavan, K.V., 1972. *Japan's relations with Southeast Asia: 1952–60*, Somiya Publications, Bombay.

Millar, T.B., 1991. *Australia in War and Peace*, The Australian National University Press, Canberra.

Nishihara, M., 1975. *The Japanese and Sukarno's Indonesia: Tokyo–Jakarta Relations, 1951–1966*, University Press of Hawaii, Honolulu.

United Nations, 1962. *Yearbook of the United Nations*, Columbia University Press in co-operation with the United Nations, New York.

Watt, A., 1968. *Australian Foreign Policy 1935-66*, Oxford University Press, Melbourne.

Acknowledgments

The author wishes to thank Professor Alan Rix, Professor Bill Tow, Dr Karim Najjarine and Trevor Wilson for comments on an early draft of this paper. The author alone is responsible for any errors or short-comings.

3 THE JAPAN-AUSTRALIA PARTNERSHIP IN THE ERA OF THE EAST ASIAN COMMUNITY

CAN THEY ADVANCE TOGETHER?

Takashi Terada

Australia's engagement with East Asia and the Pacific was widely perceived to be its overriding foreign policy priority during the 1980s and 90s, especially when Prime Ministers Hawke and Keating were in power. Australia was actively engaged in regional economic diplomacy. The partnership with Japan functioned successfully as part of Australia's strategy through their joint initiatives in establishing regional economic institutions such as the Pacific Economic Cooperation Council (PECC) in 1980 and the Asia Pacific Economic Cooperation (APEC) forum in 1989, each serving as catalysts in promoting Australia's regional engagement at that time. These regional institutions were designed to promote economic cooperation with member states and, more symbolically, to nurture togetherness with them by tackling common problems and pursuing shared goals such as trade liberalisation in the region. Sharing a view with Australia that the stability and prosperity in East Asia and the Pacific was a vital national interest, Japan—Australia's largest trading partner—consistently supported Australia's engagement policy. The significance of Japan's supportive role in Australia's engagement was fully acknowledged by Australia, as declared in Australia's first *Foreign and Trade Policy White Paper* that 'the partnership with Japan will have a decisive bearing on

Australia's overall standing in East Asia and [Australia's] degree of participation in regional affairs' (Commonwealth of Australia 1997:60).

However, the foreign policy priorities and approaches of the Howard government were perceived to be distinctive from those of the Hawke and Keating governments. Conspicuous differences stemmed from Howard's deliberate design and implementation of his foreign policy which placed a higher priority on security issues, attached more significance to relations with the United States and the United Kingdom, and promoted bilateral trading arrangements in lieu of regional institutions. Enormous changes emerged in East Asia after Howard came into power in 1996. The Asian financial crisis, the aftermath of continued economic and political uncertainty, especially in Southeast Asia, the historic transition to democracy and decentralised rule in Indonesia, and East Timor's independence movement were all intermingled in the articulation of his foreign policy. For domestic political reasons, Howard also displayed indifference to the feelings of Southeast Asians, as seen in his 'pre-emptive strike' statement made in December 2002, which indicated that he was prepared to order pre-emptive strikes in Southeast Asia to prevent terrorists' attacks against Australia. These characteristics helped create a general impression in East Asia that Australia had turned away from engagement with the region, despite the Howard government's frequent statements about Australia's continuing interest in strengthening relations with East Asia. This foreign policy approach under Howard can be characterised as 'inconsistent engagement', representing a divergence between foreign policy statements and actual implementation.

One of the most striking features of this 'inconsistent engagement with East Asia' was that there was no regional institution that Australia could utilise to promote its foreign policy. Australia's exclusion from ASEAN+3— which in recent years became more institutionalised—and the declining significance of the Asia Pacific Economic Cooperation process (APEC) highlighted the absence of a useful foundation for Australia's further engagement with East Asia, and at once symbolised Australia's growing isolation in the region. This also meant that Japan and Australia lacked a common foreign policy grounding in regionalism, an essential component that had characterised the Australia-Japan partnership over several decades.

With Japan as a major player in East Asian regionalism, Australia's increasing indifference towards East Asian affairs and its declining presence could be seen as detrimental to the Japan-Australia partnership.

Since winning a fourth term in October 2004, however, Howard has directed his foreign policy focus towards forging closer relations with East Asia by vigorously pursuing bilateral and regional diplomacy. This is evidenced by Australia's improved relations with Indonesia and Malaysia, two Southeast Asian countries that had a history of overt criticism of Howard's regional policy approaches. Even his former political rivals such as John Hewson (*Australian Financial Review*, 3 December 2004) and Paul Keating (*Sydney Morning Herald*, 4 April 2005) acknowledge the achievements Howard made through his later diplomacy in East Asia, including the announcements on the launch of free trade agreement (FTA) negotiations with ASEAN and China.

This chapter aims to examine the implications of the rise of East Asian regionalism for the Australia-Japan partnership. In particular, it investigates whether both nations can sustain their partnership, which evolved around regionalism over a number of decades, exploring the upsurge of Japan's interest in East Asian regionalism and examining Australia's foreign policy under the Howard Government. A clear regionalist approach was missing during the Howard government's first three terms (1996–2004), but his government demonstrated a keener interest in furthering relations with East Asian countries and promoting East Asian regionalism since late 2004. The change in Australia's stance on East Asia was well accepted by the region, allowing Australia to participate in the first East Asian Summit, held in Kuala Lumpur in December 2005.

Rise of East Asian regionalism

Regionalism is a concrete manifestation of regional consciousness perceived by members because it needs a boundary to differentiate insiders (members) from outsiders (non-members). A regional concept that establishes a particular geographical boundary is necessary for any instance of regionalism. The concept of East Asia as a region is relatively new. Until the appearance of the abortive East Asian Economic Caucus (EAEC) idea, which was put forward by Prime Minister Mahathir of Malaysia in the early 1990s, there was no strong conceptual framework for regionalism in East Asia as a whole. What was significant in Mahathir's EAEC proposal was that he introduced the concept of East Asia, integrating Northeast Asia and Southeast Asia into one regional unity. Most of these countries had previously been involved in 'Asia Pacific', 'Southeast Asian', or 'Pacific' regional institutions for economic cooperation, including APEC, the Pacific Economic Cooperation Council (PECC), or ASEAN. It was difficult for regional countries to accept the 'East Asia' concept initially because other regional institutions, especially APEC, were prominent as useful regional institutions during the 1990s. Many countries in East Asia thus found it unnecessary to rush into the creation of East Asian regionalism. This was the case in Japan, whose attitude to the EAEC was lukewarm, despite Mahathir's strong expectations of its leadership role (Terada 2003).

A major reason for Japan's unsupportive stance was that Japan did not view 'East Asia' as a concept for regional cooperation. Japan instead adhered to the concept of 'Asia Pacific', which includes the Pacific nations such as the United States and Australia, as a basis for promoting regional economic cooperation. In fact, it was Japan and Australia that exercised coordinated leadership in the establishment of APEC in 1989 (Terada 1999). Japan's refusal at that time to become involved in the formation of East Asian regionalism meant that there was insufficient critical driving force towards creating East Asian regionalism. Yet later it was to be Japanese Prime Minister Junichiro Koizumi (2002a) who started urging regional countries to 'act together and advance together', envisaging the creation of an East Asian community in a major speech in Singapore in January 2002. Koizumi's insistence on the creation of a community in East Asia triggered other East Asian leaders to follow Japan's initiative. This is partly because Japan, previously non-committal towards the EAEC, now became one of the most enthusiastic supporters of East Asian regionalism and even displayed its readiness to lead the creation of an East Asian community.

A regional institution around which the community in East Asia is expected to revolve is the ASEAN+3 framework established in 1997 in Kuala Lumpur, as Koizumi suggested in his Singapore speech, to make 'the best use of (ASEAN+3) to secure prosperity and stability' in East Asia. As in Europe, institutionalisation of ASEAN+3 is expected to be crucial to successful community building and coordinated management of a variety of emerging regional problems in East Asia. Japan's strong involvement in the ASEAN+3 process and its advocacy of an East Asian community have been milestones for East Asian regionalism, given Japan's initial hesitation to become involved in the EAEC. Regional cooperation on the ASEAN+3 basis is now extending to such areas as an emergency communications network among the energy ministers, the creation of an East Asian rice reserve system, a framework action plan to prevent and control SARS (severe acute respiratory syndrome), and a new oil reserve system to prepare for possible petroleum shortages arising from instability in the Middle East. Japan has found the development of these cooperative schemes in East Asia useful as vehicles encouraging the establishment of an East Asian community. The crux of the argument lies in the fact that Australia was excluded from these emerging regional cooperation schemes in East Asia, underlining the lack of an effective regional mechanism where Japan and Australia would exercise policy coordination for regional cooperation as they did in the case of PECC and APEC.

The Australia-Japan partnership and APEC

The history of the development of Asia Pacific economic cooperation is important in the evolution of Australia-Japan relations. Regional economic cooperation was a significant national interest for both countries, and both were encouraged to cooperate in building new institutions in the region. Major regional economic institutions such as the Pacific Trade and Development Forum (PAFTAD), the Pacific Basin Economic Council (PBEC), PECC, and APEC were the products of initiatives taken jointly by Japanese and Australians. Although the interests of both countries in promoting regional economic cooperation were distinctive, certain elements drew the two countries together in these institution-building endeavours. The most conspicuous element was diplomatic complementarity between the two countries. Japan's attempt to conquer the Asia Pacific region in World War II and its subsequent rapidly growing economic presence were obstacles to its involvement in regional economic diplomacy. Australia's traditional ties with Britain and its 'White Australia' policy initially made it difficult for Australia to be accepted by other regional countries. These historical and cultural disadvantages led Australia to strive all the more in its regional diplomacy, while Japan's economic presence and its cultural and historical closeness to other Asian countries were useful to Australia's regional diplomacy. On the other hand, Australia's non-threatening middle-power status, underpinned by its lesser economic presence, and its active and dexterous diplomacy, compensated for Japan's more muted regional diplomatic role. This partnership—wherein each compensated for the other's shortcomings—functioned well in the establishment of PECC and APEC (Terada 2000).

When APEC emerged as a major regional institution in 1989, it represented the achievement of maturity and success in the Australia-Japan relationship because Japan and Australia had played key roles in its establishment. APEC has adequately proven the viability of a 'merger' between two distinct nations, which complemented each other to overcome their national shortcomings. Together they represented a formidable regional force, particularly as both countries continued to cooperate in the development of the APEC process. The APEC Leaders' meeting, the highest level meeting within the APEC framework, stemmed from ideas floated by Australian Prime Ministers Hawke and Keating, which Japan strongly supported.[1] Describing an episode where the United States urged Australia to join a movement for encircling Japan with 'a network of free-trade arrangements' in 1992, Keating (2000:33–4) clearly stressed that this option was not in Australia's interest and wrote 'we did not benefit from approaches that discriminated against Japan', due in part to Australia's trade surpluses with Japan. Even though this rejection invited bitter reactions from the United States, it was based on Keating's desire to convey a message to Australia and the region that 'there was a shift in our approach to Asia', a symbol of which was Australia's keener engagement in regionalism such as APEC. At the 1995 APEC Leaders' Meeting in Osaka, Japan and Australia were in conflict over the inclusion of areas like agricultural products for achieving the Bogor Declaration, but they reached a compromise in the course of bilateral meetings convened to resolve the problem; the meeting between Prime Minister Keating and Minister for International Trade and Industry Hashimoto was especially critical in achieving this (Terada 2000).

However, APEC is perceived to have lost its functional momentum after the Asian financial crisis and its failure to advance the Early Voluntary Sectoral Liberalisation (EVSL) program. A view has emerged that APEC has failed to deliver on its core trade liberalisation goal (Ravenhill 2001), although the targets for trade liberalisation are still down the track and there is some time before they have to be met. Japan managed to entice some ASEAN countries to support its stand on ruling out the inclusion of agriculture in EVSL by offering substantial aid in the wake of the Asian financial crisis at the 1998 APEC meeting in Kuala Lumpur. Australia's Trade Minister Tim Fischer was 'underwhelmed at the Japanese failure' (*The Australian*, 16 November 1998). These developments reflected the increasingly distinctive Australian and Japanese approaches to trade liberalisation, especially over the treatment of agricultural products. They also foreshadowed that the Australia-Japan partnership might eventually be frustrated over regional economic cooperation, especially over trade liberalisation projects.

Howard's indifference to East Asia in his foreign policy and his sporadic regional commitments had the effect of undermining the viability of APEC and its ability to exercise regional economic leadership. All Australian prime ministers from the early 1970s—Whitlam (1981), Fraser (1984), Hawke (1994) and Keating (2000)—displayed a special interest in regional economic institutions and took decisive steps to give effect to this interest. Australia's leadership in regional institution building was, historically, a positive signal of Australia's engagement with East Asia and the Pacific, both to the region and at home. Former foreign minister Percy Spender (1969:195) commented that 'our future to an ever-increasing degree depends upon the political stability of our Asian neighbours, upon the economic well-being of Asian peoples and upon understanding and friendly relations between Australia and Asia'. This statement epitomises what has come to reflect Australia's comprehensive and consistent interests in engagement policy. Yet, as Dalrymple states, while Labor governments tried to 'minimise the perception of differences between Australia and East Asia through the postulation of convergence, the Howard government was comfortable in portraying Australia as, in effect, permanently and irreparably separate from East Asia' (2003:156). Simon Crean, then Opposition Leader, targeted the inconsistency of Howard's foreign policy on regional engagement: 'the Howard Government's decision to shift foreign policy away from the processes on regional engagement and to focus exclusively on bilateralism has undermined 50 years of bipartisanship in this country' (*Sydney Morning Herald*, 5 May 2002).

It was Hawke's and Keating's vision that APEC would become a major economic driving force in the region, accelerating the movement towards regional trade liberalisation and ensuring the continual prosperity and security of the region. But with Keating's demise in 1996, the importance of APEC as the symbolic organisation of Australia's regional engagement and the main vehicle to promote regional trade liberalisation was relegated to the periphery in Australia's political sphere. The Howard government's distancing of itself from East Asia was also strongly criticised by Australian academics and former senior diplomats. For instance, Ross Garnaut, Peter Drysdale and Stuart Harris, long-standing experts on politics and economics in East Asia at the Australian National University, wrote an article to *The Australian* (7 November 2001) in their joint names, demonstrating that Australia's relations with the region became 'more fragile and less productive than at any time for several decades'. Richard Woolcott, former Secretary of the Department of Foreign Affairs and Trade, also criticised Howard's inability to carefully and skilfully handle Australia's relations with its neighbours, especially Indonesia: 'it is painful to encounter the extent to which Howard is widely seen in our region as a narrowly focused domestic politician, uninterested in and uncomfortable with Australia's Asian and Pacific neighbours' (*Sydney Morning Herald*, 6 November 2001).

From the perspective from Japan, APEC's ineffective trade liberalisation program in part prompted Japan to become more enthusiastic in pursuing and formulating other regional and bilateral arrangements. The fact that both Japanese foreign and trade ministers did not attend the 2002 APEC Mexico meeting strengthens the perception that Japan placed more priority on ASEAN+3 than on APEC. In short, while ASEAN+3 has become more institutionalised and ideas for the establishment of an East Asian community including a regional integration scheme have been more vigorously pursued by many countries in the region, APEC—which Japan and Australia once commonly regarded as the principal regional organisation—came to be widely seen to be 'crisis-stricken, becalmed or adrift' (Webber 2001:339).

Trade liberalisation schemes without 'the Pacific' nations

One of the important implications of APEC's ineffective trade liberalisation program is that member states have instead promoted bilateral arrangements to attain further trade liberalisation, a trend that involves Japan and Australia as well. More significantly, these moves towards trade liberalisation can also be associated with ASEAN+3 forming a kind of an East Asian free trade agreement that excludes the Pacific nations such as the United States and Australia. In effect, while Australia was disengaged from East Asia, Japan, along with China, became a linchpin in the FTA movement in East Asia by employing the so-called 'multilayered trade policy', focused on the pursuit of bilateral and regional FTAs that would complement the World Trade Organization (WTO)-based multilateral attempts to facilitate the endeavours towards global trade liberalisation. Symbolically, this trade policy approach of Japan triggered a domino effect of FTAs in East Asia. For instance, China's interest in concluding FTAs is believed to have been spurred by Japan's interest in an FTA with South Korea, announced in October 1998. This move by Japan and South Korea led China to feel isolated from the FTA movement in East Asia. China ultimately joined this movement by proposing an FTA with ASEAN in October 2000, which was officially agreed on in November 2001.

Koizumi's 2002 proposal for a Japan-ASEAN Comprehensive Economic Partnership Agreement, which would include FTA elements, was a response to the China-ASEAN FTA proposal. The Japan-Singapore Economic Partnership Agreement (JSEPA), signed in 2002, prompted Malaysia and Indonesia, initially the least enthusiastic about bilateral FTAs in the region, to develop their own FTA proposals with Japan (Terada 2006). China's and Japan's FTA approaches to ASEAN also contributed to South Korea's developing an interest in pursuing the same path when, at the 2004 ASEAN Economic Ministers' meeting in Jakarta, South Korea agreed with ASEAN to complete an FTA by 2009. These developments reflected the growing push for the completion of FTAs with ASEAN by Japan, China and South

Korea, paving the way for the eventual establishment of an East Asian FTA through the possible consolidation of the existing bilateral and regional FTAs in the region.

The 2003 ASEAN+3 summit meeting in Bali witnessed a number of statements and speeches that stressed the desirability of East Asian cooperation, including a region-wide FTA. This seemed to represent significant progress in the institutionalisation of ASEAN+3. Chinese Premier Wen Jiabao proposed that research be undertaken for the establishment of a free trade area in East Asia, signifying China's interest in promoting greater integration between the 13 East Asian economies. South Korean President Roh Moo-hyun underscored the desirability of further promoting exchanges of people and information in East Asia that would encourage even wider regional integration. Singapore Prime Minister Goh Chok Tong asked Japan and China to seek to negotiate a bilateral FTA with a view to the creation of an East Asian FTA, reflecting a general view in the region that the movement towards an FTA between these two nations was a missing link in the recent proliferation of FTAs in East Asia (*Nihon Keizai Shimbun*, 8 October 2003).

The ineffectiveness of APEC also led to Japan's decision to abandon its pursuit of 'open regionalism', an approach to which Japan had committed itself over many years in line with the non-discriminatory provisions of the GATT (Article 1). Instead, Japan developed its interest in discriminatory bilateral and regional trading arrangements under GATT Article 24. Japan's commitment to open regionalism, in an attempt to seek consistency between regionalism and multilateralism, subsequently became the benchmark of APEC's trade liberalisation approach. Open regionalism is based on most-favoured nation (MFN) treatment, which was set up within the GATT system to avoid trade discrimination against third states by granting equal treatment to all. When a regional economic institution fostered trade liberalisation among its members, controversy would arise as to whether the benefits gained through liberalisation within the region would be applied to outsiders or not. Maintaining consistency with the non-discrimination principle of GATT Article 1 was therefore an issue in any regional policy approach that would be considered by Japan. Importantly, developing the concept of open regionalism was a joint undertaking between the Japanese and Australian academics over the decades; the Japanese coined the term and set up the basic framework, and Australians developed the concept with empirical research (Terada 1998). For instance, Peter Drysdale (1988:237–38), who discussed the concept at the 1980 Pacific Community Seminar in Canberra with Saburo Okita (former Japanese Foreign Minister and architect of Asia Pacific Economic Cooperation), had in 1968 attended the first PAFTAD meeting, which discussed the feasibility of a Pacific Free Trade Area (PAFTA), an idea proposed by Kiyoshi Kojima, elaborated the concept he then called 'regionalism without discrimination'. Drysdale justified creating an Asia Pacific regionalism based on unconditional MFN by arguing that 'the concentration of Pacific countries' trade within the Pacific is such that most of the benefits from trade liberalisation on an MFN basis are likely to accrue within the region'. In fact, in 1965 the ratio of intra-regional trade among nations in Asia and the Pacific accounted for 46.8 and 51.9 per cent in exports and imports, respectively, and these figures rose to 64.6 and 62.5 per cent in 1987 (cited in Garnaut 1997:148). This is essentially how some of the basic ideas for the subsequent creation of APEC were conceived in Japan and Australia.

Some time later, however, Noboru Hatakeyama (1996), former Vice Minister of International Affairs at the Ministry of International Trade and Industry (MITI) and subsequently Chairman of Japan External Trade Organisation (JETRO), began to promote FTAs as an option for Japan's international trade policy, insisting that Japan should consider a trade policy that involved bilateral and regional arrangements despite these arrangements being discriminatory. This is an approach that Japan itself had long criticised. While stressing that FTAs were 'legal' as stipulated in GATT Article 24, Hatakeyama suggested that Japan should confront the reality of growing bilateral and regional FTA networks in the world and remove the 'taboo' surrounding Japanese trade policy over many years by pursuing a 'multilayered' trade policy. Hatakeyama (1996) wrote that Japan was not a 'saint', implying that Japan should also be allowed, like other countries, to have FTAs. Hatakeyama (personal interview, 10 April 2003, Tokyo) later added that 'it was good in the end that the multilayered approach would allow Japan to make more options for promoting trade liberalisation'. These propositions gradually came to be shared by many officials in MITI after Mexico and South Korea approached Japan for FTAs in late 1998, at the same time as the concept of open regionalism was gradually losing its policy relevance and validity within the Ministry. Japan's growing interest in the pursuit of bilateral and regional FTAs—with their legally binding provisions for the reciprocal exchange of preferences which discriminate against non-partner countries—marks a distinctive departure from APEC's approach to non-discriminatory and globally-oriented regional integration that Japan strongly supported over many years.

Significantly, this paradigm shift in Japanese trade policy did not originally entail the possibility of concluding an FTA with Australia, which also pursued FTAs vigorously. It is true that Howard was able to persuade Koizumi to set up an FTA study group to examine the feasibility of such an agreement when he visited Japan in May 2005. But it was believed that an FTA with Australia, one of the world's largest agriculture exporters, would inevitably provoke a strong resistance from Japan's agricultural pressure groups and politicians, who rely on farmers' votes for their elections and who oppose liberalisation of key agricultural sectors such as rice, beef, wheat, or sugar. Indeed, Japan still maintained substantially high tariffs on those products, for example rice (778 per cent), sugar (325 per cent), wheat (252 per cent) and beef (50 per cent) (*Nihon Keizai Shimbun*, 7 November 2005). Even Japan's FTA with Singapore—which hardly exports any agricultural products to Japan—contained a provision for only a 14 per cent increase in the number of Japan's zero-tariff commitments with regard to agricultural products. Moreover, the content of this commitment had already been negotiated within the WTO framework, meaning that there were no agricultural products in the JSEPA from which Japan agreed to remove tariffs (Terada 2006). This fact underlines the infeasibility of the Japan-Australia FTA. As a senior official of the Ministry of Agriculture, Forestry and Fisheries stated: '[s]hould Japan be able to forge a FTA with Australia, it could do so with all of the countries in the world' (personal interview 11 July 2002, Tokyo). This suggested that Japan and Australia, between whom an FTA was seen as highly unlikely to materialise, would not easily maintain their partnership in promoting regional economic integration in East Asia, even if Australia intended to join the movement towards the formation of an East Asian FTA.

The Australia-Japan partnership in an East Asian community

As a nation that was pursuing the concept of 'Asia-Pacific' or 'Pacific' regionalism, Japan was previously uninterested in joining regional institutions that excluded 'Pacific' nations. This was evident in Japan's strong insistence on America's inclusion in the first APEC meeting, despite Australia's hesitation over the establishment of APEC (Terada 1999). Japan supported Australia's inclusion in East Asian regionalism, as seen in its announcement in April 1995 that 'it would not participate in the informal ASEAN 7+3 meeting at Phuket unless ASEAN invited Australia and New Zealand as well' (cited in Leong 2000:78). Japan was also supportive of Australia's membership in the Asia-Europe Meeting (ASEM) that initially comprised the then 15-member European Union and 10 Asian countries. Prime Minister Hashimoto (1997) explicitly reiterated this position during his visit to Canberra in April 1997: '[w]e should like to do our part for that ... We are taking this task on ourselves, as we would like you to join ASEM as a member of the Asian side.'

Yet, for Japan to continue to recognise the significance of the Japan-Australia partnership, Australia needed to be more explicitly committed to engagement with East Asia. When Japan expressed its support for Australia's participation in ASEM, there was 'uncertainty how hard Australia wanted to push its bid' for its ASEM membership and Australia's 'soft-pedalling' approach to membership confused and concerned Japan (*Australian Financial Review*, 28 April 1998). Moreover, Japan was concerned about Australia's declining influence in East Asia and its deteriorating relations with Indonesia and Malaysia, the key members of ASEAN who occasionally blocked Australia from joining regional institutions. For instance, Malaysia was behind the exclusion of Australia from the 1996 ASEM Bangkok summit and warned that including Australians 'would be like admitting Arabs to the European Union' (*Sydney Morning Herald*, 4 March 1996). Indonesia, together with Malaysia, was pivotal in ASEAN's rejection of Australia's proposal of a FTA among ASEAN, Australia and New Zealand in October 2000 (*Age*, 7 October 2000).

At stake in terms of the actual organisational links between ASEAN+3 and an East Asian community that Koizumi proposed is whether Australia as well as New Zealand should be included in any activity associated with ASEAN+3. Koizumi said in his Singapore speech (2002a): '[t]hrough this cooperation, I expect that the countries of ASEAN, Japan, China...Australia...will be core members of such a community.' Yet Australia—whose relations with ASEAN countries, especially Malaysia and Indonesia, were strained until late 2004, when the leaders of both countries decided to visit Canberra to promote bilateral relations—was not expected by many in the region to be a natural member of the community. In fact, when Koizumi proposed an East Asian Community in his trip to Southeast Asia in January 2002, he faced difficulties in convincing ASEAN leaders, especially Prime Minister Mahathir, that Australia should be included in the community (*Australian Financial Review*, 10 January 2002). The fact that Australia has not become a member of ASEAN+3, despite Koizumi's advocacy, represented a discrepancy on the point of Australia's participation between already existing regional institutions and an envisaged regional community. Koizumi said in his Sydney speech in May 2002, 'I do not believe it is always the best policy to set up new organisations or institutions to build a community (Koizumi 2002b).' He did not touch on ASEAN+3, the significance of which he stressed in his Singapore speech a few months before, somewhat contradicting his earlier approach to the establishment of a community in East Asia. The Tokyo Declaration, launched by Koizumi and his ten ASEAN counterparts in December 2003, mentions creation of an East Asian Community as a significant goal, but it does not include any statement about membership. It says, 'to build an East Asian community which is outward looking...upholding Asian traditions and values, while respecting universal rules and principles [would be important].' This may reflect a view that, although the community is outward looking—suggesting that any country can join it—any potential member should possess or understand Asian traditions and values.

However, it remained questionable as to whether Australia displayed sufficient understanding of these so-called Asian traditions and values, as former Australian diplomat Dalrymple once argued: 'Australia's cultural differences with its neighbours would increasingly appear too manifest, and its identification with the US and Europe too close, to be reconciled with the forces driving East Asian regionalism' (2003:150). In fact, Australia's interest in exposing itself to a debate on its understanding of Asian political, social, and cultural values in association with the development of East Asian regionalism had previous been clearly rejected by Alexander Downer, the Australian Foreign Minister, in his address at the 2000 Asian Leaders Forum in Beijing, when he sought to draw a 'distinction between cultural regionalism and one based upon practical considerations of trade and economic relationships' (*Straits Times*, 29 April 2000). Appearing to be at odds with Australia's long-term regional policy approach, the central implication of Downer's remarks was that Australia did not see itself as belonging culturally and socially to the East Asian regional entity and that ASEAN+3 was not useful as a way of promoting Australia's national interest. Regional doubts about Australia's participation in East Asian regionalism, partly caused by the Downer statement, lingered as a result.

In the meantime, in Japan, the groups responsible for foreign and trade policymaking tended to see Australia's unfriendly relations with Southeast Asia as detrimental to Japan's regional policy. Japan became increasingly interested in ASEAN+3 rather than APEC in its foreign and trade policies, and began pursuing bilateral FTAs with major East Asian nations to strengthen general economic relations with them. There was no policy framework for Australia to be involved in this foreign and trade policy approach, and this indicated that Australia's significance in Japan's total foreign and trade policy was declining. It was true that Japan was still Australia's largest export market and the third largest foreign investor in the early 2000s, but the relationship was perceived not to be advancing soundly. For instance, a Japanese report, presented in the 2001 Australia-Japan Conference in Sydney, which 'likened the Japan-Australian relationship to an "ageing marriage" represents a view that the bilateral relations might become 'one in which both are satisfied with maintaining the *status quo*, while having no real interest in one another' (cited in Rumely 2002:3). This raises the important question of why Koizumi advocated the inclusion of Australia in his proposed East Asian community at a time when Australia was perceived to be detached from East Asia in its foreign policy.

There were other policy groups in Japan who believed in the usefulness and effectiveness of the partnership with Australia in achieving Japanese national interests. According to a senior official of the Ministry of Foreign Affairs, who declined to be named (personal interview, 9 April 2003, Tokyo), three significant elements affect the Australia-Japan partnership in East Asian regionalism: a tendency to fear China's possible predominance within ASEAN+3 and East Asia as a whole; security issues emerged as a more significant policy area in the bilateral relations with the United States, subsequently leading to the establishment of the trilateral defence talks among Japan, the United States, and Australia, thus enhancing Australia's presence in Japan's security policy; and the consideration that the United States had expressed concern about the rise of China as detrimental to American interests in East Asia. In short, the rise of China was a new factor that reconnected Japan and Australia in more strategic and political arenas, and the United States hope that both nations would play a checking role against China. US concern over China derives, for instance, from China's military build-up, as emphasised by US Defense Secretary Donald Rumsfeld, who believed that China's improved ballistic missile system would allow Chinese missiles to 'reach targets in many areas of the world...Since no nation threatens China, one wonders: Why this growing investment? Why these continuing large and expanding arms purchases?' (cited in *Straits Times*, 5 June 2005) Importantly, such a stark view on China's increasing military spending as threatening the delicate security balance in East Asia was widely shared by Japanese leaders including then Foreign Minister Machimura and Defence Agency Minister Ohno, as was seen in their talks at the US-Japan 2+2 Consultative Committee in May 2005.

According to a Ministry of Foreign Affairs official (personal interview above), some top senior officials in the Ministry believed that Japan would be isolated within an East Asian framework, in which most of the members are developing countries, whereas China could be seen as the leader of this group. Ministry officials believed that Japan would face a difficulty in injecting considerations that reflected the perspectives of developed countries. For these reasons, these officials hoped that Australia would see the need to join Japan in an attempt to be more committed to creating better relations with Southeast Asia, with which China has also been engaged in making cooperative relations. Hitoshi Tanaka, a Vice-Minister, who was one of these senior officials in the Ministry of Foreign Affairs and had been responsible for drafting Koizumi's Singapore speech, commented on Japan's need to have Australia participate in East Asian cooperation

> [i]n my heart I truly hope Australia will participate in the East Asia summit…We have worked very hard to make it possible. We are doing this not for Australia's sake, but for Japan's sake. We need you…I have a very strong feeling about our cooperation with Australia and I have been advocating it for a long time (*The Australian*, 28 May 2005).

The development of this policy stance indicates that there have been competing views on Australia among Japanese policy makers. Asian specialists in MOFA were said to oppose the inclusion of Australia, mainly because Japan has been engaged in strengthening the relations with ASEAN, as was evident in its efforts to organise the 2003 Japan-ASEAN Commemorative Summit in Tokyo; also, the inclusion of Australia, with its troubled relations with some ASEAN members, was considered not to be helpful. The Ministry of Economy, Trade and Industry (METI), whose primary interest has revolved around an FTA with ASEAN or its individual members, also did not welcome Australia's involvement as a result. Initially, METI promoted the idea of an East Asian Free Business Zone that did not envisage Australian membership. Given these divergent views on Australia within Japan and the region, Japan hesitated before revealing the intended membership of the proposed East Asian community—to be included in the Tokyo Declaration—as an agenda that Japan and ASEAN should promote in concert. This was simply because Tokyo could predict ASEAN's opposition to Australia's inclusion and thought it inappropriate to cause problems with ASEAN in a commemorative ceremony by making public its proposal to include Australia in the membership of an East Asian community (personal interview with a senior METI official, 24 December 2003, Tokyo). Japan's proposition that Australia should be a core member of an East Asian community was based on a condition it hoped Australia would meet, namely a fundamental transformation in

Australia's foreign policy orientation in order to change the negative view of Australia held by some East Asian countries, and Koizumi's Singapore speech partly aimed to convey such a message to Australia. Japan had difficulty adjusting government policy over the treatment of Australia at home, and internationally ASEAN's opposition to Australia's involvement in East Asian regionalism made it difficult for Japan, the first nation that proposed Australia's inclusion in the East Asian community, to make a strong push in this direction.

New developments in Australia's engagement policy

Since winning his fourth election in October 2004, Howard seems to have focused on East Asia more directly. Howard can already claim some achievements, including improving the previously strained relations with Indonesia and Malaysia through his swift and generous rescue packages for the Indonesians who suffered from the earthquake and tsunami in December 2004, and also through Indonesian and Malaysian leaders' visits to Canberra in April 2005. The achievements also include reaching agreements on the launch of FTA negotiations between Australia, New Zealand and ASEAN, as well as launching several bilateral FTA arrangements, including one with China. These foreign policy developments in Australia's relations with East Asia created a new opportunity for Japan to forge a stronger partnership with Australia in community building in East Asia.

Australia's involvement in the FTA networks in East Asia—given that Australia had already concluded the trading arrangements with Singapore and Thailand—could help Australia's entry into the movement towards the creation of an East Asian community. In a practical sense, FTAs can integrate markets, facilitate investment, and promote the exchange of business people among the signatories, an element that helps Australia to be recognised as an integral member of the region. Australia's sound economic growth over the decade has contributed to its being an attractive FTA partner, as is evidenced by Malaysia's interest in an FTA with Australia. In addition, Howard's participation in the summit meeting with ASEAN leaders in November 2004 in Laos—in which the three parties agreed to begin talks towards the creation of an FTA among ASEAN, Australia, and New Zealand (AFTA-CER)—was important as a positive sign of Southeast Asian countries' greater receptiveness to Australia's engagement policy. It is noteworthy that this meeting was held on the occasion of the ASEAN+3 Meetings, of which Australia is not an official member, even though the AFTA-CER FTA proposal was once rejected in 2000, mainly because of Malaysia's opposition.

The issue of Australia's commitment to East Asian cooperation also surfaced during heated debate on Australia's membership in the inaugural East Asian Summit in Malaysia, December 2005. Australia initially gave the cold shoulder to ASEAN's request that it sign the ASEAN Treaty of Amity and Cooperation (TAC), on the grounds that it was perceived to be a remnant of the Cold War and bore little relevance to the contemporary regional order. But ASEAN, especially Malaysia, the host of the Summit, insisted that signing the TAC should be a precondition of Australia's participation in the Summit. Australia hesitated to sign the TAC, which included the principle of non-interference in the affairs of other countries, a linchpin of ASEAN's political values. This was because Australia feared that its diplomatic reach would be restricted if it could not assist the United States to promote human rights and democracy in Southeast Asia. Moreover, Howard's pre-emptive strike statement in the wake of the terrorist attack in Bali in December 2002 appeared to contradict this principle. So Australia's eventual decision to sign the TAC indicated that it placed higher value on participation in the Summit than on Howard's personal political faith. This decision was a key to East Asia's full acceptance of Australia as a fellow member.

Downer had at one stage ruled out Australia's interest in the ASEAN+3 framework, as mentioned above, but other Australian leaders attempted to overturn this position. Treasurer Peter Costello stated, '[w]e would love to have ASEAN Plus Four. We have pursued it and we will continue to pursue it' (cited in *Far Eastern Economic Review*, 5 June 2003). Downer ultimately discarded his previous doubts about ASEAN+3 and worked hard to persuade Howard to sign the TAC so that Australia could be admitted to the inaugural East Asian Summit. ASEAN+3 and East Asian Summit can serve to 'provide a framework for demonstrating East Asian influence and leadership on regional and international affairs' (Drysdale 2003:12), enabling East Asian leaders to identify common positions more easily and to articulate them more effectively in multilateral institutions such as WTO and the United Nations. Australia's decision to sign the TAC, overturning its previous position suggests that the significance of this argument has been acknowledged by Australian political leaders.

The birth of East Asian regionalism involving Australia, initiated by Koizumi, was to be realised through the organisation of the East Asian Summit, held in Malaysia in December 2005. Japan, as well as Singapore and Indonesia, supported Australia's membership in the summit. This encouraged Australia to sign the TAC, a precondition for it to be invited to the Summit. Like Australia, Japan at one time hesitated to sign the TAC, as Prime Minister Koizumi stated in the 2003 ASEAN+3 meeting in Bali: 'I believe it is possible for Japan to strengthen its ties with ASEAN in the future without Japan signing the treaty. I think we have the understanding of ASEAN members on this point' (cited in *Asahi Shimbun*, 16 December 2003). However, China's announcement that it had signed the treaty influenced Japan's subsequent decision to do so. Importantly, before its decision to sign it, Japan had examined the impact and implications of the Treaty for its foreign policy, especially the US-Japan alliance system, and the result of the analysis was delivered to Australia through its Embassy in Tokyo (personal interview with a senior official of MOFA, 14 June 2005, Tokyo). It was Foreign Minister Nobutaka Machimura who suggested to his counterpart, Alexander Downer, in their meeting in March 2005, that Australia sign the TAC which, Machimura argued, would not cause any serious problem for Australia's foreign policy (*The Australian*, 6 August 2005).

The movement in Australia's regional diplomacy in recent times was a welcome development for Japan, which had been worried about Australia's inconsistent engagement with the region, especially after Howard came into power in 1996, as outlined above.

Japan and Australia have been also engaged in strengthening their bilateral relations, especially in security and defence areas. Japan's generous and crucial contribution to help fund the multinational force in East Timor (INTERFET), which was led by Australia, was a good case of cooperation between the two nations in political and security areas. Welcoming Japan's contribution of some hundreds of engineers in East Timor, as part of peacekeeping efforts in the former Indonesian province, Howard (2002) said that 'We see that kind of security involvement of Japan in the region in an extremely positive light.' This proposition is a foundation on which Australia's consistent and bipartisan support for Japan's bid to be a permanent member of the Security Council of the United Nations has been built.[2] In February 2005, in response to requests from Japan as well as the United States, Australia decided to despatch its troops to Iraq to protect Japanese Self-Defence Forces (SDF) there. In May 2005, the trilateral strategic dialogue among the United States, Japan, and Australia was upgraded to a ministerial-level forum involving the three Foreign Ministers. The highlight of both nation's interest in forging closer strategic ties is the formal declaration of security cooperation, launched by Howard and Abe in March 2007. This may be a symbolic attempt to formalise the bilateral cooperation on security, as seen in Cambodia and East Timor previously, but the declaration and the subsequent coverage of it in major Japanese newspapers, which was very rare previously, reinforced a view among the Japanese that Australia was now the second closest strategic partner after the United States. Japan's initial interest in inviting Australia into its proposed East Asian Community is partly motivated by Japan's wish to check China's growing political influence in the region, as well as its long-term regional partnership with Australia. These developments can be seen as a means of achieving the common strategic interests that the three countries share.

Japan's agreement to set up a feasibility study for a bilateral FTA (a development that sounds perplexing at first glance, as Australia is one of Japan's largest agricultural exporters) can be seen as reflecting Koizumi's desire to take Australia's trade interest more seriously as a sign of Japan's gratitude for Australia's deployment of troops to Iraq to protect Japan's SDF units (*Nihon Keizai Shimbun*, 26 April 2005). It also reflected Japan's intention to strengthen relations with Australia more comprehensively despite the political difficulties the FTA would cause at home. Accordingly, should the Japan-Australia FTA occur, it might be Japan's first bilateral FTA that is promoted primarily on the basis of political and strategic considerations rather than economic considerations. It can be argued that, in the era of the East Asian Community, the Australia-Japan partnership should be built on such a substantive and solid framework, as this will reinforce the wider strategic and economic interests shared by Japan and Australia in more stable and resilient ways.

Conclusion

Historically, the Australia-Japan partnership was strengthened through the activities undertaken towards the realisation of economic institutions in the Asia-Pacific region, and it was the partnership with Japan that helped to promote Australia's engagement with the region. Yet Howard's early disengagement with regional institutions, including APEC, and growing indifference towards his Southeast Asian partners placed the function of the Australia-Japan partnership under uncertainty, and this view was further strengthened by Japan's keener commitment to East Asian regionalism like ASEAN+3, which excluded Australia.

However, the partnership was strengthened by incorporating more strategic elements following the emergence of China. If China's interests in improving and strengthening its relations with ASEAN and its further commitment to the formation of an East Asian community were seen as a way of China creating its own sphere of influence in East Asia, this would be counterproductive to America's regional interests. So the role of the bilateral partnership between Japan and Australia, both key regional US allies, was to counter the emergence of China's ambition to dominate the region. However, a complicating factor is the fact that China's substantially growing economy means that both Japan and Australia have a strong interest in forging better economic relations for the sake of their economic growth. The fact that China was the world's largest importer of iron ore and wool in 2004 explains Australia's keener interest in the FTA with China. The fact that China has replaced the United States as Japan's largest trading partner illustrates its closer mutual economic interdependence with China, prompting many Japanese business leaders to request Prime Minister Koizumi not to visit the Yasukuni Shrine so that this major cause of the bilateral tensions would not hamper the smoother economic ties.

Therefore, the separation of strategic and political issues from economic and business interests in attempts to deal with the rise of China might be a key to the successful formation of an East Asian community. For instance, in their meeting in Washington in July 2005, Howard was reported to have turned down Bush's request that the United States and Australia work together to 'reinforce the need for China to accept certain values as "universal"' on the grounds of Howard's approach towards China which was 'to build on the things that we have in common, and not become obsessed with the things that make us different' (*Straits Times*, 19 August 2005). This indicates Australia's reluctance to contain China strategically in East Asia especially in the East Asian Summit, in line with US interests. However, as long as Japan maintains extremely high tariffs on Australia's key agricultural exports, it is highly unlikely that Japan and Australia would be able to conclude a bilateral FTA, suggesting that both nations lack a basis for future joint initiatives in promoting regional economic integration in East Asia. Moreover, the divergence of Japanese and Australian approaches to agricultural liberalisation also makes it difficult for them to forge a partnership in the WTO Doha Round negotiations, which has been hampered by differing tariff reduction proposals among key members including Japan and Australia. Given that Australia has been committed to improving its strained relations with Indonesia and Malaysia about which Japan had long worried, a key factor for restoring the bilateral partnership—in both regional and global bodies—is whether Japan can compromise over its highly protected agricultural products.

The 'isolation' factor has been a backdrop to Australia's commitment to regional institutions (Terada 2000), so the emergence of East Asian regionalism and the declining significance of APEC highlighted the lack of useful mechanism on which Australia could rely for avoiding its isolation in the region. In this sense, if Australia were admitted to the gradually expanding array of meetings, working groups, and cooperative linkages within ASEAN+3, it would be able to create networks of the responsible officials in relevant ministries such as trade, industry, or finance and the ways in which they are associated with their counterparts in other member economies. As these intra- and inter-governmental interactions and networks between government agencies in East Asia will become more entrenched among members, they can be instrumental in nurturing a sense of 'togetherness' among those officials, including Australia. They are also useful in identifying common policy interests among members.

Given the fact that the existence of different levels of policy discussions on the basis of their shared interest in regional economic cooperation played a significant role assisting Japan and Australia in their initiatives in Asia Pacific regionalism, this movement also should involve academic as well as business exchanges. The intellectual assets represented by those policy networks, which sustained the leadership role of both nations in institution building in the Asia Pacific region, can provide a platform for both nations to think through the evolution of the East Asian community idea and the relationship of East Asian cooperation arrangements in the new regional policy environment that faces both countries in the twenty-first century.

Notes

1   Aware of 'the fact that East Asia was the only part of the world not to have a regular Summit of leaders,' Hawke was encouraged to propose such a meeting within APEC in mid-1991 (Mills 1993:195); yet Hawke's prime ministership was taken over by Keating late that year, and Keating instead proposed the leaders' meeting in April 1992. Keating had canvassed the idea with major regional leaders including Japanese Prime Minister Kiichi Miyazawa, who officially supported the idea during his visit to Canberra in April 1993. This idea was later adopted by US President Clinton when the United States hosted the APEC meetings in Seattle in 1993.

2   Prime Minister Hawke officially supported Japan's permanent membership of the UN Security Council as early as 1990, in one of the earliest expressions of support Japan received in this regard (Terada 2000:192).

References

Commonwealth of Australia, 1997. *In the National Interest: Australia's Foreign and Trade Policy White Paper*, Canberra.

Dalrymple, R., 2003. *Continental Drift: Australia's search for a regional identity*, Ashgate, London.

Drysdale, P., 1988. *International Economic Pluralism, Economic Policy in Asia and the Pacific*, Allen & Unwin, Sydney.

——, 2003. 'Regional Cooperation in East Asia and FTA Strategies', paper delivered at IIPS Conference on Building a Regime of Regional

Cooperation in East Asia and the Role which Japan Can Play, Tokyo, 2–3 December.

Fraser, M., 1984. 'Pacific Community: Further Steps', Robert Downen and Bruce Dickson (eds), *The Emerging Pacific Community: A Regional Perspective*, Westview Press, Boulder.

Garnaut, R., 1997. *Open Regionalism and Trade Liberalisation: An Asia-Pacific Contribution to the World Trade System*, Allen & Unwin, Sydney.

Hashimoto, R., 1997. 'Reforms for the new era of Japan and ASEAN: for a broader and deeper partnership', Speech delivered in Singapore, 14 January.

Hatakeyama, N., 1996. *Tsusho Kosho: Kokueki-o Meguru Drama* [International Trade Negotiations: Dramas concerning National Interests], Nihon Keizai Shimbun-Sha, Tokyo.

Hawke, R.J.L., 1994. *The Hawke Memoirs*, William Heinemann Australia, Melbourne.

Howard, J.W., 2002. 'Opening Statement' at the Joint Press Conference, Sydney Australia.

Japan External Trade Organization, 2003. *Survey of overseas business activities,* Japan External Trade Organization, Tokyo.

Japan, Ministry of Economy, Trade and Industry, 2004. *White paper on small and medium enterprises,* Ministry of Economy, Trade and Industry, Tokyo.

____, 2006. *White paper on international economy and trade,* Ministry of Economy, Trade and Industry, Tokyo.

Japan, Ministry of Finance, 2003. *Trade statistics,* Ministry of Finance, Tokyo.

Japan, Ministry of Foreign Affairs, 2003. *Official development assistance white paper,* Ministry of Foreign Affairs, Tokyo.

Keating, P.J., 2000. *Engagement: Australia Faces the Asia-Pacific*, Pan Macmillan, Sydney.

Koizumi, J., 2002a. 'Japan and ASEAN in East Asia: a sincere and open partnership', Speech delivered in Singapore, 14 January.

——, 2002b. 'Japan and Australia toward a Creative Partnership', speech delivered in Sydney, 1 May.

Leong, S., 2000. 'The East Asian economic caucus: "formalised" regionalism being denied', in Hettne, B., Inotai, A. and Sunkel, O. (eds), *National Perspectives on the New Regionalism in the South*, London.

Mills, S., 1993. *The Hawke Years: the story from the inside*, Viking, Ringwood,

Ravenhill, J., 2001. 'Australia and the global economy', in J. Cotton, and J. Ravenhill (eds), *The National Interest in a Global Era: Australia in world affairs 1996–2000*, Oxford University Press, London.

Rumely, D., 2002. 'Beyond the Pacific Rim Strategy: Japan-Australia Relations in the 21st Century', a paper delivered at Japan, Canada, and the Pacific Rim: Trade, Investment, and Security Issues Conference, University of British Columbia, 27 March.

Spender, P., 1969. *Exercises in Diplomacy: the ANZUS Treaty and the Colombo Plan*, New York University Press, New York.

Terada, T., 1998. 'The origins of Japan's APEC policy: Foreign Minister Takeo Miki's Asia-Pacific policy and current implications', *Pacific Review*, 11(3):337–63.

——, 1999. *The genesis of APEC: Australia-Japan political initiatives* Pacific Economic Papers, No. 298, December, The Australian National University Canberra.

——, 2000. 'The Australia-Japan partnership in the Asia Pacific: from economic diplomacy to security cooperation?', *Contemporary Southeast Asia*, 22(1):175–98.

——, 2001. 'Directional leadership in institution-building: Japan's approaches to ASEAN in the establishment of PECC and APEC', *Pacific Review*, 14(2):195–220.

——, 2003. 'Constructing an East Asian concept and growing regional identity: from EAEC to ASEAN+3', *Pacific Review*, 2:251–77.

——, 2006. *The making of Asia's first bilateral FTA: establishment of the Japan-Singapore economic partnership agreement and regional implications*, Pacific Economic Papers No. 354, The Australian National University, Canberra.

Webber, D., 2001. 'Two funerals and a wedding? The ups and downs of regionalism in East Asia and Asia-Pacific after the Asian crisis', *Pacific Review*, 14(3):339–72.

Whitlam, E.G., 1981. *A Pacific Community*, Harvard University Press, Massachusetts.

4 JAPAN'S QUEST FOR FREE TRADE AGREEMENTS

CONSTRAINTS FROM BUREAUCRATIC AND INTEREST GROUP POLITICS

Hidetaka Yoshimatsu

In the 1990s, regional economic arrangements including free trade agreements (FTAs) became a popular way of promoting trade liberalisation and market integration. Japan, as an economy possessing exceptionally diverse export markets, had long taken a cautious stance on regional economic arrangements with a discriminatory nature. The Japanese government deemed economic arrangements with specific countries as contradicting the spirit of the General Agreement on Tariffs and Trade (GATT)/ World Trade Organization (WTO) as well as stunting the growth of overall trade.

However, intensive moves worldwide towards FTAs and regionalism have prompted Japan to reconsider its basic trade policy stance. Only in the late 1990s, did the Japanese government begin to shift the emphasis of its trade policy from multilateral to bilateral and regional arrangements. In part of this shift, in January 2001 Tokyo embarked on formal negotiations with Singapore about the formation of an FTA, signing the Japan-Singapore Economic Partnership Agreement (JSEPA) one year later. This move was followed by bilateral FTA agreements with Mexico, Malaysia, the Philippines, and Thailand, and negotiations with South Korea, Indonesia, and others.

Indeed, international forces constituted the initial factor that induced the Japanese government to reconsider its basic trade policy and promote bilateral FTAs. At the same time, domestic politics influenced the manner and speed with which the government's initiatives in FTAs were realised. Two factors are particularly important. The first is the preferences and behaviour of central government bureaucrats. In Japan, trade negotiations have been undertaken by four ministries: the Ministry of Economy, Trade and Industry (METI), the Ministry of Foreign Affairs (MOFA), the Ministry of Agriculture, Forestry, and Fisheries (MAFF), and the Ministry of Finance (MOF). These ministries tend to develop specific preferences that are incorporated into their concrete actions. The second factor is the influence of major domestic interest groups. A shift from the multilateral-oriented to the bilateral-centred trade policy has significant distributive effects on various segments of the domestic society. Accordingly, major interest groups have developed particular preferences and sought to have them accepted in the policymaking process.

This chapter argues that bureaucratic politics and interest group politics have impinged on the initiation and evolution of FTA policy in Japan. While inter-ministerial conflicts inhibited the Japanese government from pursuing a clear-cut approach on FTA policy and negotiations, demands from major interest groups exercised a critical influence over the start and progress of an FTA with a particular country. Before examining the development of Japan's FTA policy in detail, the following section provides a brief overview of bureaucratic politics and interest group politics in Japan.

Japan's FTA policy and trade politics

In the late 1990s, the Japanese government began to shift its stance on trade policy from an emphasis on multilateralism to stressing regionalism. In 1998, METI began internal discussions about new trade policy, and revealed its new policy orientation in its 1999 White Paper (Munakata 2001). In line with this change, in January 2001 Tokyo embarked on formal negotiations with Singapore over the formation of an FTA, signing the JSEPA one year after. Then, Japan signed the Japan-Mexico FTA in September 2004, followed by the conclusion of a similar agreement with

Malaysia in December 2005 and the Philippines in September 2006 (Table 4.1). Japan expanded the target of its FTA partners by beginning governmental negotiations with the Association of Southeast Asian Nations (ASEAN), Indonesia, Brunei and Chile.

While the Japanese government shifted its basic stance on trade policy, this shift did not produce apparent and smooth policy outcomes. The Japanese government did not at the outset, as a whole, set up a clear-cut vision for a new trade policy, and some of its new initiatives took a long time to put in place. Why did Japan show such an indecisive and rather awkward attitude towards trade policy? In order to address this question, we need to highlight two factors that affect continuity in reactive trade politics: bureaucratic politics and interest group politics.

In Japan, the parliamentary political system is practised and the cabinet led by the Prime Minister constitutes the senior executive organ. Since political appointees such as the ministers and senior vice-ministers turn over in a short time-span, ministries are run in practice by career officials, headed by the vice ministers and secretaries. Accordingly, bureaucrats have

Table 4.1   **Japan's negotiation of FTAs to April 2007**

Partner	Negotiations	Signature	Effective
Singapore	1/01–10/01	1/02	11/02
Mexico	11/02–3/04	9/04	4/05
South Korea	12/03–ongoing	n.a.	n.a.
Malaysia	1/04–5/05	12/05	7/06
Philippines	2/04–11/04	9/06	n.a.
Thailand	2/04–9/05	4/07	n.a.
ASEAN	4/05–		
Indonesia	7/05– 11/06	n.a.	n.a.
Chile	2/06– 9/06	3/07	n.a.
Brunei	6/06– 12/06	n.a.	n.a.
Gulf Cooperation Council	9/06–ongoing		
Vietnam	1/07–ongoing		
India	1/07–ongoing		

Source: Compiled by the author from data on the Japanese government website.

considerable autonomy and discretionary power, particularly with regard to internal organisation and personnel decisions. Moreover, central government bureaucrats are highly talented and disciplined elite officials with many years of service in the same ministry. They dominate the policymaking process by drafting virtually all legislation, controlling the national budget, and retaining significant amount of information necessary for formulating public policy (Johnson 1982, 1995; Campbell 1989). Thus, bureaucratic politics constitutes a major element in Japanese policymaking.

Bureaucratic politics in Japan is characterised by sectionalism—turf battles among ministries. This characteristic derives from various factors. The historical origins of sectionalism lie in conflicts among the south-western clans in the early Meiji era. Institutionally, the structure of each ministry is determined by the establishment law of each agency, and the code of conduct for each ministry is produced under this law. This legal system has deepened the gap between the ministries (Muramatsu 1994). Furthermore, limitations on resources given to each ministry have intensified sectionalism. Ministry-centred competition enabled the government to maximise the mobilisation of limited resources by way of severe inter-ministerial competition in the political market for policy innovation (Muramatsu 1996). From a broader perspective, bureaucratic conflicts had much to do with the weak power of the Prime Minister and the cabinet. Both the Prime Minister's Office and Cabinet Secretariat traditionally had weak capabilities with small staff, most of whom were bureaucrats, not personal appointees, often being entrenched in the sectionalism of their home ministries (Mulgan 2000).

The second factor that prevented the Japanese government from adopting a decisive stance on trade policy is interest group politics. Some scholars of international political economy postulate that trade policy is a function of interests and capabilities of interest groups that compete each other for greater benefits or incomes and form political coalitions to attain this objective. Theoretical and empirical interests have been directed towards clarifying conditions under which particular groups develop particular preferences for trade policy. Some observers have focused on factors of production such as labour and capital, as central factors in creating different policy preferences (Rogowski 1989). Others have highlighted sectoral or firm-based factors as keys to develop particular policy preferences (Ray 1981; Milner 1988; Frieden 1990). The characteristics of sectors—including the number of firms or workers in an industry, an industry's size or geographic concentration—have been regarded as critical factors in affecting concrete policy preferences and outcomes of trade politics.

As far as the representation of interest groups in Japanese policymaking is concerned, some scholars argue that the influence of traditional interest groups such as big business, labour and farmers declined as Japan moved to its catch-up goal and its matured economy produced more diverse interests in the society (Curtis 1999). However, the political influence of these traditional interest groups still matters, especially in the fields where a bureaucratic agency, relevant Liberal Democratic Party (LDP) politicians, and interest groups constitute the so-called 'sub-governments'.[1] This sub-governmental triangle is an exclusive policymaking institution, which is often insulated to a large extent from the influence of other political actors (Otake 1979). In the sub-governments, interest groups have influenced the evolution of public policy by forging tie-ups with relevant politicians in the ruling parties.

Reactive FTA politics before 2003

Japanese trade negotiations are conducted by various representatives from the Ministries of Foreign Affairs, Industry, Trade and Economy, Agriculture, Forestry and Fisheries, and Finance. Ministerial rivalries and bureaucratic conflicts have often impeded the Japanese government from formulating consistent and cohesive trade policy in a timely manner. This problem has been repeated over the handling of agricultural products in FTA negotiations between MAFF on the one hand and MOFA and METI, on the other. MOFA and METI considered that close trade linkages through FTAs were inevitable trends. It was METI that led a shift in trade policy from multilateralism to bilateralism. When METI officials began to investigate the importance of bilateral FTAs in the late 1990s, they regarded FTAs as effective measures to motivate government officials and private actors to promote structural reforms of domestic industries (Oyane

2004:58). In October 2002, MOFA published guidelines for FTAs, *Japan's FTA Strategy* (MOFA 2002). In these guidelines, MOFA maintains that 'unless we take a stance linking FTAs to economic reforms in Japan, we will not succeed in making them a means of improving the international competition of Japan as a whole'. Accordingly, both ministries acknowledged that some pains resulting from the formation of FTAs would be unavoidable for promoting structural reforms.

However, MAFF was cautious about including agricultural products in the purview of FTAs. MAFF's views on FTAs were revealed in several official documents. In a paper regarding the JSEPA released in August 2001, MAFF stated that given the current situation of Japanese agriculture, tariffs relating to agriculture, forestry and fisheries should be discussed at the WTO negotiations, and that further tariff reductions should not be made at negotiations for individual FTAs (MAFF 2001). In July 2002, MAFF issued a formal position paper entitled *Japan's Food Security and Agricultural Trade Policy: Focusing on FTAs*. MAFF stated that, in committing to an FTA, it is necessary to pay due attention to food security in Japan and to avoid negative impacts on efforts to implement structural adjustment. The report also states that FTAs will give minimal direct benefits to the agricultural sector (MAFF 2002). MAFF considered the potential benefits of FTAs in light of the agricultural sector alone, not the entire Japanese economy.

While MOFA and METI adopted a concerted stance over the necessity of market opening even in internationally weak sectors, they had different views over concrete approaches to FTAs. In the 2002 FTA guidelines, MOFA argued that Japan should give priority to FTAs with South Korea, ASEAN and Mexico. MOFA's basic direction was the same as METI's. However, there were differences in concrete strategies between the two ministries. For instance, MOFA's strategy for ASEAN was to create bilateral economic partnership individually, and begin a process of expanding these agreements to one between Japan and ASEAN as a whole. As for China, MOFA supported a strategy of continuing to closely monitor the country's fulfilment of its WTO obligations and the status of overall bilateral relations before determining Japan's policy. METI hoped to pursue the conclusion of an FTA with ASEAN as a whole. METI's policy orientation was understandable given that the ministry has striven to assist economic integration and industrial cooperation in ASEAN, which would then serve to the interests of Japanese firms operating in the region. As for China, METI included the country into its concept of the 'East Asian Business Zone'.[2]

Trade frictions have often occurred in policy fields where the major interest groups and their supporters in political circles could play a vital role in policymaking. This interest group politics was prominent in the initial stage of Japan's FTA policy. A driving force to promote some of FTAs was exercised by Nippon Keidanren (the Japan Business Federation, hereafter referred in this article as Keidanren), the most influential peak business association in Japan.[3] Keidanren became the main player who raised the position of Mexico in Japan's FTA strategy. Mexico was one of the most active countries in the promotion of FTA networks. Mexico signed the North American Free Trade Agreement (NAFTA) in 1992 and expanded its FTA networks to encompass Latin American countries in 1994. As of December 2002, Mexico had concluded FTAs with 32 countries covering regions from the American Continent through Europe to the Middle East. US firms had already secured access to the Mexican market through NAFTA, as did the Europeans after the FTA between Mexico and the European Union (EU) came into force in July 2000. Japanese manufacturing firms and trading houses suffered from serious negative effects from these moves. The absence of an FTA with Mexico forced Japanese firms to pay duties on key imports products from Japan and excluded them from bids on government procurement in the country.

Given the above conditions, Keidanren demanded a prompt conclusion of the Japan-Mexico FTA (JMFTA). In April 1999, the federation issued a report entitled *Report on the Possible Effects of a Japan-Mexico Free Trade Agreement on Japanese Industry*. This was the first comprehensive report that examined the likely effects of the FTA on bilateral trade and Japanese investment in Mexico, and identified problems needing to be resolved. Furthermore, Keidanren directly lobbied senior government officials in both countries to conclude the FTA at an early date. When the members of the federation's Japan-Mexico Economic Committee met with Herminio Blanco Mendoza, Minister of Commerce and Industrial Development, in

July 1999 and August 2000, they made a formal request that the Mexican government begin FTA negotiations as swiftly as possible. Furthermore, Nobuhiko Kawamoto, the head of the Japan-Mexico Economic Committee, met with Takeo Hiranuma, then Minister of METI, immediately prior to Hiranuma's visit to Mexico in January 2001, and requested the Japanese government to conclude the JMFTA as soon as possible (Tsuchida 2001). The federation's persistent lobbying persuaded the Japanese government to consider the JMFTA issue seriously. In particular, the federation forced the government to take necessary actions by demonstrating the serious damage being caused to Japanese firms' businesses with Mexico by the absence of the FTA with the country.

Interest group politics had regressive influences on Japan's FTA policy. The *norin zoku* ('agricultural tribes') in the LDP had vital influence in initiatives and negotiations over a series of FTAs.[4] A major reason why Japan chose Singapore as the first partner for an FTA was that the country exported a minimal amount of agricultural products. Singapore's exports of agricultural products, such as dairy products and cut flowers, made up only 3 per cent of Japan's imports from the country. Nonetheless, the treatment of the agricultural sector became a controversial issue during the negotiations because MAFF asserted that agricultural products should be excluded from the target of an FTA. The Japanese government as a whole was anxious about international criticisms of excluding the entire range of agricultural products from the FTA with Singapore. Accordingly, the government adopted a policy to list agricultural products whose tariffs were virtually zero as 'tariff zero products'. Some 460 items became the target under this method.

The peculiar treatment of agricultural products in the JSEPA had much to do with political pressure. In early August 2001, MAFF explained detailed policies for agricultural products in an FTA with Singapore at the LDP's Research Commission on Trade in Agriculture, Forestry and Fishing Products, and confirmed that tariffs affecting agricultural and fishing products would not change as a result of the FTA. However, commission members argued that tariffs on agricultural products should only be discussed at the WTO and that it was necessary to examine effects of an FTA with Singapore on Japan's proposed FTA negotiations with Mexico and South Korea.[5] LDP commission members had a strong preference for discussing tariffs on agricultural products at the WTO because they feared that once Japan made concessions on market liberalisation in an FTA with Singapore, it would be forced to make the same concession to other countries. Eventually, on the same day as the third round of negotiations, when the Japanese government hoped to reach a virtual agreement with Singapore, the LDP formally approved the government policy.[6] A government official who was involved in the negotiations recalls that 'there was strong pressure from the LDP and the farm lobby on the government not to agree to make any further liberalisation of the agricultural market in negotiating an FTA with Singapore'.[7]

The FTA negotiations with countries that had larger agricultural exports to Japan then became more controversial. A typical example is Japan's FTA with Thailand. In September 2002, the Japanese and Thai governments set up a working group to discuss FTA issues. Since Thai Prime Minister Thaksin Shinawatra planned to make a visit to Tokyo in June 2003, both governments hoped to use his visit as an occasion to launch formal FTA negotiations that would conclude by the end of 2003. However, the LDP's *norin zoku* objected to full-scale negotiations because Thailand was expected to demand the liberalisation of rice imports and free trade in chicken. The MOFA officials in charge of FTA policy lobbied the *norin zoku* to agree to the conclusion of the FTA within 2003, but they met furious opposition.[8]

The FTA talks with Mexico were also problematic. At a meeting of the LDP's Research Commission on Trade in Agriculture in May 2003, commission members reached a consensus that an accord that would bring benefits to both Japan and Mexico should be pursued and that Japan should not agree to an easy compromise. They also decided that exceptional items should be established in an FTA. At a meeting in August 2003, the commission reaffirmed that important exceptions should be allowed.

Strong lobbying by the agricultural groups occurred behind the scenes. When the initiation of the full-scale FTA negotiations with Thailand became a critical issue, agricultural groups intensified their lobbying of the *norin zoku* and LDP executive members. In April 2003, the Central

Union of Agricultural Cooperatives (Zenchu) distributed to the LDP members a brochure entitled *Requests Regarding FTA Talks with Thailand, Mexico and Other Countries*. In the brochure, the association expressed vehement opposition to FTAs, stating that it was premature to begin negotiations with Thailand and that the Mexican request to liberalise tariffs on agricultural imports was unacceptable. At a meeting of the LDP's Research Commission on Trade in Agriculture in May 2003, Isamu Miyata, chairman of Zenchu, asserted that a transition to formal negotiations for an FTA with Thailand would not be permitted because this would ignore the preferences of those who would suffer serious damage if FTAs were implemented, namely those in the agricultural, forestry and fishery sectors.[9] Eventually, the Japanese government failed to agree on the start of negotiations for the FTA with Thailand during Thaksin's visit.

When negotiations on the FTA with Mexico entered their final stage, agricultural groups again became increasingly active. At a meeting of the LDP's Research Commission on Trade in Agriculture in September 2003, Zenchu's executive director adamantly opposed concessions to Mexico involving tariff cuts for all farm products.[10] In early October, Zenchu chairman Miyata held a meeting with senior LDP executives, and demanded that pork be listed as an exclusion item in the FTA with Mexico.[11] The LDP members, *norin zoku* in particular, were attentive to the demands of agricultural groups because a general election was expected before June 2004. Clearly, when LDP members called for postponing formal FTA negotiations with Thailand and the adoption of exceptional items in the FTA with Mexico, these were responses to demands by the agricultural groups that could influence the retention of their elected positions.

In brief, bureaucratic politics and interest group politics constituted major obstacles to the smooth formation and implementation of trade policy in Japan. The fragmented structure of the Government on trade issues and the lack of coherent interests and policies among bureaucrats virtually prevented the government from formulating cohesive and persistent trade policy preferences. The protection of specific sectors due to opposition from interest groups and their political supporters often impeded the smooth development of FTA initiatives.

Nuanced changes in FTA politics after 2004

In the previous section, we outlined how Japan's reactive trade policy and indecisive commitments to any new policy had much to do with bureaucratic politics and interest group politics.

An objective source of bureaucratic politics lies in the fact that no single entity had the authority and power to make decisions that span multiple ministries. In order to overcome this problem, the coordinating role or leadership of the Prime Minister had long been called for. In this respect, the reorganisation of government ministries in January 2001 contributed to enhancing the power of the Prime Minister and the Cabinet. The Cabinet Secretariat increased its authority by assuming the role of planning and drafting important national policies. This was one of the major points that bureaucrats strongly resisted during the consultations over administrative reform. The existing ministries did not want the Cabinet Secretariat to plan and draft bills in their own jurisdiction (Shinoda 2004). The secretariat also strengthened its functions by the expansion of senior positions. Five new posts (three Assistant Chief Cabinet Secretaries, one Cabinet Public Relations Secretary and one Director of Cabinet Intelligence) were established as special positions directly appointed by the Prime Minister.[12]

Moreover, the Prime Minister demonstrated his determination to improve coordination among the ministries. In February 2002, Prime Minister Koizumi ordered an expansion of personnel exchanges among the ministries, aiming to increase the ratio of exchange in some 1,400 senior posts from 3 per cent in 2004 to 10 per cent in 2007. In summer 2004, 14 ministries and agencies exchanged officials for 40 new posts in addition to the 47 existing posts. This initiative was expected to overcome the shortcoming of vertically structured ministries and to promote more coordination among the ministries.

The Prime Minister and the Cabinet Secretariat also began to play more coordinating roles in trade policy formation and negotiations in various ways. For instance, the Prime Minister became more willing to intervene directly in the trade negotiation process. A typical example was negotiations over an FTA with Mexico. The Japanese government strongly hoped it could reach an agreement on the FTA when Mexican President Vicente Fox visited Tokyo in October 2003. Accordingly, Tokyo proposed a bold cut in tariffs on pork imported from Mexico at the final stage of negotiations. However, both governments failed to agree, largely due to a difference of view over the access quota for Mexican orange juice. In early November, a mission comprised of senior officials from METI and MAFF had a meeting with the Mexican government representatives, but no progress was made. In late November, Prime Minister Koizumi dispatched Shotaro Yachi, a Deputy Chief Cabinet Secretary, to Mexico City in a bid to break the impasse in the FTA negotiations. Cabinet Secretariat officials were part of the mission, but officials from relevant ministries such as METI and MAFF were excluded on the basis of instructions from the Prime Minister. That this action was exceptional is shown by the fact that Hosei Norota, Chairman of the LDP's Research Commission on Comprehensive Agricultural Administration, criticised this move as leading to 'dual diplomacy'.[13]

Prime Minister Koizumi continued his efforts to strengthen the participation of the Cabinet Secretariat in coordinating issues over trade policy among ministries. Koizumi himself considered that the lack of coordination among ministries was a main cause of failure in negotiations with Mexico. Accordingly, several measures were adopted in order to overcome this problem. In December 2003, Koizumi ordered the institutionalisation of meetings of FTA-related ministries under the Deputy Chief Cabinet Secretary. At the meeting, Directors-General from 14 relevant ministries were in attendance. Furthermore, Prime Minister Koizumi created the Council of Ministers on the Promotion of Economic Partnerships. Council members from 15 government agencies held their first meeting in March 2004, and discussed Japan's overall FTA policy at their second and third meetings in September and December. At the third meeting in December 2004, the Basic Policy towards Further Promotion of Economic Partnership Agreements (EPAs) was announced. The policy identified the value of EPAs in the development of Japan's foreign relations, the attainment of Japan's economic interests and the promotion of structural reforms, and positioned EPAs as a mechanism to complement the multilateral free trade system centring on the WTO. The policy was accompanied by criteria for identifying countries and regions with which EPAs were to be negotiated.

These two institutions aimed to strengthen systems that overcome miscommunication and bickering within the different government branches. In particular, the Basic Policy was important because it was virtually the first coordinated government policy for FTAs and EPAs. Although each ministry had issued its own FTA policy, there was no integrated policy as the Japanese government.

The formation of cross-ministry institutions had positive effects on each ministry's posture towards FTAs. In November 2004, MAFF made public its policy guidelines (Promotion of EPAs with Other Asian Countries in the Field of Agriculture, Forestry and Fisheries Green Asia—EPA Promotion Strategy). The new guidelines were explicit in proclaiming that 'EPA efforts...will be promoted in a positive way.' It then listed six points in promoting EPAs: i) stabilising and diversifying the sources of food imports into Japan; ii) ensuring the importation of safe food; iii) promoting the export of Japanese brands of agricultural products; iv) developing a business environment for the food industry; v) resolving problems like poverty in rural areas; and vi) conserving the global environment and ensuring the sustainable use of resources. MAFF defined the value of FTAs by referring to the expansion of exports of Japanese agricultural products and the maintenance of the people's food safety.

The institutionalisation of the ministers' meeting forced MAFF to reconsider its previous approach. Before the basic policy towards EPAs was announced at the Council's meeting, each ministry needed to clarify its own policy stance. MAFF maintained an extremely cautious approach about including the agricultural sector in FTA talks, formulating a list of strict criteria for FTA negotiations. Other ministries had formulated their approach to FTA policy stressing the promotion of FTAs with East Asian countries. MAFF was in a difficult policy position as most East Asian countries aimed to conclude FTAs that expanded agricultural exports to Japan. Eventually, MAFF formulated new policy guidelines with a focus on Asian countries.

Despite moves to overcome inter-ministerial conflicts, bureaucratic politics remained a major issue for Japan's FTA policy. As the FTA negotiation emerged as a crucial policy issue for Japan, relevant ministries began to strengthen their internal organisations that sought to implement this policy. In November 2003, MAFF established its FTA Headquarters for formulating strategies for FTA negotiations. Under the headquarters, five country-specific teams were organised. In August 2004, MOFA reorganised its FTA/EPA Office into the Regional Economic Partnership Division, increasing the number of staff from 30 to 40. METI also established its Economic Partnership Division with some 80 staff.[14] These moves intensified rivalries among ministries and led to less coordination in FTA negotiations.

This influence was seen in the Japan-South Korea FTA (JKFTA). During the Asia-Pacific Economic Cooperation (APEC) summit meeting in October 2003, Prime Minister Koizumi and Korean President Roh Moo-hyun agreed to launch formal negotiations for a JKFTA, and the first round of negotiations took place two months later. However, talks were stalled after late 2004, largely due to political tensions caused by Prime Minister Koizumi's visit to Yasukuni Shrine. At the same time, internal differences over negotiation style within the Japanese government impinged on the deadlock. METI and MAFF had different ideas about negotiating the JKFTA. While METI asserted a negotiation style of exchanging demands from each government first, MAFF supported a strategy of presenting the concession lists each other first.

In April 2006, METI announced its New Global Economic Strategy. One of two pillars of the strategy was the East Asian EPA concept.[15] The concept aimed at launching a comprehensive economic partnership agreement among ASEAN members, China, South Korea, India, Australia and New Zealand regarding investment, intellectual property rights, and economic cooperation in addition to tariff reductions. The creation of a region-wide FTA network would assist Japanese manufacturing firms under METI's jurisdiction that had formed production networks throughout East Asia.

However, other ministries displayed chilly attitudes towards the East Asian EPA concept. For instance, Shoichi Nakagawa, who had changed his ministerial post from METI to MAFF in October 2005, criticised the concept at the press conference just after it was announced by METI.

Nakagawa claimed that METI's concept was unexpected and many matters should be settled before launching such a concept.[16] From MAFF's standpoint, the East Asian EPA concept, which included Australia, a major exporter of agricultural products to Japan, should have been formulated with due consideration to the influence on the domestic agricultural market. MOFA was also sceptical about the concept from the viewpoint of Japan's relations with the United States, which was excluded from the concept, and coordination with the ongoing bilateral FTA negotiations.

It was an urgent matter for Japan to formulate a regional FTA strategy once China launched its aggressive regional economic policy. In fact, the concept behind Japan's strategy derived from METI's concern with the rising regional role of China, which had proposed the establishment of a study group for an FTA among ASEAN members, China, Japan and South Korea at the ASEAN+3 Economic Ministers meeting in September 2004. METI hoped to show Japan's leadership in regional FTA policy by expanding the possible membership to 16 countries to the regional FTA and broadening the fields targeted in the agreement.[17] However, contrary to normal bureaucratic practice in Japan, METI did not undertake prior consultations concerning the East Asian EPA concept with other ministries. METI had little interest in conducting satisfactory discussions, and the Council of Ministers on the Promotion of Economic Partnership did not function effectively.

Significant changes in attitudes towards trade policy began to emerge in the moves and influence of the interest groups and their supporting politicians. Keidanren gradually intensified their activities in support of FTAs. A particularly important move was its use of the resumption of political donations as leverage to exert influence on politicians. In January 2003, Keidanren revealed its plan to commence discussions about the resumption of political contributions, and this move strengthened the federation's bargaining position against politicians. Keidanren organised meetings with the LDP's senior executives where its officials explained the damage that lack of FTAs by Japan caused to Japanese industry. When the federation's senior officials met with the LDP's top executives in June 2003, the LDP members welcomed the federation's decision to resume political contributions. Keidanren members referred to the FTA issue and obtained positive responses from the party.[18] Coincidentally, one month after this meeting, the LDP set up the Select Commission on FTAs. Keidanren also linked the provision of political donations to the parties' commitments to its preferred policies. One of the ten priority policy items was 'the promotion of commercial, investment and economic cooperation policies responding to intensive global competition'. Keidanren's strong commitment to FTAs was the main content of this item.

Keidanren's activities made LDP politicians recognise FTAs as a vital policy issue by detailing the negative effects resulting from the lack of FTAs on Japanese business activities and the Japanese economy. For instance, 'Promotion of EPA/FTA Strategy'—the policy guidelines that the LDP's Select Commission on FTAs launched in February 2004— included a phrase that 'we need to take account of preventing and breaking up situations where Japan suffers diplomatic and economic drawbacks from the lack of an FTA'. This was precisely the point that Keidanren forcefully argued in relation to the necessity of an FTA with Mexico.

Keidanren also took the lead in expanding the target countries for FTAs. In April 2006, the Japanese government officially announced that it would start FTA talks with the Gulf Cooperation Council (GCC), and the first negotiation meeting was held in Tokyo in September 2006.[19] The close linkages with the GCC through an FTA were important in terms of energy security because Japan gets 75 per cent its crude oil from GCC members. Japan's moves were rather slow given that China started FTA talks with the GCC in April 2005 and the EU did in March 2002.

Importantly, Keidanren was the primary actor urging the government to enter into FTA negotiations with the GCC promptly. In September 2005, the federation issued a policy proposal—Call for Early Launch of Negotiations for Japan—GCC Economic Partnership Agreement. The paper stated that 'Japan must actively pursue a comprehensive EPA with the GCC. Such an agreement should include not only elements of an FTA but also cover the energy sector and the improvement of the business environment. The conclusion of such an agreement would be of crucial strategic importance to the historically amicable diplomatic relationship between Japan and the Middle Eastern countries' (Nippon Keidanren 2005). Keidanren hoped to avoid a repetition of the experience where

Japanese firms suffered substantial economic losses due to the lack of an FTA with Mexico.

As already explained, the agricultural sector was the most serious constraint upon Japan's new trade policy, and Zenchu was the actor leading moves against the inclusion of the agricultural sector in FTAs. However, the association eventually began to be more realistic towards FTAs. Before formal negotiations FTAs with Asian countries were launched, an informal study group comprising representatives from the government, business and academia engaged in a deliberation of possible effects and problems of the FTAs. Zenchu sent its officials to these study groups as representatives from Japanese business circles. In the meantime, Zenchu began intensive internal discussions about the impact of FTAs on Japanese agriculture. In February 2004, the association issued a report entitled *JA Group's Basic Ideas Concerning FTAs with South Korea, Thailand, the Philippines, Malaysia, and Indonesia*. The 54-page report was still cautious about the conclusion of FTAs, but it represented substantial progress in that Zenchu had actually investigated the concrete impact of FTA arrangements on Japanese agriculture from various viewpoints. Moreover, the report stressed the need for a public dissemination program in order to make the agricultural groups' basic stance on FTAs better understood by the members and the public.

In line with this new orientation, Zenchu intensified its own public relations activities to disseminate its basic approach on FTAs to the Japanese public. An important event in this respect was a summit meeting with Keidanren, a long-honoured enemy over trade policy. At this meeting in February 2004, Chairman of Zenchu Isamu Miyata explained to Chairman of Keidanren, Hiroshi Okuda, the necessity of 'offensive' strategies such as export expansion for Japanese agriculture. The association then determined that April–June 2004 would be months during which it would conduct intensive public relations activities such as convening study groups and symposiums. Zenchu's public relations activities even went beyond borders. When a special seminar of the Asian Farmers' Group for Cooperation was held in Manila in mid-March, Association representatives attended and stressed that FTAs should not pursue trade liberalisation alone, but must involve agricultural cooperation in areas such as food safety and rural development.[20] In March and April, the Association sent a 30-member mission to the Philippines and Thailand to exchange views with senior government officials in the two countries and explain Japan's conditions for FTA negotiations.

These changes in attitudes on the part of the agricultural groups were partially caused by new shifts in their support for politicians from the LDP. Some of the *norin zoku* gradually departed from advocating the simple protection of the domestic farm market from international competition. These *zoku* can be called the 'internationally oriented *zoku*' who consider the protection of Japanese agriculture from a broader and international perspective. They are different from the conventional *zoku* who tend to act to defend narrow interests of agricultural groups. Former Agriculture Ministers, Yoshio Yatsu and Shoichi Nakagawa, are two representatives of the newly emerging *zoku*.

The internationally oriented *zoku* directly influenced the evolution of FTA policy and negotiations. In April 2003, Nakagawa and Yatsu met with Koizumi, and stressed the importance of FTAs. Koizumi was reportedly influenced through this discussion about FTAs.[21] They also played a crucial role in leading the conclusion of an FTA with Mexico. Nakagawa, who had become the Minister of METI in the cabinet reshuffle in September 2003, sought to lead the negotiations over the Japan-Mexico FTA to a smooth conclusion by coordinating agricultural and trade policies and interests. As noted earlier, the Japanese government made concessions by cutting tariffs on pork in October 2003. Some LDP members criticised this bold measure at a meeting of the party's Research Commission on Trade in Agriculture, Forestry and Fishery Products. Yoshio Yatsu, the Secretary-General of the commission, asserted that the commission members agreed to leave the matter to the executives of the commission, and the Government undertook negotiations in close liaison with commission executives and agricultural producers.[22]

In summary, the fundamental characteristics of sectionalism in Japanese bureaucratic politics have remained almost unchanged. However, the Prime Minister has deepened his recognition of shortcomings caused by sectionalism and of the need to provide more coordination among ministries. As a result, the Cabinet Secretariat intervened in trade negotiations processes and set up institutions that cut across the ministries.

New moves also emerged in interest group politics. While pro-FTA interest groups gradually increased their influence, anti-FTA groups became more realistic in handling the FTA issues and were more tolerant of FTAs. As for the agricultural issues, internationally oriented *zoku* gained influence in the policymaking process.

Conclusion

This chapter examined the evolution of Japan's FTA policy by examining trends in domestic politics. In particular, it considered the influence of bureaucratic politics and interest group politics.

Japan was behind other countries in initiating bilateral FTAs due to its commitments to multilateralism. After a policy shift from multilateralism to bilateralism in the late 1990s, Tokyo intensified its own internal deliberations on FTAs and expanded the number of countries who would be party to the agreement. However, the new trade initiatives, in general, did not lead to smooth policy outcomes. The Japanese government failed to establish a clear-cut vision for FTAs, and the negotiation process often took longer than expected. The bureaucratic politics and interest group politics had much to do with this result.

The Japanese government failed to formulate and implement comprehensive and consistent external economic policy largely because of rivalry and factionalism among relevant government agencies. METI, MAFF and MOFA adopted diverse policy stances on FTAs. MAFF was extremely reluctant to promote FTAs that would lead to the liberalisation of the long protected agricultural market. METI was an active promoter of FTAs that would produce significant benefits to Japanese manufacturing exporters. MOFA tended to consider FTA issues from the broader perspective such as the stable relationship with the United States.

Interest group politics exercised a vital influence over the evolution of Japan's FTA policy. The Japanese Government was obliged to be passive towards FTAs due to strong opposition to market liberalisation from agricultural interest groups and their supporting politicians. Agricultural groups successfully impeded the progress of negotiations of FTAs with Mexico and Thailand. On the other hand, Keidanren spearheaded the evolution of the FTA with Mexico through various measures. In its position papers, the federation explicitly demonstrated the negative effects that the absence of an FTA with Mexico had on the performance of Japanese firms operating in that country. It then lobbied government officials and ruling politicians to begin negotiations for an FTA. These activities encouraged government officials to consider the adoption of an FTA strategy more seriously and to take necessary actions to this end.

Some evolution occurred also in both bureaucratic politics and interest group politics. The Koizumi administration made efforts to promote inter-ministerial coordination and intensified direct involvement of the Cabinet Secretariat in FTA issues. Moreover, cross-ministry institutions were set up to promote smooth coordination among relevant ministries. Such moves surely contributed to the advancement of FTA policy by drawing flexible responses from MAFF. However, the fundamental characteristics of fierce inter-ministerial rivalry remained unchanged. As for interest group politics, Keidanren increased its leverage in political circles by resuming political donations. Agricultural groups became more realistic in handling the FTA issues. They changed their strategy from stubborn opposition to stress on public relations activities to gain public understanding about its stance on FTAs.

Notes

1   Sub-governments are defined as 'small groups of political actors, both governmental and nongovernmental, that specialise in specific issue areas' (Ripley and Franklin 1984:8).
2   The concept of the East Asian Business Zone was formally introduced in the White Paper on International Trade and Industry 2003.
3   *Nippon Keidanren* was founded in May 2002 through the merger of the Japan Federation of Economic Organisations (*Keidanren*) and the Japan Federation of Employers' Association (*Nikkeiren*).
4   *Zoku* (tribe or clan) are 'LDP Diet members who exert, formally or informally, a strong influence on specific policy areas mainly at the LDP's Policy Affairs Research Council' Inoguchi and Iwai 1987:20).
5   *Nihon Nogyo Shimbun*, 10 August 2001.
6   *Nihon Nogyo Shimbun*, 4 September 2001.
7   *Japan Times*, 23 November 2001.
8   *Nihon Keizai Shimbun*, 1 August 2003.
9   *Nihon Nogyo Shimbun*, 31 May 2003.
10 *Nihon Keizai Shimbun*, 9 September 2003.
11 *Nihon Nogyo Shimbun*, 3 October 2003.

12   At this reorganisation, the Cabinet Office was established by merging most part of the Prime Minister's Office with the Economic Planning Agency, with an eye to providing greater assistance and support to the Prime Minister and Cabinet.
13   *Asahi Shimbun*, 12 December 2003.
14   *Nihon Keizai Shimbun*, 27 July 2004.
15   The other pillar was the establishment of a policy coordination entity in East Asia to be modelled after the Organisation for Economic Cooperation and Development (OECD).
16   Press Conference by Shoichi Nakagawa, Minister of Agriculture, Forestry and Fisheries, 7 April 2006. Available at http://www.kanbou.maff.go.jp/kouhou/060407daijin.htm.
17   *Asahi Shimbun*, 28 July 2006.
18   *Nihon Keizai Shimbun*, 17 June 2003.
19   The GCC member countries are United Arab Emirates, Bahrain, Saudi Arabia, Oman, Qatar, and Kuwait.
20   *Nihon Nogyo Shimbun*, 13 March 2004; *Japan Agrinfo Newsletter*, 21, 9 May 2004.
21   *Nihon Keizai Shimbun*, 9 December 2003.
22   *Asahi Shimbun*, 21 November 2003.

References

Campbell, J., 1989. 'Bureaucratic primacy: Japanese policy communities in an American perspective,' *Governance*, 2(1):5–22.

Curtis, G.L., 1999. *The Logic of Japanese Politics: leaders, institutions, and the limits of change*, Columbia University Press, New York.

Frieden, J.A., 1990. *Debt, Development, and Democracy: modern political economy and Latin America, 1965–1985*, Princeton University Press, Princeton, NJ.

Inoguchi, T. and T. Iwai, 1987. *'Zoku Giin' no Kenkyu* (Research on 'tribal Diet men'), Nihon Keizai Shimbunsha, Tokyo.

Johnson, C., 1982. *MITI and the Japanese Miracle: the growth of industrial policy, 1925–1975*, Stanford University Press, Stanford.

——, 1995. *Japan, Who Governs? The Rise of the Developmental State*, Norton, New York.

Ministry of Agriculture, Forestry and Fisheries (MAFF), 2001. *Shogaikoku tono jiyu boeki kyotei no kento jokyo oyobi nichi/shingaporu keizai renkei kyotei ni okeru norin suisanbutsu no toriatsukai ni tuite*, (On the treatment of agricultural and fisheries products in the Japan-Singapore Economic Partnership Agreement and in considering free trade agreements with other countries) (August). Available at http://www.maff.go.jp/wto/wto_fta.htm.

———, 2002. *Wagakuni no shokuryo anzen hosho to nosanbutsu boeki seisaku: jiyu boeki kyotei wo megutte*, (Japan's food security and trade policy on agricultural and fisheries products in connection with free trade agreements) (July). Available at http://www.maff.go.jp/sogo_shokuryo/fta_kanren/seisaku.pdf.

Milner, H.V., 1988. *Resisting Protectionism: Global Industries and the Politics of International Trade,* Princeton University Press, Princeton, NJ.

Ministry of Foreign Affairs (MOFA), 2002. 'Japan's FTA Strategy,' (October). Available at http://www.mofa.go.jp/mofaj/gaiko/fta/senryaku.html.

Mulgan, A.G., 2000. 'Japan's political leadership deficit', *Australian Journal of Political Science*, 35(2):183–202.

Munakata, N., 2001. '*Nihon no chiiki keizai togo seisaku no keisei*' The formation of Japan's regional economic integration policy), in N. Munakata (ed.), *Nitchu Kankei no Tenki A Turning Point of Japan-China Relations*), Toyo Keizai Shinposha, Tokyo.

Muramatsu, M., 1994. *Nihon no Gyosei: Katsudo gata Kanryosei no Henbo* (Japan's Public Administration: the transformation of the active bureaucratic system), Chuo Koronsha, Tokyo.

———, 1996. 'Post-war politics in Japan: bureaucracy versus the party/parties in power' in M. Muramatsu and F. Naschold (eds), *State and Administration in Japan and Germany*, Walter de Gruyter, Berlin.

Nippon Keidanren, 2005. 'Call for Early Launch of Negotiations for Japan-GCC Economic Partnership Agreement', September 13. Available at http://www.keidanren.or.jp/english/policy/2005/060.html.

Otake, H., 1979. *Gendai nihon no seiji kenryoku keizai kenryoku* (Political and economic power in contemporary Japan), Sanichi Shobo, Tokyo.

Oyane, S., 2004. *Higashi Ajia FTA: Nihon no seisaku tenkan to chiiki koso* (East Asian FTA: Japan's policy change and regional concept), *Kokusai Mondai*, 528(March):52–66.

Ray, E., 1981. 'Determinants of tariff and nontariff trade restrictions in the US', *Journal of Political Economy*, 89(1):105–21.

Ripley, R.B. and Franklin G.A., 1984. *Congress, the Bureaucracy, and Public Policy*, 3rd ed., The Dorsey Press, Homewood, Illinois.

Rogowski, R., 1989. *Commerce and Coalitions: how trade affects domestic political alignments*, Princeton University Press, Princeton, NJ.

Shinoda, T., 2004. *Kantei Gaiko: Seiji Ridashippu no Yukue* (Diplomacy by Prime Minister: Tracing political leadership), Asahi Shimbunsha, Tokyo.

Tsuchida, N., 2001. '*Nichiboku Jiyu Boeki Kyotei wo Meguru Kokumin Reberu no Gironwo*' (Searching for national level discussions about the Japan-Mexico Free Trade Agreement), *Economic Report,* April). Available at http://www.bizpoint.com.br/jp/reports/oth/nt0104.htm.

5 OPEN, SECURE, INFLUENTIAL?

CONTEMPORARY ISSUES IN JAPAN'S

INTERNATIONAL ECONOMIC ENGAGEMENT

Christopher Pokarier

Open borders facilitate economic prosperity but entail risks. Whilst the promotion of further economic openness remains a formal objective of Japanese government policy, this imperative is tempered by politically salient national security concerns that are both broad in scope and deeply complex. Since 2000, a series of diverse and significant negative events—such as terrorism, crime, disease, and economic nationalism abroad—have impacted upon the perceived risks of open borders and reliance upon international supply chains. These developments have given rise not only to demands for specific public policy and private sector initiatives in response to such perceived threats, but have also contributed to a general attitudinal climate in which policy measures to guard 'national interests' find ready legitimacy. Economic openness is not inevitable, being strongly contested domestically.

Japan's deep international economic engagement presents a challenging confluence of contemporary risk management issues, but these are easily appropriated by domestic protectionist interests and old-fashioned nationalists. Expansive, and heightened, national security concerns have led to Japan's scope for influencing its international environment becoming a more explicit object of policy. Japan exhibits strong concerns about being what may be termed 'open, secure, and influential' in its international economic engagement. This chapter explores the imperatives behind, the deep tensions within, and the prospects for, these aspirations.

Japan's recently more uncertain international political environment, and its policy responses, have been well explored from conventional security perspectives. The threat of cross-border terrorism, regional tensions involving a rising China, an autarkic and paranoid North Korea, and a more self-confident Russia impact on Japanese perceptions of national security. Japan's historical concern with resource security has renewed currency with the rapid growth of China and India as rival customers for energy and raw materials, in a context of a near global resurgence in economic nationalism in relation to the resources sector. More generally, the ever-growing dependence of the Japanese corporate sector on cross-border supply chains, foreign production locations and markets make the attenuation of threats to such cross-border business operations a growing concern for Japanese firms and policymakers. Threats include political and regulatory risk, infrastructural limitations, inadequate protection of property rights, crime and corruption, and growing competition for essential business inputs (energy, basic materials, human resources, rights to technology and brands etc.). Other operating risks emanate from the physical environment, such as natural disasters, from the scale, connectivity and mobility of modern human environments—such as contagious disease and other phyto-sanitary threats—and from growing political awareness of issues of environmental sustainability.

From a business perspective, impacts of diverse negative events such as the SARS epidemic, terrorism, mad cow (BSE) disease, and natural disasters are experienced by firms directly through operational disruptions and, indirectly, through the responses—measured or otherwise—of managers, insurers, investors and regulators. From a public policy perspective, many of these cross-border risks are compounded by national rivalries, principally intra-regional. International cooperation is less than fully forthcoming for joint efforts to address cross-border risks to national welfare. National pursuit of supply chain certainty through forward integration abroad (such as through controlling equity stakes) and controls at home, collectively may compound perceived overall uncertainty in the international business environment. Many of the contemporary international risk issues are characterised by a high level of technical complexity; with understandings shared amongst international networks of experts—often state employees— across regions. This has significant implications for the scope and nature of public policy prescriptions, the forms of international cooperation, and raises important questions about the efficacy of bilateral and regional approaches.

The international mobility of many contemporary knowledge-intensive Japanese enterprises makes salient a much broader set of policy preferences than when Japan was primarily an exporter of manufactures. For instance, foreign investment regulation (including those pertaining to cross-border mergers and acquisitions), intellectual property and corporate law regimes, product and business regulation, and tax treatment of royalties and license fees can impact as heavily on firms abroad as tariff regimes. The imperative for policy reciprocity, in turn, potentially makes these same issues contentious within Japan. Whilst change in Japan's preferred loci of negotiations—from multilateral to bilateral initiatives—attracts much attention, equally important is the shift in Japan's priority issues.

Leading Japanese enterprises potentially are significant contributors to the resolution of apparent conflicts between the imperatives for fewer barriers to international trade and more secure societies. Japanese firms are leading providers of information and communications technologies (ICTs), especially hardware, that may permit the simultaneous facilitation of desirable cross-border mobility whilst strengthening capacities for legitimate border protection. In the aftermath of 9/11 the US government has given unprecedented policy and financial support to technological applications aimed at enhancing homeland security. Applications providers, in turn, are scrambling to meet this opportunity, and to align products and systems with established corporate demands for more efficient ICT-enabled cross-border supply chains. The pursuit of 'traceability' through radio frequency identity systems (RFIDS) (also known as IC tag) and e-documentation symbolises this heady pursuit of simultaneous efficiency and accountability. Japan is, potentially, at the forefront of this technologically enabled pursuit of a secure but open society.

Consequently, Japan potentially has much to contribute internationally: commercially, through aid for capacity building; and through positive demonstration effects. Yet the scope for creative policy responses might be heavily constrained by residual structures of interests, and the heightened risk averseness and uncertainty avoidance commonly associated with mature economies, an aging demographic make-up, and perhaps with established patterns of Japanese values.[1] Efficiency with assurance (assurance of security and/or effective attenuation of unavoidable but bearable risks) is the key, still not well understood, objective.

Much of the large literature on the determinants of Japan's trade and other policies impacting on its international economic engagement looks primarily to the nation's domestic environment (for example, Mason 1992; Warren 1997). Whilst developments in the international environment are profoundly important, and have contributed significantly to policy change, such influences are generally manifested through a domestic political economy (for example, Yoshimatsu 2000, 2003). Good accounts abound of the roles of private interest politics, bureaucratic interests and turf wars and, somewhat less systematically, public interest ideas concerning national economic development, in shaping policy outcomes. They accord with a substantial international literature, both comparative and country-specific, that examines the domestic politics of trade protectionism (Odell 1990; Milner and Yoffie 1989). The role of countervailing domestic private interests in promoting foreign trade liberalisation in various countries is also well understood; as is the interdependent nature of trade policies and structures of domestic economic interests (Milner 1988; Rogowski 1989; Odell, 1990; Simmons 1994). Although these studies emphasise the concrete material interests of domestic constituencies, the important role of ideas and imperfect information as an explanatory variable is also recognised (Breton 1964; Anderson and Garnaut 1987; Machan 1992). Consumers, and sometimes even producer interests, may have an imperfect understanding of their interests (Bates and Krueger 1993).

The discussion that follows in this chapter assumes an important explanatory role for both private interests, including those manifested by and through public institutions, and public interest ideas. The potentiality of political and policy entrepreneurship for reform can be readily conceptualised in these terms; as the Koizumi administrations attested to the importance of (Mulgan 2000, 2002). Ideas have independent explanatory power in relation to policy outcomes because information and cognitive limitations are systematic, as the recent theoretical work of eminent economic historian Douglass North (2005) prioritises. Of particular relevance to this chapter is stability and change—sometimes rapid change—in the *perceived* security of private and national economic interests. North sees economic performance as principally a function of the quality of a society's institutions, broadly defined, and a principal objective of such institutions is a perpetual, and often fruitless, desire to deal with uncertainty (in the Knight-Ellsberg sense; see Moss 2002:40–43).

Open?

Early globalisation discourses about an inexorable move towards 'a borderless world', as in the title of Ohmae's (1990) influential book, were rather naïve (Wolf 2002). Despite increasing international regulatory cooperation and binding international agreements, sovereign national borders still fundamentally delineate authority in distinct economic governance systems. Certainly technological innovation has further enabled various forms of cross-border mobility, and the competitive commercial adoption of these transport and communications technologies has dramatically lowered, over time, the costs of such mobility. The direct consequence has been a dramatic quickening in the pace of growth of cross-border mobility of all factors of production: 'globalisation' as popularly discussed.

For convenience's sake, the many forms of cross-border mobility may be simply classified as involving the following types of flows: goods, services, financial and corporate transactions, information, and people. A distinction is drawn between cross-border financial flows and corporate mobility, the latter referring to cross-border shifts in legal residence of a corporate entity or to a move, or extension abroad, of the networks and hierarchies of control that firms represent. Significantly, most international mobility involves the crossing of public borders through the means of private channels, be it via privately provided transport, communications, payments or service infrastructures. Yet, crucially, new technologies need not necessarily weaken the capacity of states to enforce borders. They will impact significantly on the means available and necessity to do so. The ready accessibility of modern border-spanning private channels creates new national vulnerabilities, and hence political imperatives for effective border enforcement. At the same time, recognition of the profound economic and social benefits of open borders creates imperatives for efficient and minimalist policing of borders.

Japan ranks quite highly in aggregate measures of globalisation, reflecting the formidable performance of its leading enterprises in global markets and its international political engagement. Dreher's (2006) KOF index of globalisation, ranked Japan 21st in 2000, although the 2007 ranking had Japan at 40th overall (Swiss Institute of Business Cycle Research, KOF 2007). The World Economic Forum's Global Competitiveness Report 2006–2007 has Japan ranked 7th; reflecting its emphasis upon endowments (such as a rigorous education system and advanced social infrastructure) rather than openness *per se* (World Economic Forum 2007).

With certain sectoral exceptions, most notably in agriculture, Japan has very low average tariff rates. Of course, formally open borders are only part of the story. It may be that beyond open borders nonetheless lie closed domestic worlds. Indeed, the formal opening to foreigners of certain industries and organisations may not be particularly threatening to established domestic interests because established practices discourage or frustrate new entrants—domestic or foreign. Japan ranked well behind the United States and Germany (as EU surrogate) in Wolf, Levaux and Tong's (1999) mid 1990s assessment of the practical openness of particular economies to foreign enterprises; metrics derived through extensive surveys of executives and qualitative assessments in relation to the three countries plus South Korea and China. Indeed, on technical barriers such as testing and certification, restrictions to entry and the like, Japan ranked least open amongst the five economies. Japan was consistently ranked third across ten attributes of foreign investment openness (Wolf et al., 1999). In the decade to 2007 there has been incremental micro-economic reform in many sectors, but it remains to be demonstrated that Japan's relative openness in relation to NTBs has improved while, as will be seen below, there are signs of regression in relation to some forms of foreign investments.

Barriers may be attitudinal as much as regulatory or organisational. Richard Florida (2005:68) may be over-simplifying things somewhat when he argues, in his influential work on the mobility of 'creative class', that 'openness is the real motor force of economic growth'. He nonetheless raises challenging questions with his insistence that openness means much more than the absence of formal barriers to new participants, ideas and approaches. Openness also entails a substantial cultural dimension.[2] There are no ready comprehensive metrics when the socio-cultural dimensions of economic openness are considered. The Dreher/KOF indices are notable for the incorporation of a composite measure of social globalisation; such proxy measures of social openness being still remarkably rare given the enormous debate over the nature and social impacts of globalisation (Koster 2007). The KOF 2007 social globalisation had Japan at 54th; although methodological issues may result in a significant under-estimation of the extent of inbound information flows to Japan and convergence of tastes.

Yet strikingly, Florida's 'Global Creativity Index' ranks Japan second only to Sweden, followed in turn by Finland and the United States (Florida 2005:156). Florida's index is a composite measure based on the '3 Ts of economic growth'—technology, talent and tolerance—with Japan being particularly strong in the first two. Much of Florida's work though is predicated on concerns that the United States, in particular, is dissipating its own established strengths in those two dimensions through declining tolerance, especially in relation to the inward mobility of people, as freshly perceived threats to national security become politically salient. It is to the Japanese experience of the contemporary security-openness quandary that we now turn.

Secure?

This section first considers perceived security, security and threats as both perceived and empirical phenomena, and the scope for profound disconnects between them. Contemporary Japanese concerns about the national security dimensions of open borders fall into two broad categories, which the following discussion deals with in turn. The first may be described generally as the risks entailed in a prosperous dependence upon cross-border transactions. These primarily relate to supply chain security, and resource security in particular, and vulnerabilities associated with reliance upon foreign production locations and markets. The second category entails threats from abroad associated with particular forms of inward cross-border mobility. To reiterate, the inflows with which such threats may be associated entail the general areas of goods, services, corporate, financial and informational flows, as well as human flows.

Perceived security

Central to perceived security is the presence or otherwise of sensed threats, judged abilities to avoid them, or at least attenuate their (by definition, negative) impacts, and capacities and preparedness to bear any such residual impacts. Posner (2004:120–2) explores the 'economics of attention' to explain the inevitably limited capacities of individuals to give attention to diverse risks and their varying probabilities; with the consequence that risks 'available to the mind' owing to recent occurrence gain greater attention. They have lower 'imagination costs' than less frequent negative events, reflecting 'the tendency of people to attach disproportionate weight to salient, arresting events'; an insight that accords directly with psychologists' concept of the availability heuristic (Posner 2004:122, 169). The mass media, in turn, can identify and amplify the cognitive impacts of events amongst large audiences that are typically national in orientation. Benedict Anderson's (1983) profound insight into how nations are essentially 'imagined communities', given that no citizen knows more than a tiny proportion of her fellow citizens, and the role of the media in that imagining, is of direct relevance to the expansive nation of national security under consideration here. Many of the recently perceived cross-border risks that are by-product of economic openness would manifest in negative impacts on a relatively small proportion of individuals, whom it is unlikely most citizens would ever know personally. Yet through the entrepreneurship of certain actors—media, political, rent-seekers or others—the perceived threat may become politically salient.

Japan, and indeed many other nations, has experienced, since 2000, a substantial number of 'arresting events'. Moreover, it is hypothesised here that these come on top of a gradual rise in risk averseness associated with economic maturation (Moss 2002) and an aging demographic. Moss (2002:290), in a masterful study of the expansion of the role of the American state as 'the ultimate risk manager', noted that 'beginning around 1960, policymakers not only demonstrated unprecedented interest in addressing a wide range of risks facing the average citizen but also revealed a new affinity for risk management policies of all kinds'. This 'security for all' exposed the state to significant potential financial liabilities, potentially compounding moral hazard problems (Moss 2002). This is consistent with North's insight, noted earlier, that economic institutions have evolved as peoples endeavoured to deal, often ultimately fruitlessly, with uncertainty. Heightened popular risk perception could bring political pressures upon governments to attenuate perceived threats; without commensurate understandings or acceptance of the opportunity costs of trying to do so with the often blunt policy instruments available to the state.

Prosperous dependence and security

Japan's growing concerns about resource security are certainly not just perceptual; they are clearly evidenced in the sharp rises in energy and minerals prices since 2003. This has not been an entirely unmitigated bad for corporate Japan. Some firms, such as Mitsubishi Corporation, who took equity stakes in foreign resources projects in the past, have achieved dramatic capital gains and dividend returns on those stakes. Often initially taken to underpin long-term procurement contracts (effectively bond posting) or for partial control, these stakes had some of the 'forward defense' attributes noted above. Yet Japan's longer-term resource security is an overriding concern for the Japanese Government as China proactively seeks such equity stakes in the development of new resource projects. Combined with a resurgence of economic nationalism in Russia and Latin America, ongoing governance problems in Africa, renewed instability in the Middle East, and rising demand from India and other emerging economies, Japan faces significant challenges. Disagreement with China over test drilling in disputed waters has provided a potent 'arresting event', if high gasoline prices and Middle East instability were not already enough to make resource security a broadly salient threat.

Detailed discussion of Japan's recent resource security initiatives is beyond the scope of this chapter. Suffice it to note that there is considerable public-private sector coordination for renewed 'resources diplomacy' and alternative energy projects, amongst other initiatives. For instance, key coal industry stakeholders have been involved in an extensive study with the Queensland state government and Australian industry participants to address both infrastructure bottlenecks and promote the development of clean coal technologies. Yet this also highlights a particular policy dilemma facing the Japanese Government: its championing of greenhouse gas emission reductions since its decisive hosting of the 1997 UN Climate Change negotiations brought the Kyoto Protocol into being. Japan has joined, along with China, India and South Korea in the joint Australia-US initiative, the Asia-Pacific Partnership on Clean Development and Climate, which had its inaugural ministerial meeting on 12 January 2006 (www.asiapacificpartnership.org; *The Australian*, 13 January 2006; *Yomiuri Shimbun*, 13 January 2006). This is despite other lead members seeing it as an alternative to ratification of the Kyoto Protocol.

Broader supply chain security and efficiency issues have become more important to Japan as its firms increasingly source and produce abroad for global markets, including Japan's own. It is increasingly recognised that costs associated with inefficiencies or monopoly in port and associated multi-modal transport infrastructures can dwarf the trade-reducing effects of tariff protection. This is recognised in an issues paper on the liberalisation of logistics services submitted to multilateral trade negotiators earlier in 2004 by Australia amongst others (Australia 2004b). Transaction costs for cross-border trade remain relatively high for the Asia Pacific as a whole, compared to OECD averages (Wilson 2006). Issues include port efficiency, documentation requirements, extent of IT infrastructure and inter-operability throughout cross-border supply chains and the like (World Bank 2005). Japan has been an active proponent of reform and capacity-building in these areas through APEC and other regional forums although, as shall be seen below, it remains in need of further regulatory reform and enhanced corporate practice at home.

Although observers of Japan's shift in priorities to bilateral agreements frequently refer to these as free trade agreements, Japan's preferred terminology of economic partnership agreements (EPAs) is significant, not just because it was less antagonistic towards domestic agricultural issues (Terada 2006). Nippon Keidanren, the key domestic constituency for trade liberalisation at all levels, takes seriously the wide range of non-tariff issues that Japanese negotiators have pursued concessions on. For instance, Japan's agreement with Malaysia, formally concluded in December 2005, covers investment, services trade, intellectual property issues and competition policy (*Daily Yomiuri*, 12 December 2005). Mutual recognition of regulatory standards is another significant policy preference; once that mirrors European Union developments a decade before. Some of these issues 'beyond tariffs' have a long pedigree; with matters such as tax treaties and visa rules having figured prominently in negotiations between Australia and Japan in the mid 1950s in the lead-up to their landmark Commerce Agreement of 1957 (Australia, DFAT 1997). For Japan's global firms, these basic issues matter a great deal. For instance, in February 2006 Japan and the United Kingdom agreed to a revised tax treaty that reformed source country taxation on dividend payments from a subsidiary to the parent firm abroad; including exemptions for royalty income from trademarks and patents. At the same time, reducing tax evasion was a joint objective; highlighting the desire of states to strengthen their enforcement capacities while acting to facilitate international business (*Daily Yomiuri*, 4 February 2006).

At the failed Cancun ministerial meeting Japan placed great importance on the 'Singapore issues' of multilateral investment rules, trade facilitation measures (such as customs and trade procedures), transparency in government procurement and common competition policy rules (WTO 1998, 1999; Tanaka 2004). Investment provisions, along with competition issues, were strongly opposed by developing countries and yet were Japan's highest priority. Such a policy preference was consistent with the interests of Japanese enterprises operating abroad. Yet the 'Singapore issues' could also serve as a shield against criticism for the failure of multilateral negotiations over the refusal of Japan and the EU to make substantial concessions on agriculture. One senior Japanese official has since effectively acknowledged this while asserting that all countries sought to use the intractable Singapore issues in such a fashion (Tanaka 2004). The politics of the 'old trade issues' remain intractable in sensitive sectors in Japan, Europe and the United States, and are the main reason for stalled multilateral negotiations.

Salient inbound risks

Most types of cross-border inflows into Japan are currently perceived by at least some policymakers and commentators as presenting distinct risks to national welfare. Tough new anti-money laundering provisions have seen tighter controls imposed on both the international operations of banking service providers in Japan, and new identification verification requirements for domestic cash deposits. Only cross-border information flows are generally seen in a thoroughly benign light. Interestingly, Japan is distinguished from many other nations by its lack of protectionist measures in media contents—especially broadcast and cinema markets (although foreign control of a broadcaster is prohibited and the Japanese language affords a degree of natural protection in the case of contents). Risks associated with imports of goods, foreign investment bringing corporate control, and the presence of foreigners entail particularly salient issues.

Goods mobility

Contraband is always of concern, not least given the proximity of Japan's neighbours and the astonishing track record of North Korea's involvement in the cross-border smuggling of drugs. Enhancement of Japan's shipping interdiction capacities has been pursued through joint military and policy training with the United States and Australia in particular. Smaller scale anti-smuggling measures are also important. Enforcement of a total import ban on North Korean products, imposed in response to nuclear and missile tests, resulted, for instance, in arrest of a Chinese merchant-ship crew in late March 2007 for falsely declaring North Korean clams as of Chinese origin (Kyodo/*Daily Yomiuri*, 1 April 2007).

International concern about cross-border shipping as a terrorist vector has arisen given the huge volume of cargo and ship movements, with much of the seaborne shipping being under flags of convenience, and the complex interface of port operations and various domestic transport and other infrastructures (Barnes 2004; Australia, DFAT 2004). As of 1 July 2004 maritime shipping has been subject to new security measures—the International Ship and Port Facility (ISPS) code—mandated by the International Maritime Organisation (IMO) in cooperation with the World Customs Organisation (WCO). It addresses basic shipping security and is entailing significant compliance challenges and costs for the global industry (Barnes 2004). Far more onerous however are the United States' voluntary measures, the Container Security Initiative (CSI) and the Customs-Trade Partnership Against Terrorism (C-TPAT). The latter envisages a security and prescreening regime for entire supply chains and would place US customs officials in foreign ports (OECD 2003). It requires close working relationships between firms, host governments and US agencies and has potentially significant implications for cross-border trade. The concerns for Japan are currently more pertaining to the imposts on Japanese exporters and shippers to the United States, and less upon Japan's own import clearance regime. US developments nonetheless provide a significant reference point for Japan's own border security initiatives, as is clearly seen in the case of passenger movements discussed below. The US approach to security essentially has two dimensions: 'pushing the border out' and 'profiling out', the latter being aimed at concentrating limited resources for inspection and monitoring upon cross-border movements that may entail the highest risk (Riley 2005:589).

Japan is in a relatively strong position as a potential lead developer, implementer, and international supplier of advanced technology-based e-border and cross-border supply chain management systems that may help to resolve the seeming contending imperatives for more efficient cross-border flows and for enhanced border security. Japan is richly endowed with private sector providers of information and communications technology-based (ICTs) hardware and applications, such as Hitachi Ltd, with its advanced hardware infrastructure capacity and leading place in the rapidly growing RFID IC-tag business. The latter is central to advanced inventory management and supply chain traceability systems. Japanese firms are also leading providers in scanning and sensor technologies, data storage architecture and so many other relevant high technology applications. There is an ostensibly supportive policy environment, under such banners as e-Japan and a 'ubiquitous computing society', since at least the time of the Mori government in 2001, yet in practice public sector agencies involved in border enforcement could do much more. Given the cross-border nature of perceived threats, the international government-to-government coordination challenges are immense if even just some of the potential of ICT applications (for trade efficiency with border security) is to be realised.

Given the pattern of Japan's trade, and the primacy of the Asia Pacific in its firms' production networks, regional coordination will be crucial and the most efficient locus of negotiation and cooperation in relation to international trade security. Trans-shipment is a striking feature of regional goods flows, and multi-location production in industries such as consumer electronics is so common, that a mainly bilateral approach within the Asian region to the issues will be insufficient. Japan has been a strong supporter of recent initiatives in APEC in relation to counter terrorism (APEC 2003a), including strengthening the APEC Counter Terrorism Task Force. Simultaneously, APEC adopted a regional trade and financial security initiative within the Asian Development Bank to support projects related to port security and other measures to guard against the economic and social costs of terrorism (APEC 2003a). The APEC leaders' statement of November 2005 addressed counter-terrorism measures, including voluntary tests of airport vulnerabilities. Yet APEC still remained mindful of its founding mission to facilitate trade and regional economic integration; adopting a statement of resolve to realise simplified customs procedures whilst strengthening border security *(Daily Yomiuri,* 17 November 2005).

As noted above, Japan has been a strong supporter of regional initiatives to enhance port and other supply chain infrastructure and efficiency in the Asia Pacific region. Yet Japan itself has been in need of port reform, streamlining of documentation requirements, and more electronic enabling of the export-import function amongst both businesses and agencies. Japan has lagged well behind both leading European economies, as well as efficient open Asia Pacific economies such as Singapore. Japan's direct port charges are among the highest in the world and diminish both Japan's competitiveness as an export production location and its market accessibility for foreign-made goods (Tanaka 2004). Compliance with the full US agenda on port and logistics security could significantly compound these costs, as would any future Japan-specific security initiatives. Prime Minister Abe sought to address some of the port inefficiencies late in 2006, announcing a series of reforms, including more efficient documentation and 24-hour operations for certain facilities.

Cross-border goods trade may substantially increase the risk of cross-border flows of biohazards—to people, to economically and socially important agriculture, and to species diversity. Consequently, sensitive trade issues, at multilateral, regional or bilateral levels, are increasingly concerned with the contested science of threats. Quarantine matters, and related consumer protection issues, have had a strongly bilateral dimension, reflecting the usual pattern of direct shipment of perishables. This is also partly because restrictions often arise under existing administrative arrangements and can be reformed without new legislation. However, such issues would be resolved more easily if countries were to follow scientifically rigorous risk assessment and management practices that enjoy multilateral standing.

Japan's response to identification of a single case of Bovine spongiform encephalopathy (BSE) (or 'mad cow disease') in the United States in December 2003 is illuminative of the complex domestic political economy of phyto-sanitary measures. An immediate ban on US beef was imposed, which remained in effect until December 2005, when Japan concluded a bilateral deal with the United States that applied much tougher restrictions than applied in the United States.[3] Japan had demanded a comprehensive BSE-testing program for all herds in the United States (*Japan Times*, 9 July 2004). A ban on US beef was re-imposed in early 2006 after a shipment from the United States was found to contain backbone material, but was then lifted in July after official Japanese inspections of certified US export processing plants (*Daily Yomiuri*, 31 March 2007). Japan's initial ban had a dramatically negative impact on Japanese beef importers and end users such as the large *gyudon* (beef bowl) chain Yoshinoya, having ended a trade worth US$1.4 billion in 2003 (*Daily Yomiuri*, 31 March 2007).

Although Japanese beef producers gained some modest short-term benefits from the ban, ironically more significant was the boost to the reputation of Australia as beef provider as Japanese users featured it in their advertising. Japan's own BSE cases presented a challenge to the existing bureaucratic politics of agricultural policy as it clearly pitted domestic producers' interests against the cause of consumer protection, placing bureaucrats and legislative supporters of producer interests in a difficult position. Anticipating official granting of safety status to US beef by the UN World Organisation for Animal Health (OIE) in May 2007, the US Agriculture Secretary called on Japan to ease its restrictive provisions for US beef imports swiftly (31 March 2007). The issue brings to the fore the issue of Japan imposing more stringent standards than international organisations, taking up the counsel of international communities of experts, have adopted.

Services

Japan's general progress on services liberalisation has been well explored elsewhere, as has such reform's capacity to stimulate economic growth more generally (see, for example, Mattoo, Rathindran and Subramanian 2006). Motoshige Itoh has recently identified public services, health care, food services and education as areas where reform remains difficult, but is needed. The call by private sector members of a government panel for 'open skies' aviation deals and 24-hour operations at Haneda (Kyodo/ *Daily Yomiuri*, 29 March 2007) touched on a sensitive area of infrastructure in which national security concerns can readily be deployed in defense of established interests. In late March 2007, a Construction and Transport Ministry advisory panel issued a report to the Government recommending strict measures—regulatory and firm-based—to prevent foreign investors having significant shareholdings in Japan's three major international airport operators. Narita International Airport Corp., Chubu Centrair International Airport Corp. and Kansai International Airport Co. are to be privatised through public floats. The report declared that: '[i]t is necessary to prevent foreign entities from obtaining control and investment funds from conducting hostile takeovers' as the airports constitute 'social infrastructure indispensable to the nation's economic activity and citizens' life' (Kyodo/*Daily Yomiuri*, 29 March 2007).

Corporate mobility

As this case suggests, inbound corporate mobility—principally captured statistically through figures on inward FDI and mergers and acquisitions involving foreign firms—continues to provoke insecurities in Japan. This is despite powerful positive examples provided by the likes of the Renault-Nissan corporate alliance that revitalised the once-ailing Japanese automaker (Ghosn and Ries 2005). Merger and acquisition activity involving Japanese firms abroad actually outstripped that involving foreign firms in Japan in 2004 and 2005 and, overall, inward FDI into Japan is strikingly low by comparison with other OECD economies.

Hostile corporate control events, once exceedingly rare in Japan, have become more common (Milhaupt 2005; Nottage 2006). The Japan Ministries of Economy, Trade and Industry (METI) and Justice released guidelines for defensive measures against hostile takeover bids in 2005, around the rather nebulous notion of 'corporate value', which they saw as something analytically distinct from shareholder value (Whittaker and Hayakawa 2007:20). Subsequent legislative changes to company law in May 2006 gave incumbent managers more latitude to enact takeover defences. This was principally because of more liberal provisions relating to the issue of special class shares, new rights plans that would exclude a bidder, and the use of 'golden shares' (Whittaker and Hayakawa 2007:21).

A 2006 Nikkei survey revealed that some 70 per cent of responding executives were considering adoption of takeover defences (*Nikkei Weekly*, 29 March 2007). NTT and airlines have defences in place, primarily directed at foreign investors seeking control (Kyodo/*Daily Yomiuri*, 29 March 2007). Striking too is the support that the managements of targeted firms can draw from sections of the mass media; itself a recent loci of controversies over unsolicited bids for corporate control by domestic industry outsiders, principally from new media/internet entrepreneurs. In 2005–6 Japan was transfixed by the hostile move on Fuji Television by internet firm Livedoor and its controversial then-president Takefumi Horie. The role of the US investment banking institution, Lehman Brothers, in providing finance to Livedoor attracted critical scrutiny from both populist politicians and some media commentators.

The American investment fund, Steel Partners Japan Strategic Fund (Offshore), has been a lightning rod for criticism of the role of foreign investors. Steel Partners launched unsolicited bids for several firms, including Yushiro Chemical, Soto Co. and Myojo (*Forbes*, 29 March 2007). The bids all failed, but were nonetheless profitable as Steel Partners were able to sell down partial stakes in the firms at substantial premium, following alternative 'white knight' bids solicited by the boards of the targeted firms. In the case of Myojo, it was absorbed by larger domestic rival Nissin. Yet Steel Partners' move on leading brewer, Sapporo Holdings Ltd, ran into interesting difficulties, where its board won approval from a majority of shareholders for defensive measures (*Nikkei*, 29 March 2007; *Forbes*, 29 March 2007). These shareholders included a considerable number of individual investors, who may have foregone short-term capital gain as a consequence.[4] Appeals to attitudes concerning the distinctive attributes of Japanese firms, and an element of economic nationalism, seem to have been effective for management.

The Fuji–Livedoor dispute and Steel Partners cases have prompted intense discussion in Japan about markets for corporate control, shareholder value norms, and their appropriateness or otherwise in Japan. The *Yomiuri Shimbun*, a leading conservative daily, editorialised vociferously against such non-Japanese practices, vulture-like hedge funds, and a culture of so-called 'mammonism'. The antipathy to foreign ownership and control evidenced in the Construction and Transport Ministry advisory report on privatisation of major airports, cited earlier, was strikingly at odds with Japan's professed objectives in international negotiations. To date, such multilateral negotiations have shown no prospects for success while those at the bilateral level have involved partners that were unlikely to be significant sources of direct investment to Japan.

People mobility

The dual themes of openness and security, and potential tensions between them, are readily observed in policy developments and public discourse over the presence of foreigners in Japan, on both temporary and longer term bases. Whilst the entry of foreigners in Japan has long been associated—probably quite excessively—with the risk of crime, several violent crimes and instances of pickpocket and burglar gangs in the early 2000s compounded such fears. The events of 9/11, and the United States' subsequent adoption of a strict advance passenger movement alert systems, fingerprinting on arrival, profiling, and its push for wide adoption 'smart' biometric passports, have significant changed Japanese policy dynamics on migration controls. Taking a lead from the new US measures, Japan passed legislation implementing many similar measures. Whether the new ICT applications are utilised to simply enhance the efficiency of border policing—at the expense of the comfort of foreigners travelling to and from Japan—or whether they also offer benefits to the affected will be a significant test of the resolve of policymakers to realise secure but relatively open borders. ICT applications have the potential to simplify significantly the currently arcane alien registration system, as well as applying for visa extensions that currently entails considerable inefficiency and frustration for applicants.

In Japan, as elsewhere, SARS was a potent 'arresting event' in relation to the perceived risks of international mobility. Concerns about cross-border transmission of disease are not limited to inbound foreigners, given the high international mobility of Japanese. Health issues are inevitably regional and multilateral given the multidirectional mobility of people across borders. The threat of a pandemic, with devastating direct social as well as economic costs, entails profound technical and policy complexity. Clumsy anticipatory responses themselves may have profoundly negative economic impacts. The APEC Leaders' and Ministers' meetings in Bangkok (APEC 2003a, 2003b) endorsed the Health Security Initiative in the wake of SARS and of a US-Singapore initiative to create a regional emerging disease intervention centre in the latter. In November 2005, APEC members in Busan agreed to the establishment of a list of 'available and funded' experts on bird flu and like influenza pandemics, to a joint desk-top simulation exercise testing readiness, and to building capabilities for rapid responses to pandemics in their early stages. The statement pledged members 'to effective surveillance, transparency, and openness and close domestic, regional and international coordination and collaboration' (*Daily Yomiuri*, 20 November 2005). Around the same time, the G7 also agreed to closer cooperation on the bird flu threat (*Daily Yomiuri*, 20 November 2005). Significantly, APEC members also committed to information exchange on border screening procedures and controls, with a view to minimising adverse impacts on trade and travellers (*Daily Yomiuri*, 20 November 2005).

It is a formal object of policy to promote substantial growth in inbound international student, researcher and specialised labour mobility. Motivations for this include their potential role as an impetus to the invigoration of the organisations that host them, synergistic effects leading to the creation of new knowledge resources, and longer-term linkages that might enhance Japan's international influence. Somewhat controversially, Japan's Economic Partnership Agreement with the Philippines created a precedent for concessions on access for professional service providers. The agreement allowed for a quota of nurses from the Philippines, subject to professional qualifications and Japanese language requirements being met.

New concerns about guarding knowledge resources from theft by foreign employees and visiting researchers have become publicly salient. In 2004, the Ministry of Education, Culture, Sports, Science and Technology (MEXT) issued a formal advisory to universities about access to certain sensitive technologies by foreign researchers and students. Media attention focused in early 2007 on the particular case of a Chinese employee at Toyota-related firm, Denso, which was found to have copied a large number of component blueprints. Popular concerns about Chinese espionage—official and industrial—were much heightened by the suicide of a Japanese diplomat in China after he reportedly was entrapped through a romantic liaison. In March 2007 significant media attention was being given to the case of a Maritime Self-Defense Force petty officer who was found to be in possession of a hard disk containing advanced Aegis destroyer radar data after police searched his home following an allegation that his wife, a Chinese national, was in violation of immigration law (*Yomiuri Shimbun*, 31 March 2007). Subsequent reports suggested that long-standing data mishandling at a training centre had, in fact, led to a number of unapproved SDF staff being in possession of the data.

In recent years there have been explicit official policy statements in relation to the contribution that long-term foreign residents and permanent migrants may make to Japan, both in terms of addressing specific skills shortages and contributing to the general problem of Japan's rapidly aging demographic profile. In fact, as Dr Robert Feldman notes, the economics of an aging society in Japan are so severe that they cannot be resolved primarily through inward migration (Feldman 2004). Domestic human resource productivity must play the primary role, although he notes that foreign human resources—through either management know-how or simply an infectious desire to work and achieve—may help stimulate that. Yet many Japanese firms are still a long way from changing human resource recruitment and promotion systems that would allow Japan to attract and retain the international human resources mooted in official policy statements. In a positive vein, there was strong media interest in 2006 data showing that more than one in a dozen marriages in Japan were to foreign citizens, with a ratio of nearly one to eight in the Tokyo region. This may prove to be an impetus to discussion about Japan's growing diversity and what it means for national interests.

Influential?

In a system of sovereign nation states, threats to national interests originating beyond national borders can be addressed only through appeals to the mutual interests of foreign public and private actors where present, or through exercising influence over them. Japan's scope for international influence in relation to the issues discussed above has two dimensions. Firstly, reflecting the technical complexity and the consequent importance of communities of expertise, is the open question of Japanese influence in these specialist international circles. That also gives rise to consideration of the international standing of Japanese universities and other research institutions, and to the issue discussed above of what are the appropriate loci of international negotiation on particular issues impacting on, or arising from, economic integration. Secondly, broader issues of Japan's 'soft power' arise. That, in turn, raises the continuing domestic and international political difficulties surrounding Japan's modern history in the region, as well as how the politics of domestic interest groups may impact adversely on Japanese influence abroad.

Specialist influence

The previous section noted the complexity of many of the contemporary perceived threats to national welfare associated with Japan's international economic engagement. This complexity has two dimensions: inherent technical difficulty and then the complexity entailed in designing, implementing and assessing policy responses to it. Relevant policy communities have a distinct demography, reflecting networks and clusters of expertise that span organisational types and, in specialist academic circles at least, national borders. Frequently, members of these policy communities will have strong shared norms that may shape the set of conceivable policy options (Atkinson and Coleman 1992).

An illuminating instance of the dynamics potentially involved here is provided by Japan's July 2003 defeat in a WTO Dispute Settlement Body ruling on a case brought by the United States against Japan for its ban on American apples.[5] Japan utilised quarantine provisions to prevent the imports on the grounds of a risk of the apple blight disease being transmitted to domestic apple production. The panel report did not accept that Japan had established such a risk as it was obligated to do under the agreement on phyto-sanitary measures adopted at the conclusion of the Uruguay Round. A review of the transcripts of the final hearings is illuminating in showing how risk issues were dealt with by the expert witnesses and how the Japanese case appeared not to be informed by those established risk assessment and management concepts (WTO 2003).[6] Yet the considerable size and status of the Japanese delegation in attendance testifies to the importance that was placed on the WTO panel report by Japanese policymakers (WTO 2003) One of the expert witnesses in the case concluded that the original SPS agreement had specified the Principle of Managed Risk which should have led signatories to establish a formal risk management policy and, by implication, appropriate capacities to realise it (WTO 2003).[7]

Recent supply crises involving the beef, poultry and pork industries might be transformed into a positive force over the longer term if there is effective state-private sector collaboration within Japan and with suppliers abroad to implement mutually accepted risk management methodologies and tracing technologies. Greater consumer confidence can be invoked, to the benefit of foreign and Japanese stakeholders in such international supply chains. Moreover, states have a significant capacity to attenuate or compound the disruption to international supply chains entailed in critical incidents, not only through border controls but also through their control of major medical, scientific and analytical capacity as well as state authority itself. Many firms and other private institutions, for instance, relied solely on the official advices issued by home governments and international agencies on basic matters such as staff travel after the outbreak of SARS and heightened concerns about terrorism. While international regulatory cooperation, under the aegis of multilateral, regional and bilateral initiatives, has certainly been enhanced in recent years, there is still a long way to go before a true 'international policy community' can be said to exist. The Japanese civil service needs enhanced risk assessment and management capacities as well as more personnel with the skills set necessary to function as effective long-term interlocutors with their counterparts in relevant foreign agencies.

Japan's 'soft power' and regional challenges?

Complex external threats, especially arising through and because of transnational private organisations, require the cooperation of many foreign individuals, diversely situated organisationally, to address them. Nye (2004) argues for the importance of 'soft power' in a nation being able to secure that cooperation. METI (2003a, 2003b) has recently made much of the role of exports from Japan's cultural industries in enhancing the nation's 'soft power'—'Brand Japan' in Foreign Minister Aso's words— and the positive economic 'ripple effects' to other Japanese industries and organisations abroad.[8] Japan's official FTA strategy statement asserted, rather blithely, that resulting economic linkages would give 'rise to a sense of political trust among countries that are parties to these agreements, expanding Japan's global diplomatic influence and interests'[9] (MOFA 2002).

Japan's standing as a net exporter and major beneficiary of the multilateral trading system means it risks dissipating international influence in protecting uncompetitive domestic producers in remaining protected sectors. World Bank research revealed significant gaps between the perceived openness and efficiency of particular national business environments—as measured in influential surveys such as that by AT Kearney—and realities as judged by World Bank analysts (World Bank 2004). This suggests an important role—of an essentially public goods nature—for the effective national projection to international business communities, and the media and public agencies relating to them. The Japan Export Trade Organisation (JETRO) has long been well-resourced and committed to such a function, yet the broader lesson remains that perception management is imperative.

Japan's greatest economic and political challenges lie in engagement with emerging China. As the discussion above attests, an emergent China is a significant consideration in a number of Japan's established and emerging security concerns, broadly defined. Japanese exports and investment to China have surged (*Asian Wall Street Journal*, 23–25 July 2004:A3). China presents significant competition to Japan in raw materials and energy markets, as well as in related shipping and other business services. China is very relevant to contemporary Japanese cross-border crime and public health concerns. While Japan's official FTA strategy flagged a vision of future mutual economic partnership between Japan, China, Korea and ASEAN, a 'wait and see' policy on an FTA with China was enunciated (MOFA 2002). Achieving a comprehensive FTA with China would be immensely difficult, with a pre-requisite being an effective official dialogue that goes well beyond the recent thaw in official relations with the ascension of Shinzo Abe to the prime ministership.

The contemporary cross-border risk agenda can only be addressed through international cooperation and negotiation, the loci of which must be driven by the nature of each of the issues at stake. It must also be recognised that the scope for trade-offs will vary greatly depending on the nature and number of parties at the table; the level of the international game impacts on the domestic political calculus for governments. In their review of the state of the Australia-Japan bilateral relationship, de Brouwer and Warren (2001) concluded that while the locus of negotiations over the removal of tariffs and other major formal trade barriers should be at the multilateral level, important trade facilitation initiatives could nonetheless be pursued at the bilateral and regional level. Some of the issues at the interface of trade and security will inevitably be first dealt with at a bilateral level—albeit with the United States rather than the countries with which Japan pursues free trade agreements.

Conclusions

Established structures of producer, legislative and bureaucratic interests have interacted historically to present apparently formidable barriers to a major change in Japan's foreign economic policy preferences. Nonetheless, the Japanese economy, through both long established dynamics of policy liberalisation and private sector initiative, has become deeply integrated into the Asia Pacific regional and global economies. Key Japanese constituencies for further economic openness abroad—such as the Keidanren and its leading members—could do much more though to articulate the benefits of openness at home. In particular, the positive contribution that foreign investors, in free markets for corporate control, might make to corporate value in Japan needs to be prioritised.

Japan is sufficiently endowed with technical expertise to make a significant contribution to resolving the apparent dilemmas of national economic openness and security. The suite of contemporary risk issues, ranging from terrorism to disease and including immigration and crime, has made 'border protection' highly political salient in many countries. Some political entrepreneurialism tapping community concerns in Japan is inevitable. As in past political controversies over the costs and benefits of trade and FDI, there is a crucial role for independent rigorous assessments of the real risks presented by cross-border movements of goods and people and the opportunity costs of heavy-handed restrictions. Japan's past spurious defences of non-tariff barriers on risk grounds are the stuff of legends. Japanese trade policymaking needs to be informed by a sense of the fragility of state credibility and yet the potency of state reputation in restoring confidence in the wake of a critical incident.

As Yoshimatsu in this volume and other authors have shown, bureaucratic turf wars on 'traditional' trade issues in Japan remain rife, underpinned as they are by private interest politics and institutional inadequacies that make strategic policy initiatives difficult both to formulate and to implement. With effective political leadership, the new security, risk and border protection agendas could provide an impetus to inter-agency coordination and strategic planning. This would not only see the issues dealt with more effectively, but might also provide some scope for transcending particularistic interests in favour of national interest-maximising trade policy preferences. Ideally, leading civil servants would use the technical complexity and new analytics of the risk issues involved to take on a 'bureau shaping' role. Dunleavy (1992) recognised that this was fundamental to executive actors in Anglo-American societies becoming drivers of bureaucratic reform itself and broader economic reform. Without that leadership, entrenched protectionist interests might appropriate the new currency of cross-border risk to frustrate some of the market liberalisation initiatives arising from bilateral and, one hopes, multilateral negotiations.

Notes

1   It is not the intention of the author to extrapolate from the influential work of Hofstede (2001) on comparative values, in which Japanese were found to exhibit relatively very high levels of 'uncertainty avoidance' (as he used the term) on average, to the political economy of cross border mobilities. Much more conceptual and comparative empirical work would be required before any such conclusions could be drawn.

2   In Florida's (2005:72) words: 'Since every human being has creative potential, the key role for culture is to create a society where that talent can be attracted, mobilised and unleashed. All of this turns on an expansive, open, and proactively inclusive culture…Open culture is a spur to innovation, entrepreneurship, and economic development'.

3   US standards require the removal of brains, spinal cords, backbones and other risk material from cattle aged 30 months or older, while the more restrictive Japanese provisions imposed a 20-month age threshold. That agreement was nonetheless controversial in Japan (*Daily Yomiuri*, 31 March 2007).

4   The Sapporo poison pill and related defence measures nonetheless required annual reaffirmation by shareholders, suggesting that management needs have at least some regard for shareholder value.

5   Japanese agriculture bureaucrats and legislative backers seem determined to strengthen their hand *vis-à-vis* major food suppliers such as the United States and Australia on phyto-sanitary issues wherever possible. In 2005 the ministry announced a new project, and associated pubic consultation process, to examine the environmental and economic impact of introduced species.

6   The US submission wryly observed of Japan's much-emphasised distinction between 'direct' and 'indirect' evidence of a risk, with the latter being sufficient to justify restrictive measures, that what mattered of evidence was 'whether it was scientific' (WTO 2003:24).

7   The advising expert was Dr Ian Smith, Director-General of the European and Mediterranean Plant Protection Organisation in Paris. He noted that submissions in the apple case, as in some others, had focused solely on the Principle of Minimal Impact. Yet the Principle of Managed Risk created as part of the International Standards on Phyto-sanitary Measures states that 'because some risk of introduction of a quarantine pest always exists, countries shall agree to a policy of risk management when formulating phyto-sanitary measures'. Coupled with Standard No. 11 that stated 'since zero risk is not a reasonable option, the guiding principle for risk management should be to manage risk to achieve the required degree of safety that can be justified and is feasible within the limits of available options and resources'. Smith concluded that 'on the basis of this principal it should be possible to manage risks which are open to some uncertainty' (WTO 2003:220).

8   The 'soft power' concept was first developed by Joseph Nye and has recently been applied to discussions of the United States in particular in the wake of September 11 and the Iraq conflict. Popular and official interest in Japan's soft power was provoked by an article in *Foreign Policy* by MacGray (2002) on Japan's 'gross national cool'. The general 'brand state' notion was proposed by van Ham (2001) in an equally influential article in *Foreign Affairs*.

9   Moreover, it was declared that FTAs would 'increase Japan's bargaining power in WTO negotiations' without clarifying how or to what ends such leverage, if it was in fact attained, might be deployed (MOFA 2002).

References

Anderson, B., 1991. *Imagined Communities: Reflections on the origin and spread of nationalism*, revised edition, Verso, London.

Anderson, K. and Garnaut. R., 1987. *Australian Protectionism: extent, causes and effects*, Allen and Unwin, Sydney.

Asia Pacific Economic Cooperation Forum (APEC), 2003a. 'Bangkok Declaration on Partnership for the Future', 11th APEC Economic Leaders' Meeting. Bangkok.

____, 2003b. 'Fifteenth APEC Ministerial Meeting Joint Statement', 18 October, Bangkok. Available at http://www.apec.org/apec/documents.

____, 2004. 'APEC agrees to new measures to enhance agricultural biosecurity', Media report issued by the APEC Agricultural Technical Cooperation Working Group, Chiang Mai, 19 June.

Aso, T., 2006. 'A New Look at Cultural Diplomacy: A Call to Japan's Cultural Practitioners', Speech delivered at Digital Hollywood University, 28 April. Accessed at www.mofa.go.jp.

Atkinson, M. and W.D. Coleman, 1992. 'Policy Networks, Policy Communities and the Problems of Governance', *Governance*, 5(2):154–80.

Australia, Department of Foreign Affairs and Trade (DFAT), 1997. *The Australia-Japan Agreement on Commerce 1957*, Australian Foreign Policy series, AGPS, Canberra.

——, 2004. *Combating Terrorism in the Transport Sector: economic costs and benefits*, Economic Analytical Unit, Canberra.

Australian Government, 2004a. *Enforcement of Business Regulations and Commercial Laws in the APEC Region*, Report submitted to the APEC Ministers Responsible for Trade Meeting, Pucon, 6 June.

Australian Government, et al., 2004b. *Logistics Services: Communication from Australia, Hong Kong, China, Nicaragua, Switzerland, the Separate Customs Territory of Taiwan, Penghu, Kinmen and Matsu*, Room document distributed at the CTS Special Session on 2 April.

Barnes, P., 2004. 'Security risk management issues in maritime trade: An analysis', Paper presented to the 2004 Academy of International Business (AIB) Southeast Asia Regional Conference, 5–6 August, Macau.

Bates, R.H. and Krueger, A.O., 1993. 'Generalizations arising from the country studies', R.H. Bates and A.O. Krueger (eds), *Political and Economic Interactions in Economic Policy Reform: evidence from eight countries*, Blackwell, Cambridge:444–72.

Breton, A., 1964. 'The economics of nationalism', *Journal of Political Economy*, 72(4):377–78.

de Brouwer, G. and Warren, T., 2001. *Strengthening Australia-Japan Economic Relations*, Department of Foreign Affairs and Trade, Canberra.

Dreher, A., 2006. 'Does globalization affect growth?: Evidence from a new index of globalization', *Applied Economics*, 38(10):1,091–10.

Dunleavy, P., 1992. *Democracy, Bureaucracy and Public Choice: Economic Explanations in Political Science*, Prentice Hall, New York and London.

Farrell, R., 1997. *Japanese foreign direct investment in real estate 1985–1994*, Pacific Economic Papers, 272, October, Australia-Japan Research Centre, The Australian National University, Canberra.

Feldman, R.A., 2004. 'Immigrants: Torrent or Trickle', Morgan Stanley Equity Research Japan, 7 January.

Florida, R., 2005. *The Flight of the Creative Class: the new global competition for talent*, Harper Business, New York.

Ghosn, C. and P. Ries, 2005. *Shift: inside Nissan's historic revival*, Currency/Doubleday, New York.

Hofstede, G.H., 2001. *Culture's Consequences: comparing values, behaviors, institutions, and organizations across nations*, 2nd Edition, Sage, Thousand Oaks.

Japan, Ministry of Economy Trade and Industry (METI), 2003a. '*Contentsu sangyo no kokusai tenkai to hakyu koka*' at *Keizai Sangyo Sho Shomu Joho Seisakukyoku, Bunka Joho Kanren Sangyoka*, (International Development of the Contents Industry and its Ripple Effects), available at www.meti.go.jp.

____, 2003b. '*Contentsu sangyo kokusai senryaku kenkyukai – Chukan torimatome*', (Interim Report on International Strategy for the Contents Industry), METI, Tokyo, available at www.meti.go.jp.

Japan, Ministry of Foreign Affairs, 2002. 'Japan's FTA Strategy', Economic Affairs Bureau, October, Tokyo.

____, 2003. *Diplomatic Blue Book 2003*, Government of Japan, Tokyo.

____, 2004. 'APEC Counter-Terrorism Capacity Building Initiative: Japan's new assistance package to South East Asia', June, Tokyo.

MacGray, D., 2002. 'Japan's gross national cool', *Foreign Policy*, May–June.

Machan, T.R., 1992. 'Politics and ideology: do ideas matter?', *The Mid-Atlantic Journal of Business*, 28(2):159–67.

Mason, M., 1992. *American Multinationals and Japan: The political economy of Japanese capital controls, 1899–1980*, Harvard East Asian Monograph 104, Council on East Asian Studies, Harvard University, Cambridge, Mass.

Mattoo, A., R. Rathindran and A. Subramanian, 2006. 'Measuring services trade liberalisation and its impact on economic growth: an illustration', *Journal of Economic Integration*, 21(1):64–98.

Milhaupt, C.J., 2005. 'In the shadow of Delaware?: The rise of hostile takeovers in Japan', *Columbia Law Review*, 105(7):2,171–216.

Milner, H.V., 1988. *Resisting Protectionism: Global Industries and the Politics of International Trade*, Princeton University Press, Princeton, NJ.

Milner, H.V. and Yoffie, D.B., 1989. 'Between free trade and protectionism: strategic trade policy and a theory of corporate trade demands', *International Organization*, 43:239–72.

Moss, D.A., 2002. *When All Else Fails: government as the ultimate risk manager*, Harvard University Press, Cambridge, Mass.

Mulgan, A.G., 2000. 'Japan's political leadership deficit', *Australian Journal of Political Science* 35(2):183–202.

_____, 2002. *Japan's Failed Revolution: Koizumi and the politics of economic reform*, Asia Pacific Press, The Australian National University, Canberra.

North, D.C., 2005. *Understanding the Process of Economic Change*, Princeton University Press, Princeton, NJ.

Nottage, L., 2006. *Nothing new in the (North) East?: Interpreting the rhetoric and reality of Japanese corporate governance*, Pacific Economic Papers No. 359, Australia-Japan Research Centre, The Australian National University, Canberra.

Nye, J.S., 2004. *Soft Power: the means to success in world politics*, Public Affairs/Perseus, New York.

Odell, J., 1990. 'Understanding international trade policies: an emerging synthesis', *World Politics*, 43:139–67.

Ohmae, K., 1990. *The Borderless World: power and strategy in the interlinked economy*, Harper & Collins, London.

Organization for Economic Cooperation and Development (OECD), 2003. *Security in Maritime Transport: risk factors and economic impact*, Maritime Transport Committee, Directorate for Science, Technology and Industry, OECD, Paris.

Posner, R.A., 2004. *Catastrophe: risk and response*, Oxford University Press, New York.

Ray, E., 1981. 'Determinants of tariff and non-tariff trade restrictions in the US', *Journal of Political Economy* 89(1):105–21.

Rogowski, R., 1989. *Commerce and Coalitions: how trade affects domestic political alignments*, Princeton University Press, Princeton, NJ.

Simmons, B.A., 1994. *Who Adjusts? Domestic sources of foreign economic policy during the interwar years*, Princeton University Press, Princeton, NJ.

Sassen, S., 2001. *The Global City*, Princeton University Press, New York, London, Tokyo.

Swiss Institute of Business Cycle Research, 2007. 'Press Release' 19 January 2007 and '2007 KOF Index of Globalization', accessed at www.globalization.kof.ethz.ch, Swiss Institute of Business Cycle Research, Zurich.

Tanaka, N., 2004. 'WTO Negotiations: Japan's Strategy', Presentation to Waseda University, 2 June by the Director General of the Multilateral Trade System Department, METI, Government of Japan, Tokyo.

Terada, T., 2006. *The making of Asia's first bilateral FTA: origins and regional implications of the Japan-Singapore Economic Partnership Agreement*, Pacific Economic Papers No. 354, Australia-Japan Research Centre, The Australian National University, Canberra.

van Ham, P., 2001. 'The rise of the brand state: the postmodern politics of image and reputation', *Foreign Affairs*, 80(5):2–6.

Vaile, M., 2004. 'Australia leads call for commitments on freer freight movement', Media Release, 5 April, Canberra.

Warren, T., 1997. 'The political economy of reform in services in Japan', in *The Politics of Economic Reform in Japan*, Pacific Economic Papers, No. 271, Australia-Japan Research Centre, The Australian National University Canberra: 2.1–2.23.

Wilson, J.S., 2006. 'Trade facilitation: why it matters to APEC and what next?', *APEC Economies Newsletter*, 10(9), September.

Wolf, C. Jr., Levaux H.P. and Daochi T., 1999. *Economic Openness: many facets, many metrics*, Rand, Santa Monica.

Wolf, C. Jr., 2002. *Straddling Economics and Politics: cross-cutting issues in Asia, the United States, and the global economy*, Rand, Santa Monica.

World Bank, 2004. *Doing Business in 2004: understanding regulation*, Co-publication of the World Bank, International Finance Corporation, and Oxford University Press, Washington, DC.

——, 2005. *Doing Business in 2005: understanding regulation*, Co-publication of the World Bank, International Finance Corporation, and Oxford University Press, Washington, DC. Available at www.doing business.org.

World Economic Forum, 2007. 'The Global Competitiveness Report 2006–2007, Executive Summary', World Economic Forum, Geneva. Available at www.weforum.org.

World Trade Organization (WTO), 1998. *The Impact of Investment Incentives and Performance Requirements on International Trade*, Prepared by the Working Group on the Relationship between Trade and Investment, WT/WGTI/W/56 (98–3785), World Trade Organization Washington, DC.

____, 1999. *Report of the Working Group on the Relationship Between Trade and Investment to the General Council*, WT/WGTI/3 (99–4592), World Trade Organization Washington, DC.

____, 2003. *Japan—Measures Affecting the Importation of Apples: Report of the Panel*, (WT/DS245/R), 15 July 2003, World Trade Organization Washington, DC.

Yoshimatsu, H., 2000. *Internationalization, Corporate Preferences and Commercial Policy in Japan*, Macmillan, Basingstoke.

——, 2003. *Japan and East Asia in Transition: trade policy, crisis and evolution, and regionalism*, Palgrave Macmillan, New York.

6 OUT OF THE JAPANESE INCUBATOR

I-MODE AND THE INTELLECTUAL PROPERTY

IMPERATIVE

Adam Johns

Due to a critical mass of high-tech manufacturers and the resultant intensity of domestic competition, Japan has long been a hotbed of innovation in various manufacturing and services sectors. Yet despite this potential for domestic competition to fuel international competitiveness of locally developed innovations, many Japanese firms have faced difficulties in expanding operations overseas. While exports of technology-centric manufactures have achieved considerable success, process or knowledge-intensive exports of services that are reliant on tacit communication have been more problematic for Japanese firms, despite some innovative and efficient services sector operating in the domestic market. It is not surprising thus that this deficit in trade of services has contributed to the perception that Japan's only competitive sectors are in manufacturing. This lack of competitiveness has particularly been the case when it comes to reaping a return on the intellectual property component inherent in innovations in technology, processes, and business models or systems.

This comes despite Japan having been an exemplar throughout East Asia and the Pacific as an innovator across a number of industries. Many economies in the region have long looked to Japan as the forerunner in innovations ranging from consumer electronics to automobiles, and from television programs to lifestyle goods. Yet despite this demonstration effect,[1] more intangible products such us television programs and business models have, in the past, either been imitated and adapted by local firms, or have not been exported for a number of reasons. In both situations, rents have not flowed back to Japan in an era when the economy needs to rely increasingly on its human capital and intellectual property.

In the field where telecommunications, consumer electronics, and media content converge, Japan has witnessed the unique success of mobile internet through the innovation of front-running mobile operator NTT DoCoMo and its 'i-mode' service, alongside rival services offered by KDDI and Softbank.[2] DoCoMo's i-mode is worthy of further investigation not only because of its unique success in Japan, when operators in other countries failed to launch a sustainable mobile internet service, but also because it provides a pertinent example of how a successful business model was licensed to mobile operators in countries around the world.

In the face of attempts at foreign direct investment in the US content business by Japanese consumer electronics manufacturers (Matsushita and Sony), this case highlights how Japanese firms are beginning to seek alternative revenue streams for exporting innovations not only in technological hardware and production processes, but in marketing and business model design.

The role of licensing such intellectual property has been cemented not only by the rise in recent years of licensing fees and royalties as a proportion of Japanese foreign earnings, but also by cogent Japanese government policies that recognise the value of building capacity for intellectual property creation and protecting the rights of intellectual property owners.

This chapter explores the unique success factors of i-mode, and, questioning its applicability outside of Japan, shows how DoCoMo went about licensing the business model after failed attempts at foreign direct investment. I-mode's international licensing may well be a harbinger for an increase in the licensing and export of a variety of Japanese innovations abroad that have the ability to transcend cultural specificities.

The i-mode model

Mobile internet technologies have had the potential to provide consumers with significant utility, given their ability to deliver information in a timely fashion, reduce transaction costs, and provide access to a wide variety of content. Yet until the now well-documented success of i-mode and mobile internet in Japan, mobile internet platforms in most developed countries had failed to capture consumer and industry interest. In Japan, however, mobile internet subscribers to the three major carriers' services had passed 70 million in May 2004, providing users, operators, and industry with a value-added communications channel. As of February 2007, subscribers had passed 83 million (Telecommunication Carriers Association 2007).[3]

Launched by NTT DoCoMo in 1999 to abate the slowed growth of the maturing mobile telephony market, i-mode began to garner attention from analysts, industry players, and academics outside of Japan when it attracted 10 million subscribers by mid–2000, and had 30 million subscribers by the end of 2001.[4] This resulted in a plethora of news articles and research reports as well as a significant volume of academic articles (such as Devine and Holmsqvist 2001; Jonason and Eliasson 2000), which have continued into recent years as DoCoMo began to take i-mode overseas (for example, Peltokorpi et al. 2007; Lindmark et al. 2004).

Following this success, operators across Europe and Asia have signed licensing agreements with NTT DoCoMo to offer the i-mode service in their respective markets. Yet with subscriber growth from some of DoCoMo's European partners indicating mixed results, and some operators such as Telstra in Australia and O2 in the UK announcing in July 2007 their discontinuation of i-mode, can the fundamental business model evidenced in i-mode's success in Japan be replicated in other countries, or is it simply due to socio-cultural or industry characteristics in the Japanese market?

If i-mode can in fact be transplanted to other countries, it may well become an exemplar for Japanese firms licensing their innovations abroad, given that it represents a convergence of tangible goods such as electronics manufacturing and telecommunications hardware, with more intangible products including creative content, software and technological standards, as well as marketing know-how and innovative business model design. Not only would the successful licensing of i-mode have positive spill-over effects on other Japanese firms, such as handset manufacturers and content providers, but it would also present an example of how intellectual property residing in a wide gamut of knowledge-based products can be exported.

Key features of the business model

DoCoMo's i-mode offers users (as do its rival services in Japan) an 'always on' dedicated email client and web browser by which they can access a variety of aggregated content, allowing them to browse news, check weather and train timetables, download music, buy plane tickets, update their blog, and interact with others on social networking sites. It provides a service for 'analogue' people rather than a gadget for technology enthusiasts (Matsunaga 2000).

The core of the i-mode business model can be described as creating a 'semi-open platform', that is with elements of closed, proprietary systems that offer structure and security, and open platforms that provide freedom of choice and interconnectivity (Johns 2003). The key elements to this platform are a collaborative business network between the operator and the handset manufacturer, the aggregation of content, a centralised payment mechanism, the separation between operators and content providers, freedom of access for users, and the increased connectivity these elements deliver.

Collaborative business network. The inter-firm relationships between DoCoMo (the network operator) and various handset manufacturers resulted in a highly reliable and functional technical platform. Handsets were tailored to the network operator's specifications, meaning there was no chance of incompatibility between handset capability and network-supported services. This stable operating environment was not achieved through vertical integration but through close cooperation between manufacturers, vendors, and network operators.

This 'single and indivisible relationship' (Natsuno 2000) between service provider (DoCoMo) and handset manufacturer has resulted in a win-win situation for both parties, as demand for new functions and services means an increased demand for new handsets that make these applications possible. This increases the turnover rate of handsets and improves the profitability of both actors. Thus highly customised network-specific handsets produced by popular manufacturers became necessary in order for network operators to attract and retain subscribers.[5]

Behind the reliable user interface, building an interdependent relationship with handset manufacturers allowed for the easier deployment of standard technologies. I-mode's cHTML (compact Hypertext Markup Language) was a 'simple' solution in that being a subset of HTML made it more open and widely understood. By developing cHTML and associated transfer protocols, DoCoMo implemented a language that end-users and programmers were more likely to be familiar with, as it is the *de facto* internet standard (Lunn 2001).

Furthermore, this cHTML platform was implemented over a packet-based network rather than circuit-switching technology, giving users immediate access without the need to 'dial-up', and allowing for seamless movement between web and voice usage. It also made it easier for operators to charge users for the volume of information they downloaded, not the time they were connected.

Pointing to the success also enjoyed by rival services that use different technologies, some observers have questioned the role cHTML and packet switching played in i-mode's popularity (Lindmark et al. 2004). Yet other platforms (KDDI and J-Phone/Softbank) use different technology because cHTML was developed by DoCoMo. Without the large research and development budgets, these competitors used tweaked *de facto* standards or licensed technical solutions and packaged them in a way that ultimately replicated i-mode's functionality.[6] As discussed later, the presence of a unique technology also has ramifications for the licensing of i-mode overseas.

Aggregating content. Acting as a content aggregator, DoCoMo provided access to a variety of 'official' content services through their 'iMenu' portal, affording users easy and timely access to a wide variety of content, while content providers were given easy access to markets. By restricting content that was placed on the 'iMenu', however, DoCoMo also played a monitoring role providing users with the assurance of quality. As the service provider, DoCoMo were ideally situated to play the role of aggregator between content providers and users.

Critically, the value of the i-mode services lies in the inherent market-making function of aggregation. DoCoMo do not create any content themselves, but rather organise third-party content into a user-friendly portal for users to access.[7] Aggregating content services in a portal added structure to the platform by organising content and information, thereby reducing search and decision costs while improving quality of service. Starting with 67 content providers, i-mode's iMenu had 4,245 'official sites' as at June 2004. As of February 2007, there were over 8,430 official sites for 3G i-mode users (NTT DoCoMo 2007a).

Micro-payment mechanism. According to Natsuno (2000), it was difficult for content providers to receive benefits or revenue from internet-delivered information before the entry of i-mode. Adding a centralised micro-payment mechanism allowed small subscription fees for official content to be placed on users' phone bill rather than requiring them to use another form of payment such as credit cards or prepaid cards. Instead of paying tiny fees to various content providers, subscribers have their charges aggregated on their monthly bill by NTT DoCoMo, who collects fees on behalf of providers, taking a nine per cent commission from this revenue. DoCoMo also placed restrictions on pricing strategies of content providers, limiting them to between 100–300 yen per month (Matsunaga 2000).

Encouraging third parties to develop and provide content, and users to access this content saw i-mode act as a market-place intermediary. At a time when a lack of established payment mechanisms were causing problems for 'e-commerce' and 'm-commerce' (mobile commerce) alike, i-mode's payment system added a stable and secure structure to the mobile internet platform and allowed it to be used as a viable distribution channel without the need to create a direct billing relationship between users and content providers.

Despite its success, this concept is not completely revolutionary or unique. As Matsunaga (2000) points out, telecommunications carriers have long been a proxy for the collection of fees for premium telephone information services. Similarly, subscription television operators provide users with access to a bundle of channels, and then charge on behalf of the respective content providers.

Separation from content provider. Significantly, i-mode's evolution to an e-marketplace was encouraged by ensuring independence from content providers, which facilitated a more 'level-playing field' for potential suppliers, and signalled diversity of content for users (Johns 2003). In contrast to strategies exhibited in recent years by media and telecommunications firms such as AOL TimeWarner in the United States and Telstra in Australia, the success of i-mode was assisted by DoCoMo's decision to pursue 'arms-length' transactions with upstream content providers rather than securing exclusive rights for content. Independent content providers are therefore more likely to use the platform to distribute their content as they do not perceive DoCoMo to have a vested interest in promoting the content of affiliates above their own. DoCoMo profits from commission fees, an increase in traffic, and the launch of new services rather than from holding rights to exclusive or in-house content.

Freedom of access. The fifth element i-mode exhibits is the provision of a platform without restrictions. When first introduced, i-mode users were only able to access content on the official iMenu. It appears however, DoCoMo realised that its subscribers desired the freedom to access information and content from alternative sources, and the ability to create their own web sites. Therefore, even content providers who were not on the i-mode portal could use the platform to provide information to users or to distribute their content by writing their pages in cHTML. Users were not only able to access these non-official or 'independent' sites freely, but could also create their own web pages, which DoCoMo actively encouraged. This resulted in a greater critical mass of content, which improved the platform's attractiveness and also generated revenue for DoCoMo through data charges. As of June 2004, there were 77,550 independent sites created by individuals and 'non-official' providers (NTT DoCoMo 2004). In March 2007 this figure was estimated at over 107,000 (OH!NEW? 2007).

Connectivity. Finally, a cumulative result of these factors is the increased connectivity between users. The ability to send messages via email to both fixed and mobile internet devices gave users an inter-personal communication medium not just between users on the same network or technology, but across platforms. Allowing users the freedom to access sites outside the i-mode portal provided an opportunity for self-expression and improved connectivity between users. The ability for users to create their own web pages and access those of other users resulted in a greater number of sites on the i-mode platform and facilitated community building and connectivity among users.

Hence, through this semi-open platform, i-mode reduced transaction costs, improved timeliness, and increased the value of aggregation for all participants in the value chain. Vishik and Whinston (1999) identified that aggregation of content results in a more structured, but not restricted, informational space. This appears to be the most crucial value-adding principle of the semi-open platform: to add structure but without restrictions.

Japan-specificity

Despite the key fundamentals of this business model, its transferability outside of Japan has often been questioned. Apart from the core business model, various Japan-specific factors seem to have contributed to the success of i-mode, which may limit its potential replication overseas. Many of these are well recognised. While fixed internet in Japan has now become one of the most competitive among OECD nations, evidence suggests that slow internet take-up during the introduction of mobile internet may have resulted in the absence of a comparable substitute. In particular, the legacy of telecommunications regulations had a lasting impact on the pricing and diffusion of internet services. Furthermore, the extent to which socio-cultural aspects such as commuting, and industry characteristics such as competitive media industries, contributed to the success of i-mode needs to be considered.

Low diffusion of personal computers. Despite Japan's high level of technological innovation, critics have referred to low penetration of personal computers in Japanese homes, schools, and offices during the early days of the internet (Gottlieb 2000).

The high price of portable laptop computers in Japan during the early days of internet growth discouraged their widespread use. This combined with the restricted living space in Japanese homes, which has arguably driven much innovation in device convergence, consequently resulted in a lack of space for a dedicated PC fixture.[8] Other demand-related arguments for low PC penetration in early years include difficulties in word processing in the Japanese language (Fransman 1999).[9]

On the supply side, the large sunk investments that many electronics companies had in antiquated word processor technologies may have resulted in their reluctance to abandon marketing these even after PCs had become commonplace in other countries.[10] Alternatively, as Fransman (1999) argues, a *de facto* monopoly in the PC market held by NEC (who used their own standard rather than IBM-compatible hardware) caused the Japanese PC market to grow considerably more slowly than the United States.

High cost of telecommunications. Until regulatory reform in the 1990s, Japanese telecommunications fees had been among the highest in the world (Devine and Holmqvist 2001; Anchordoguy 2001). Regulations allowed the incumbent telecommunications carrier, NTT, to effectively own the 'last mile', or the final connection to every Japanese household (McNeill 2001; Mollman 2001). Having all calls terminating and originating on NTT wires, resulted in higher costs for users.[11] The persisting NTT subscriber bond system also meant that the actual purchase of the phone line may have been the biggest expense. This constituted a significant barrier to young people and lower income earners acquiring their own private communications channel, particularly during the dial-up internet era.[12]

The Japanese Government's style of deregulatory policy also provided DoCoMo with the economic incentive to innovate. The deregulation of telecommunications resulted in the state monopoly NTT being broken up into regional and product-type companies such as NTT East and NTT West (fixed line), NTT Communications (long distance), and NTT DoCoMo (mobile). This separation of the mobile carrier DoCoMo was a key difference from most countries where incumbent networks faced the challenge of expanding mobile services without cannibalising fixed line revenues. Thus DoCoMo had a clear impetus for developing a highly competitive mobile phone service, particularly after the deregulation of the mobile telephony market in 1994.

Since the government implementation of stringent competition policy and the surge in broadband services—first via cable then in particular through ADSL (Asymmetric Digital Subscriber Line), Japan has seen dramatic increases in internet connectivity, with new market entrants being granted access to NTT's lines, and access rates fell dramatically. Data from 2002 suggests that Japan's ADSL packages consistently rank among the fastest and cheapest in the world.[13] Some argue in addition that as Japan's internet connectivity was comparable to European countries such as France, it cannot be considered as a key factor in i-mode's success (Funk 2001; Lindmark et al. 2004). Yet France also experienced below average connectivity, often attributed to sunken investments in home-grown Minitel technology (see Brousseau 2003).

While mobile telephony in Japan appears to have offered an alternative to fixed line, Funk (2001) rightly questions the degree to which mobile is a substitute for fixed internet. Despite the above discussion on the comparative attractiveness of mobile internet, it would not be accurate to say that Japanese consumers 'prefer mobile to fixed internet', or that their 'first online experience was on mobile not fixed internet'. Mobile internet (and telephony in general) also has a complementary relationship to fixed line, and neither can be said to be direct substitutes for the other, even if substitution does occur at some point. Despite current high levels of fixed connectivity, mobile internet remains popular, as it has evolved as a discrete value-added service. There are, however, socio-cultural factors that also need to be considered.

Commuting. The long commuting hours of Japanese have often been raised as a reason for the success of mobile internet (Jonason and Eliasson 2000). This travel time gives subscribers pockets of time during which they could access information and entertainment in a timely fashion (Lunn 2001). Moreover, it is possible that this reliance on and dependability of public transport initially increased the demand for mobile telephones. The necessity of commuting meant that people were both uncontactable at home or office for long periods, and were also left with time to fill.

Funk (2001) and Lindmark et al. (2004) suggest commuting time is irrelevant to the success of mobile internet in Japan, suggesting other developed nations may have equally utilised public transport systems. Yet many nations do not rely on public transport to the extent that Japan does. In Australia, for example, the comparative lack of people relying on public transportation is obvious, with just 12 per cent of the population commuting by train or bus to work in 2000 (Australian Bureau of Statistics 2000).[14] Importantly, it is not just the high usage of public transport, but also the exceptionally crowded commuting environment on public transportation in Japan that spurs the need for a compact channel for communication and entertainment.[15]

Timeliness and connectivity premium. As a result, a need for a mobile communication channel emerges, which will allow users to remain connected to their associates. Mobile telephony, and mobile internet, satisfy this need to be connected, which may in fact be more pertinent in Japan than in other countries. The improved interconnectivity of adding email to mobile phones added value that users in other countries would be unlikely to experience, given that text messages in Japan could only be used between users on the same network.

Likewise, a premium also appears to be placed on timeliness. As Ariga (1996:120) argues, the 'condensed society' aspect of Japan has spurred several 'time-saving' business opportunities that have resulted in innovative and efficient uses of time and space.

Vibrant content market. These pockets of time have resulted in an increased demand for media products such as newspapers, magazines, comics, and books. An important aspect of Japanese society is the sheer volume of information and the amount of time people devote to consuming it (Ariga 1996). Supply-side, the scale of Japan's media content industries is considerable. According to METI estimates, the broader content industry is worth 11 trillion yen, making it twice as large as the iron and steel industry and approximately half the size of the automobile industry (JETRO 2005).

Domestically, Japan has the second-largest national broadcaster and one of the largest publishing industries in the world (Tanaka 1998). Furthermore, Japan's circulation of daily newspapers is by far the largest in the world (Ariga 1996:128). Notably, half of all books published in Japan are pocket-sized paperbacks, indicating a tendency for consumers to carry books and read them when they have available pockets of time.

Magazines likewise, share the pocketbook's portability; the printing of magazines vastly outnumber the printing of books (Tanaka 1998). Given their popularity, i-mode services were designed to replicate magazines rather than fixed internet offerings (Matsunaga 2000). Again, commuting on public transport and the resulting pockets of time has undoubtedly fuelled demand for portable, informative, printed media products, and in doing so increasing this very readership.

Known in many western countries for *anime*, *manga*, and computer games, Japanese content is also well known throughout East Asia, which has long been a recipient of Japanese programming (Kawatake et al. 1996). Over 60 per cent of the animated cartoons broadcast around the world are made in Japan, with Japan's US-bound exports of animation alone being estimated at US$4.35 billion, while in East Asia 4 billion yen was generated in license sales and over 80 billion yen in sales of original manga comics (JETRO 2005).

Exportability of the model

Essentially, the i-mode model provides an end-to-end solution for device, content, delivery, and billing. The business model's semi-open nature brought structure in the form of a reliable technical platform, aggregated content and billing from subscription broadcast business models, and reduced restrictions by delivering the service across an open internet network that allowed users freedom of access and self-expression while maintaining significant separation from content providers.

While the semi-open platform evidenced in the i-mode business model is not characterised by any overt cultural specificities, its successful implementation will be affected by the unique features of individual markets. The exportability of the model, and hence DoCoMo's ability to earn money from licensing and royalty payments, also depends on its ability to have the value-added components of the business model recognised as proprietary intellectual property.

DoCoMo's forays in foreign markets. DoCoMo's initial strategy to spread their i-mode service and third generation W-CDMA standard was through direct equity investments during the mobile telecommunications 'bubble', which came at a serious cost. In 2001, DoCoMo wrote off US$7.7 billion of its overseas investments, and by late 2002, had decided to write down a further US$4.6 billion on investments in AT&T Wireless, Hutchinson 3G UK ("3"), and KPN Mobile.

DoCoMo sold its shares in AT&T Wireless to Cingular, and also sold its 20 per cent stake in "3" back to Hong Kong's Hutchinson in 2004 when Hutchinson failed to adopt i-mode as its content service for its "3" mobile network in the UK. Hutchinson's rival operator O2 launched their UK and Ireland i-mode service in 2005 after signing an agreement with DoCoMo in 2004.

Licensing to operators. Despite this series of strategic errors, DoCoMo continues to add to its list of overseas operators who are adopting i-mode. While it has invested in operators such as KPN in the past, DoCoMo appears to believe that the way to achieve less capital-intensive growth is through licensing its technology and business model rather than through direct equity investments.

The current list of i-mode licencees now includes KPN Mobile (Netherlands) and its subsidiary E-Plus (Germany), Telefonica (Spain), BASE (Belgium), Bouygues (France), Wind (Italy), Cosmote (Greece and Romania), O2 (UK and Ireland), Telstra (Australia), Far EasTone (Taiwan), Star Hub (Singapore)[16], Mobile TeleSystems (Russia and CIS), Cellcom (Israel), with Hutchinson Mobile (Hong Kong and Macau), Hutch (India), GloBul (Bulgaria), and SMART (Philippines) planned to launch services in 2007 (NTT DoCoMo 2007b).

Lacklustre subscriber figures outside of Japan have fuelled scepticism about i-mode's transferability and the ability of DoCoMo to license the technology overseas (*The Times* 2007).[17] The willingness of mobile operators to license i-mode may be questioned if i-mode were to be perceived as 'out-dated and easy to copy'. Despite the decisions of Telstra and O2 to drop the service in favour of their own 3G substitute, operators continue to sign up to carry i-mode with StarHub joining in 2005, GloBul in 2006, and Cosmote Romania, Hutchinson Mobile, Hutch, and SMART in 2007. Further, the willingness of these non-equity partners provides greater evidence of market support for i-mode rather than it being implemented by operators with which DoCoMo has direct equity investments.

As indicated above, the business model of aggregating content and payments is not as revolutionary as is its application in mobile internet markets. While licensing a technology has a more 'tangible' value proposition and historically has had clearer recourse for litigation of infringement, providing a 'technological' solution several years after its development may in fact have been detrimental to DoCoMo's attempts to license i-mode in developed nations. Yet the existence of a proprietary technology is particularly important for earning revenue from an innovation if the brand holds little value in the new market or the business model is easy to replicate.[18] This, combined with a business model that includes operator-driven handset specifications as an integral part of its success, offers significant value to offer potential licensees, even if they choose not to use the 'i-mode' brand, as did Telefonica in Spain. If O2 decides to go ahead with the launch of i-mode in Germany it is certain to be implemented under a different brand name, given that their competitor E-Plus is currently providing an internet service in the German market with the i-mode brand.

Barriers to exportability. One of the major differences likely to be encountered, technological differences aside, is the lack of the close relationship with handset makers. While there may be resistance from operators in assuming risk and from users in purchasing a network-specific handset, the absence of this collaborative relationship and operator-specified standards, this may inversely represent an opportunity for Japanese handset manufacturers to expand overseas. Many Japanese handset makers have had difficulties breaking into overseas markets, not just due to technological differences but also because of the intensity of the competition in the Japanese market. Mobile handsets have been somewhat of an anomaly in the expected pattern of industries that experience strong competition domestically being competitive in international markets. Intense competition combined with operator-controlled specifications in Japan arguably constrained manufacturers from expanding into overseas markets. Japanese makers therefore stand to do well with i-mode's expansion, as evidenced by the number of handsets NEC and other makers are adapting for overseas markets.

The second potential difference in host countries is the relationships that exist between network operators and content providers. In some European countries, the United States, and Australia, the tendency for operators to enter into exclusive agreements with content providers in order to secure content for the platform threatens to undermine a key factor of the semi-open i-mode model. Where there is a perceived lack of supply, operators may be tempted to provide content themselves or to enter into exclusive relationships with preferred providers. The need to keep the platform open to innovative providers of content may represent one of the biggest challenges to i-mode's transferability.[19]

Thirdly, given the high diffusion of prepaid mobiles (rather than the predominant post-paid contracts in Japan) i-mode billing systems would need to be adjusted to incorporate prepaid users. Overseas operators are also likely to see i-mode as a way to get prepaid users to move onto contracts, although KPN's i-mode offerings in the Netherlands and Germany appear to be available to their prepaid users.[20]

Regardless of socio-cultural differences such as commuting and high consumption of information, the business model seen in i-mode appears to be replicable outside of Japan, provided it can meet specific market needs.

Intellectual property and policy implications

This instance of DoCoMo exporting i-mode is a pertinent example of both the potential for, and the visible trend towards, Japanese firms exploiting the value of their intellectual property overseas. Just as NTT DoCoMo developed i-mode out of the need to catalyse further growth in a maturing mobile telephony market, Japanese policymakers are similarly looking to intellectual property as a key to revitalising the economy and maintaining Japan's competitiveness. This realisation of the importance of intellectual property in the economy has been underpinned by a sense that prevailing industry and policy settings in Japan have not allowed firms to fully exploit the internationalisation of their intellectual property.

While i-mode provides an instance of exporting Japanese technology and business models, the trade in television program formats offers another example of the dynamics of licensing intellectual property innovations outside of Japan. While TV program exports account for only a small amount of content exports according to METI data, it provides another example of the ability to use the intellectual property inherent in products and allow them to be adapted to local markets rather than exporting ready-made products.

The expansion of exports in other IP-based sectors

As mentioned above, Japanese programming has been exported to Asia for several decades, as has Japanese animation been sold around the world. While programming exports doubled over the 1970s to reach 4,500 hours in 1980 (Hagiwara 1995a), this figured had increased four-fold to over 19,500 hours by 1992 (Kawatake et al. 1996), indicating the exponential growth in exports, of which 58 per cent was animation. Yet METI figures estimate the value of television program exports at 5.3 billion yen in 2001, compared with 253 billion yen for game software (Hasegawa and Midorikawa 2005). Historically, Western Europe, Asia, and North America have been the largest regional markets for Japanese programming, with the largest single markets being the United States, Spain, and Hong Kong (Kawatake et al. 1996).

While there is a growing market for Japanese content, particularly with the rise of the 'Cool Japan' discourse (see McGray 2002), audiences tend to prefer local content (Hagiwara 1995b). Despite the 'cool Japan' phenomenon, an inability to adapt programs, particularly the language, is likely to reduce exportability. Furthermore, given that many nations still impose local content requirements on broadcasters, the demand for licensing innovative program formats is bound to be particularly strong. Similarly, linkages or vertical integration with local production companies may mean broadcasters prefer to produce local content rather than paying a premium for successful foreign content. Licensing formats rather than exporting programs allow local production companies to use local talent to produce content tailored for the local market and pay the Japanese originator a licensing fee.

The *Iron Chef* television program, for example, which is broadcast in 11 countries around the world (JETRO 2005), has begun licensing the program's format to overseas broadcasters and production companies. The

US remake of the show is now exported to other English-speaking countries. Similarly, ADV Films in the US announced plans for a live-action version of Japanese anime *Neon Genesis Evangelion*, while the Resident Evil series of movies has been taken from the Japanese computer game of the same name (know as Biohazard in Japan).

Japanese television industries have been recognised as having an influential role in circulating and adapting content in East Asia (Keane 2006). Yet there has been a trend in the past, prevalent particularly in Asia, for copyright holders to see their revenues 'eroded' both by piracy of their original content, and imitating of (or borrowing from) Japanese-originated formats. In the music industry, for example, pirated copies of Japanese content accounted for 17 per cent of the music software market in Hong Kong and 32 per cent of the market in Taiwan, according to a 2002 survey by the Copyright Research and Information Center (JETRO 2005). While this infringement of copyright may have ancillary benefits in other areas of the Japanese economy,[21] rents accruing to the content sector itself may be difficult to extract, either from the export market or from domestic industries that benefit from the unauthorised use of content.

There is a growing imperative to be able to repatriate rents from these innovations. This need is not only limited to content-based goods, but extends to all sectors of the Japanese economy that have an inherent intellectual property component to their products. For Japanese firms, however, it has been easier to identify, protect, and sell a tangible product such as an automobile part in international markets than it has an intangible good such as content or a business process. While there has been no shortage of innovations being cultivated in Japan, firms have often fallen short in their ability to exploit this intellectual capital overseas.

Character licensing has also seen considerable growth, and for some examples of media content, has earned copyright owners more revenue than has sales of the original content itself. *Pokemon* provides an example where a computer game also spawned a movie with 22 billion yen box office takings, and 700 billion yen from merchandising (METI figures in Hasegawa and Midorikawa 2005). The ability for intellectual property rights to be assigned to other formats, and bought and sold, indicates not only the significant potential in scope economies, but also the need for human resources that can exploit the international expansion of content, whether it is for information, education, or entertainment.

Policies to strengthen Japan's intellectual property standing

The intellectual property imperative. Rather than simply evidencing a 'hollowing out', the established trend of manufacturing shifting offshore suggests that Japan's competitive advantage lies in innovation and the development of intellectual property rather than in retaining lower-end manufacturing. Yet Japan has often had difficulty reaping the returns on its investment in intellectual property. Comparative studies, for example, indicate that while intra-industry research and development knowledge flows and spill-overs are greater in Japan than in the United States, the ability to appropriate rents from innovation has been less (Cohen et al. 2002).

It is likely therefore that a lack of capacity to protect and exploit these innovations has resulted in Japanese firms being unable to extract sufficient rents from intellectual property. This may be due to a misuse of IP by third parties, an insufficient legal framework, or the absence of professionals who are able to market intellectual property services, manage intellectual property rights, and deal with the litigation of intellectual property infringement.[22]

Japan's intellectual property strategic program. The plan for the Japanese Government to play an active role in boosting Japan's ability to exploit its intellectual property status in the world was evidenced in February 2002 with Prime Minister Koizumi's 'intellectual property super-power' speech. Since this public expression of policy intent, the government has moved with unprecedented speed in establishing a series of intellectual property-related policies (Hatakeyama 2005). The government's 2004 intellectual property Strategic Program pointed to the need to expedite Japan's transformation into an intellectual property-based nation 'by making the best use of intellectual property as a source of national wealth including patents, know-how, and content such as movies and game software' (IPSH 2004). Two years on, the program was intending to make Japan 'the most advanced intellectual property-based nation in the world' (IPSH 2006).

The Intellectual Property Strategy Headquarters (herein IPSH) was created in 2003 under the Cabinet Office.[23] Its annual whole-of-government strategic programs specify agencies and ministries to carry out action items, which aimed to develop local capacity for creating and commercialising intellectual property, and to strengthen intellectual property protection regimes. These documents demonstrate that policymakers have recognised the necessity of capacity building and plan to achieve this through a multitude of policies that promote the 'creation' of intellectual property, the 'protection' of intellectual property rights, and the ability for firms to 'exploit' the intellectual property developed in Japan both domestically and abroad.

On the 'creation' front, the government's 2006 Strategic Program aims to revitalise universities and improve their international competitiveness, to improve the mobility and diversity of researchers, and to promote research and development at universities that focuses on intellectual property creation (IPSH 2006). A significant volume of literature has focused on the poor standing of Japanese universities on the world scale, particularly at the graduate level, that need not be revisited here. But it is also recognised that a significant proportion of the patentable scientific research is conducted at universities, and the ability to allow the private sector to tap these innovations appears to be one area of the government's strategy.[24] Universities also provide an ideal environment to act as incubators as students who have acquired relevant skills prepare to make the move into the industry. Relaxing the rules for universities to increase the industry-specific skills at a post-graduate level for professionals has seen the rise of new universities such as Digital Hollywood, an industry-driven school that teaches students the skills to become digital content experts, particularly in games and animation.

The Program includes strategies to bolster 'protection' through an improved intellectual property legal framework. Some of the key policies to advance this protection are the strengthening of domestic and international legislation, and the monitoring of counterfeit goods and patent, trademark and copyright infringement. In April 2005, the Intellectual Property High Court was established to give Japanese firms streamlined access to litigation and faster resolution of IP disputes.[25] Given the well recognised lack of practising lawyers in Japan, the 2004 Program also calls for an increase in IP lawyers, to be actualised by doubling the bar exam pass rate by 2010 (IPSH 2004).

On the international front, where patent and copyright infringements are believed to considerably reduce the earning potential of Japanese firms, the government is making efforts in both multilateral forums such at the WTO, APEC, and WIPO and bilaterally with individual governments. An IPSH plan for the prevention of counterfeit and pirated goods called for a system to be established by 2005 whereby rights holders in Japan can file intellectual property rights complaints directly to the attributable countries (IPSH 2004b). Making particular reference to counterfeit and pirated goods providing funding for criminal and terrorist groups, the 2006 Program designated action agencies to cooperate with international organisations to prohibit the import of counterfeit goods.

With regard to the lack of 'exploitability', it appears there is a tendency for companies to file for patents in order to defend rather than utilise their intellectual property. The 2006 Strategic Program indicates that more than half of registered patents are not being exploited. While little data is provided in the policy statements, it has prompted the government to move to revise patent laws with the aim of allowing these innovations to be utilised rather than being no more than a listing in the Patent Office directory. Alongside this, the government plans to support international standardisation activities. Also of importance is the mention it makes of allocating resources to supporting SMEs and ventures, given their important role in innovation but their lack of resources to develop and exploit their intellectual property. While this may sound ominously like government helping larger firms to 'exploit' the intellectual property from SMEs and start-ups, the Program points out the latter's need for well trained and informed IP professionals including lawyers and consultants.

This exploitation is inextricably linked to the policy documents' concept of creation. Yet it is important for policy to focus on capacity building through the removal of cumbersome regulations combined with the development of human capital that has skill-sets to take intellectual property into the international market. While policy settings appear well-placed, there is always a danger that a policy focus on the 'creation' of intellectual property may result in either subsidies for industry on the one hand, or the government taking an over-active role in determining the allocation of private capital investments on the other.

Increases in royalties and licence fee receipts. As described earlier, this fervent policy activity has been contextualised by recent balance of payments data showing a surplus in royalties and licence fees. While still indicating a trade in services deficit on the current account, Japan's net balance for royalties and licence fees has been increasing since 1993, posting its first surplus in 2003. Since then, the item has been increasing by approximately US$1 billion per year, and at 2006 stood at a US$4.69 billion surplus according to balance of payments data from the Bank of Japan. While this is a clear indication of Japan's move towards exporting IP rather than just manufactures, it does not necessarily suggest that intellectual property-based services and content sectors are internationally competitive.

Rather, data from the Bank of Japan suggest that strengths in the manufacturing sector accounted for a large share in trade in services exports. In fact, the majority of the royalties and license fee surplus until 2005 has been attributed to strong overseas sales in these sectors, particularly automobiles and electric machinery (Bank of Japan 2006). In an analysis of 2003 trade in services data, Yamaguchi (2004) suggests these large increases in receipts have mostly been comprised of payments for trademarks and technical instruction from overseas subsidiaries of Japanese companies, rather than from licensing intellectual property to third parties.

Receipts from industrial property rights (particularly automobiles, electronics, and other industrial firms) have been in surplus since 1997, and stand in stark contrast to trade in copyrights (film, television, publishing, music), which have been in constant deficit (Bank of Japan 2006). Despite the large scale of domestic content industries, copyright payments have been around US$5 billion, compared to U$900 million in receipts, a deficit which, according to Yamaguchi, has mostly been comprised of computer-related software licensing from the United States. Literature, music, and arts comprise only 10 per cent of the deficit, according to Yamaguchi (2004). METI data from 2001 corroborates this deficit in the trade of most items: music, broadcast programs, publishing, and movies. Yet receipts from exports of game software, at a 250 billion yen surplus, would appear to negate the deficits in all other content areas.

Content industry-specific policies

While promoting the potential of the content industry, the Japanese Government appears to be well aware of the terms of trade in this sector. The 2004 intellectual property Strategy document, stated that 'intellectual property contents (works such as movies, music, animation, and game software) created in Japan are highly acclaimed throughout the world, but we cannot say that the parties concerned have made concerted efforts to develop the content business under a common philosophy' (IPSH 2004:112).

Evidently, this effort to encourage the industry to be more 'proactive' is based on both the large deficit in the trade of copyright goods, and the content industries in Japan accounting for a smaller share of GDP (2.3 per cent) than the global average (3.3 per cent). Further, with Japan's share in the worldwide content market at just three per cent in 2000 compared to the United States' 17 per cent, digital content and pop culture are increasingly being viewed as sources of potential high growth and competitive advantage within Japan (*Nihon Keizai Shimbun* 2005). Hence, the desire of the government to encourage actors in the content industry to actively increase exports is understandable.

Strategic policy objectives for content promotion. The Japanese Government has realised, albeit belatedly, the nascent value in Japan's content-related business, and may well have taken its cue from external forces signalling an interest in Japanese content (JETRO 2005; McGray 2002). The government's interest in the industry appears to stem from three sources.

First is the economic value of the industry itself. Given the domestic industry's scale being situated between steel and automobiles, the sector's contribution to the economy is clearly evident. Yet, its size also highlights the lack of success in exploiting these goods in international markets, which current Japanese IP policy is attempting to resolve.

Second is the potential for spill-overs to other sectors of the economy. As indicated in both the discussions of the i-mode model and the export of television formats, content not only lends itself to be exploited in other formats, but also fuels the consumption of complementary goods such as mobile handsets and other hardware. Further, digital content often finds applications in other industries as diverse as mining and aerospace for purposes such as exploration and training.

Third is the 'soft power' benefits derived from exported content giving overseas consumers a positive impression of Japan. The 2004 IP Strategic Program makes an explicit reference to soft power benefits, and the government may well hope that exporting content will improve the image that residents of other countries have of Japan. This would have both political public diplomacy benefits as well as the potential to make these people more likely to purchase other goods from Japan, whether electronics, automobiles, or inbound tourism.[26] Among other factors however, this is contingent on the type of content being exported from Japan, and its ability to make a 'positive' impression.

Content promotion act. In June 2004, the 'Content Promotion Act' was passed in the Japanese Diet, which applied to the content industry the same goals of promoting the creation, protection, and exploitation that guided Japan's general intellectual property strategy. This includes efforts by national and local governments to develop talent, as well as promoting the fair trade and ownership of copyrights.

According to the 2006 Strategic Program, this Act required the reinforcing of the anti-monopoly law and the revision of copyright laws to allow copyright holders to use the internet to exploit the potential of their content. On the investment front, the Act seeks to increase the available capital to the industry by changing investment laws to limit the liability of investors, and also by providing investment incentives to catalyse private sector funding. On the users side, the government pledged to explore flexible pricing systems for the sale and resale of content such as music (CDs), a marked change from the traditional standardisation of prices for content such as books and CDs.

Policy implications. The strategic program appropriately addresses the need to develop creative capacity both on the production side and within the education system to turn out graduates that can function in the global economy and sell intangible products overseas. Content providers, whether for television programs or mobile internet sites, face the challenge of not only language barriers from users (having to translate content) but also linguistic limitations of explaining the benefits of these intangible goods to potential buyers overseas. The government policy's emphasis on the need to bolster protection of intellectual property and create more spaces for intellectual property professionals, including lawyers, is also well placed.

When it comes to protecting the intellectual property inherent in content and exploiting its secondary use, copyrights are already an established system. Yet the ability to prosecute those who infringe copyrights overseas has been difficult. There does, however, appear to be a turnaround in the *status quo* that has prevailed until recently.

Firstly, governments around the East Asian region realise that they need to police intellectual property-related crimes such as piracy conscientiously if they are to successfully induce foreign direct investment in these sectors. Singapore's stringent efforts to provide protection to copyrighted works through prohibiting their illegal production and sale, for example, has undoubtedly been fuelled by its free trade agreement with the United States.

Secondly, Japanese copyright holders have become more proactive in representing their rights overseas. This has been most recently seen in the JASRAC and YouTube incident, where the Japanese copyright management organisation threatened legal action if the YouTube owner (Google) did not take measures to prevent users from posting animation and other video clips managed by JASRAC on the site. Despite the potentially positive effect that YouTube videos of Japanese copyrighted content may have for the industry, international IP agreements concluded by the Japanese Government at both bilateral and multilateral levels will undoubtedly support claimants such as JASRAC in protecting unauthorised use of Japanese IP. It is unfortunate for all parties involved that JASRAC could not see the free promotional role that YouTube could have had for its clients' content. It is likely however, that JASRAC may pursue some advertisement revenue-sharing deal with YouTube in the future.

Conclusion

DoCoMo's exporting of i-mode and the licensing of television formats are exemplars of the potential for Japanese firms to exploit the value of their intellectual property overseas. Whether i-mode will be successful in particular foreign markets will depend significantly on the receptiveness of host country industry players to the semi-open platform model. This i-mode model also has the potential to be an impetus to innovation in the creation and delivery of local content in respective markets. These benefits, and the promise of spill-over effects to other technology and content sectors in the economy, illustrate why the Japanese government is keen to have Japan migrate to the status of an 'intellectual property super-power'. This would see Japan exporting models of innovation systems that are consistent with the production of local cultural innovation.

While the government has neatly defined its strategic policy into promoting the creation, protection, and exploitation of intellectual property, the imperative to develop creative and internationalised talent suggest that policies directed toward 'creation' must be aimed at capacity building through human capital formation and modernising the intellectual property legal regime. A key lesson from 'cool Japan' may well be that open networks of well-trained creative individuals and private content enterprises are the real drivers of intellectual property development. The optimum role of the Japanese Government and of those hoping to learn from Japan is to provide an institutional framework that allows the nurturing of creativity, the freedom of private capital, and the internationalisation of training institutions.

Notes

1   While these demonstration effects are implicit across various industries throughout East Asia, official government policies in South East Asia such as *Learn from Japan* in Singapore and *Look East* in Malaysia clearly reveal the Japan's role of knowledge disseminator in the region (Atarashi 1984).

2   NTT DoCoMo is a publicly listed subsidiary of NTT Holding Company and was the incumbent mobile carrier before deregulation introduced competition. KDDI was formed from a merger between former public monopoly international telecom company KDD and mobile carriers DDI and IDO. Softbank's mobile service was formerly known as Vodafone and J-Phone reflecting the majority shareholder at the time.

3   Subscribers to mobile internet as separate to mobile phones are possibly becoming less relevant as a statistic in Japan as service subscription becomes standard.

4   As of February 2007, i-mode subscribers in Japan were at 47.3 million (NTT DoCoMo website).

5   However, this absence of handset portability gives rise to certain switching costs for the user. While mobile number portability has been introduced in Japan as recently as 2006, handsets are still network-specific in contrast to services in many other countries where handsets come equipped with interchangeable SIM cards. Users can now port their number to another network but not their handset.

6   KDDI's use of HDML, for example, was built off an early version of WAP developed by the company Phone.com (Devine and Holmqvist 2001).

7   DoCoMo have more recently announced some capital tie-ups with some content firms such as Kadokawa Group (NTT DoCoMo Press Release 2006)

8   Ariga (1996) indicates that average Japanese homes have 60 per cent of the living space of US homes.

9   Natsuno (2000) also suggests low diffusion of PCs was due to a traditional belief in Japan that as language is expressed by people, characters should be handwritten, even in business circles.

10   Gottlieb (2000) offers figures indicating 1994 was the first year PCs outsold the now antiquated word processors.

11   Prior to the introduction of ADSL and FTTH (fibre to the home) timed local calls constituted a further cost to users in Japan.

12   This system which has been in place since post-war era, originally required subscribers to pay 100,000 yen to NTT as a bond, which would be returned after 10 years. The subscriber bond system was officially abolished in 1982 according to Anchordoguy, yet various special bond systems and installation fees raised the cost of purchasing a phone line (Anchordoguy 2001). In reality, the bond (*kanyuken*) still exists, requiring a fee of less than 70,000 yen. This *kanyuken*, or 'right to use a phone line', can be bought cheaper on secondary markets. NTT now offers access through a 'lite plan' without the bond, although ongoing charges are slightly higher (as of 2004–5).

13   The Ministry of Internal Affairs and Communications (then Ministry of Public Management, Home Affairs, Posts and Telecommunications) released figures indicating that as of May 2004 32 per cent of Japanese household had broadband internet connections. Furthermore, according to InfoCom Research Inc. in the two years between 2000 and 2002, the available connection speed increased eight fold and the price halved, offering speeds unavailable even in the United States and South Korea.

14   This low figure of public transport commuters (which can be assumed to be concentrated in major cities) contrasts with more than 76 per cent of people using personal automobiles to commute (Australian Bureau of Statistics 2000). Japan census data from 2000 meanwhile indicates at least 26.4 per cent of people commute via public transport, increasing to over 57.8 per cent in Tokyo.

15   Funk argues that i-mode take-up in rural areas (with less public transportation) has been on par with that in urban areas. While this assumes that residents in rural areas are not commuting longer distances by public transport, it also ignores the tendency for fixed internet penetration, a possible substitute to mobile internet, to be lower in less urbanised areas. On a cross-national level, data supports the correlation between urbanisation and

fixed internet take-up. Controlling for per capita income, a regression of 2004 raw data from World Development Indicators yielded an R-squared of 0.915 (significant at 95 per cent confidence interval) when using urban population as an analytical weight.

16   While DoCoMo has no major equity investments, NTT Communications is a substantial shareholder of StarHub.

17   I-mode subscribers outside Japan were at 6 million as of March 2007 according to DoCoMo (NTT DoCoMo 2007b)

18   While the 'i-mode' brand has received considerable attention from industry, analysts, academics, and policymakers, the average consumer in most countries outside of Japan would not be expected to know much about i-mode. The i-mode brand, therefore, may bring little weight to the licensing agreement. Similarly, while the model of aggregating third party content and providing centralised billing services was a DoCoMo-led innovation for mobile internet, the business model itself is not revolutionary, having been used in various forms by subscription television broadcasters.

19   This may be addressed to some extent by using foreign content (assuming no language barrier exists) or encouraging user-made interactive content.

20   This existence of prepaid offerings is based on information available on web sites of European operators licensing i-mode.

21   Pirated VCDs of the TV drama *Hero* starring Takuya Kimura in China are said to have fuelled rapid sales of Japanese-made mobile phones (JETRO 2005).

22   Alternatively, it may suggest that intra-firm knowledge transfers are more commonplace amongst Japanese firms

23   At the time of its establishment, its English name was the Intellectual Property Policy Headquarters (IPPH).

24   A key government strategy to achieve this is the establishment of Technology Licensing Organisations.

25   From the Intellectual Property High Court website, it appears to deal mostly with domestic copyright infringement litigation and firms appealing patent rulings.

26   Given that tourism is a major contributor to Japan's deficit in trade in services, the government may find this argument particularly appealing.

References

Anchordoguy, M., 2001. 'Nippon Telegraph and Telephone Company (NTT) and the building of a telecommunications industry in Japan', *Business History Review*, 75(Autumn):507–41.

Ariga, M., 1996. 'Seven crucial viewpoints to understand the Japanese consumer', in S.M. Leong, S.H. Ang and C.T. Tan (eds), *Marketing Insights for the Asia-Pacific*, Heinemann, Singapore.

Atarashi, K., 1984. 'Japan's economic cooperation policy towards the ASEAN Countries, *International Affairs*, 61(1):109–27.

Australian Bureau of Statistics, 2000. 'More hazardous waste ending up in household bins', *Media Release*, 29 November Canberra. Available from http://www.abs.gov.au.

Bank of Japan, 2006. *Japan's Balance of Payments for 2005*. Available from http://www.boj.or.jp/en/type/ronbun/ron/research/data/ron0608a.pdf (accessed 30 March 2007).

Bickers, C., 2001. 'The way of the mobile warrior', *Far Eastern Economic Review*, 164:46–50.

Brousseau, E., 2003. 'E-Commerce in France: did early adoption prevent its development?', *The Information Society*, 19(1):45–57.

Cohen, W.M., Goto, A., Nagata, A., Nelson, R.R. and Walsh, J.P. , 2002. 'R&D spillovers, patents and the incentives to innovate in Japan and the United States', *Research Policy*, 31(8–9):1349–67.

Devine, A., and S. Holmqvist, 2001. 'Mobile Internet Content Providers and their Business Models', Masters Thesis, The Royal Institute of Technology, Stockholm (unpublished).

Fransman, M., 1999. 'Where are the Japanese?: Japanese Information and communication firms in an internetworked world', *Telecommunications Policy*, 23:317–33.

Funk, J., 2001. *The Mobile Internet: how Japan dialed up and the West disconnected*, ISI Publications, Hong Kong.

Gottlieb, N., 2000. *Word Processing Technology in Japan: Kanji and the keyboard*, Curzon, Richmond.

Hagiwara, S., 1995a. 'Rise and fall of foreign programs in Japanese television', *Keio Communication Review*, 17:3–26.

——, 1995b. *Gaikoku seisaku no terebi bangumi nitaisuru nihonjin no taido* [Japanese attitudes towards foreign television programs] *Mass Communication Research*, 47:180–94.

Hasegawa, F. and Midorikawa, K. (eds), 2005. *Contentsu bijinesu ga chiiki wo kaeru!* [How the Content Business Can Change Regions], NTT Publishing, Tokyo.

Hatakeyama, K. (ed.), 2005. *Odoru contentsu bijinesu no mirai* [The Future of the Chaotic Entertainment Content Biz], Shogakkan, Tokyo.

InfoCom Research Inc, 2002. *Joho tsushin outrukku 2003* [Information Communications Outlook 2003], NTT Publishing, Tokyo.

Intellectual Property Strategy Headquarters (IPSH), 2004. *Intellectual Property Strategic Program 2004,* IPSH, Tokyo. Available at www.ipr. go.jp/e_material/ip_st_program2004.pdf (accessed 28 October 2006).

——, 2004b. *Counters to Accelerate Measures against Counterfeiting and Piracy,* IPSH, Tokyo. Available from http://www.ipr.go.jp/suishin/ 041216mohou-e.pdf (accessed 21 March 2007).

——, 2006 *Intellectual Property Strategic Program 2006.* Available from http://www.kantei.go.jp/jp/singi/titeki2/keikaku2006_e.pdf (accessed 10 March 2007).

Japan External Trade Organisation (JETRO), 2005. *'Cool' Japan's Economy Warms Up,* available from http://www.jetro.go.jp/en/stats/survey/ surveys/20050509_cool_japan.pdf (accessed 12 December 2006).

Japan Ministry of Public Management, Home Affairs, Posts and Telecommunications, 2004. *Update on broadband internet subscribers in Japan,* Government of Japan, Tokyo. Available from http:// www.soumu.go.jp/joho_tsusin/joho_tsusin.html.

Johns, A., 2003. *'I-mode to sono bijinesu moderu bunseki'* [The i-mode business model: a comparative analysis]', *Journal of Public Utility Economics,* 55(2):131–38 (in japanese).

Jonason, A., and Eliasson, G., 2001. 'Mobile internet revenues: an empirical study of the i-mode portal', *Internet Research: Electronic Networking Applications and Policy, 11*(4):341–48.

Lindmark, S., Bohlin, E. and Andersson, E., 2004. 'Japan's Mobile Internet Success Story: facts, myths, lessons, and implications', *Info,* 6 (6):348–58.

Kawatake, K., Hara, Y. and Sakurai, T., 1996. *'Nihon wo chushin tosuru terebi joho no nagare'* [Japan's television information flows] in K. Kawatake and M. Sugiyama (eds.) *Media no tsutaeru gaikoku no imegi* [Foreign image presented by the Media], Keibunsha, Tokyo.

Keane, M., 2006. 'Once Were Peripheral: creating media capacity in East Asia', *Media, Culture, and Society,* 28(6):835.

Lunn, S., 2000. 'The big Mo wins in Japan', *The Australian, media section,* 9 November:13.

Matsunaga, M., 2000. '"Analog" woman hastens digital data delivery', *Japan Quarterly,* 47:23–29.

McNeill, D., 2001. 'Mission impossible for broadband providers?' *Japan Inc.*, June.

McGray, D., 2002. 'Japan's gross national cool', *Foreign Policy*, May/June, 130:44–54.

Mollman, S., 2001b. *Micro-Payment, Macro Issue*, [e-mail newsletter], Japan Inc- Wireless Watch, 20 April.

Natsuno, T., 2001. *I-mode sutorategii: sekai wa naze oikakenai ka?'* [i-mode Strategy: Why doesn't the world follow?] Nikkei BP Publishing, Tokyo.

Nihon Keizai Shimbun, 2005. *'Sangyo bunkaryoku ga hiraku 4: Poppu karuchaa contentsu o kenin'* Morning Edition, 1 January:22.

NTT DoCoMo, 2006. Press Release, NTT DoCoMo, Tokyo. Available from http://www.nttdocomo.com/pr/2006/001303.html (accessed 20 March 2007).

——, 2007a. 'Monthly Operating Data – i-mode usage', NTT DoCoMo, Tokyo. Available from http://www.nttdocomo.co.jp/english/corporate/ir/finance/subscriber/imode.html (accessed 20 March 2007).

——, 2007b. Fact Book March 2007. NTT DoCoMo, Tokyo. Available from http://www.nttdocomo.com/binary/about/facts_factbook.pdf (accessed 28 March 2007).

OH!NEW?, 2007. Online data source for i-mode independent sites, available from http://ohnew.co.jp/hepl/data/index.html (accessed 30 March 2007).

Peltokorpi, V., Nonaka, I. and Kodama, M., 2007. 'NTT DoCoMo's launch of i-mode in the Japanese mobile phone market: a knowledge creation perspective', *Journal of Management Studies*, 44(1):50–72.

Tanaka, K., 1998. 'Japanese women's magazines: the language of aspiration', in D.P. Martinez (ed.), *The Worlds of Japanese Popular Culture: gender, shifting boundaries and global cultures*, Cambridge University Press, Cambridge/Melbourne.

Telecommunications Carriers Association, 2007. Data on Mobile Telephony, Telecommunications Carriers Association, Tokyo. Available from http://www.tca.or.jp (accessed 20 March 2007).

The Times Online, 2007. *O2 puts on hold its German mobile internet plans*, 19 March. Available from http://business.timesonline.co.uk/tol/

business/industry_sectors/telecoms/article1534454.ece (accessed 24 March 2007).

Vishik, C. and Whinston, A.B., 1999. 'Knowledge sharing, quality, and intermediation', *SIGSOFT Software. Engineering Notes*, 24(2):157–166.

Yamaguchi, E., 2004. *Recent characteristics of royalties and license fees in Japan's balance of payments, Bank of Japan Working Paper Series,* Bank of Japan, Tokyo. Available from http://www.boj.or.jp/en/type/ronbun/ron/wps/data/wp04e05.pdf (accessed 23 February 2007).

7 THE DYNAMIC IN EAST ASIAN TRADE

Ligang Song, Tina Chen and Shiji Zhao

Trade has been a key component in the successful story of East Asian development since the region embarked on its modernisation drive in the 1960s. Through trade and the associated export-oriented strategy and regional economic cooperation, the East Asian economies have been connected closely with each other in climbing up the ladder of development, led first by Japan, the newly industrialising economies (NIEs), and then ASEAN, China, Vietnam, India and other South Asian countries. As a result, within a half century, the East Asia as a whole has changed from a peripheral region to one of the most dynamic and highly integrated economies in the world. The East Asian share of world trade increased from 14 per cent in 1980 to about 20 per cent in 2003, equivalent to the share of North America in world trade (Table 7.1). This has been achieved despite some negative external shocks such as oil crisis in the 1970s and exchange rate volatility, difficulties in restructuring their domestic economies, including financial opening of their economies since the 1980s, and the painful experience of the financial crisis in the mid 1990s.

The East Asian experiences demonstrated the feasibility and viability of alternative trade policies: it was no longer possible to associate comparative

Table 7.1   Share of world trade by region, 1980–2003 (per cent)

	1980	1990	2000	2003
East Asia	14.1	18.7	22.7	19.9
Japan	7.0	7.4	6.4	5.7
NIEs	4.3	7.8	10.2	6.6
ASEAN-4	2.3	2.7	3.7	3.8
China	1.0	1.7	3.5	4.9
Australia, New Zealand	1.4	1.4	1.3	1.3
North America	16.8	17.7	22.3	20.5
United States	12.3	13.1	15.4	14.4
Canada	3.6	3.7	4.2	3.9
Mexico	0.9	0.9	2.8	2.2
South America	2.8	1.7	2.0	1.9
European Union	41.0	44.0	35.4	37.7
Rest of world	23.9	16.5	16.2	18.6

Notes: NIEs: Korea, Taiwan, Singapore and Hong Kong; North America: the United States, Canada, Mexico; East Asia: Malaysia, Hong Kong, Indonesia, Japan, South Korea, China, Taiwan, Singapore, and the Philippines; Singapore is included in NIEs, not ASEAN; South America: Argentina, Brazil, Chile, Haiti, and Venezuela.
Sources: International Monetary Fund, *Direction of Trade*, Washington, DC; International Economic Databank, The Australian National University, Canberra.

advantage with reliance on primary commodity exports. And these experiences certainly put to rest the mistaken belief that developing countries relying on the international market would forever be specialised in the production of primary commodities. These experiences also put an end to the belief that developing countries could not develop rapidly when relying on integration with the international economy as 'a developing country could achieve industrialisation without relying on domestic markets to absorb almost all additional output. ... That demonstrated the fallacy of the earlier view that industrialisation could take place only through import substitution' (Krueger 1997:17).

The East Asian experience has thus stimulated some to attempt to identity the 'dynamic' factors in exporting. Das (1998) stated that looking back three decades, one finds that in several Asian economies, the structural transformation has been more or less fundamental, in that these economies have experienced a dynamic process of changing comparative advantage.

This entailed a rapid growth in their exports of manufactures as well as a changing structure of manufactured exports. This echoes the view by Krueger (1997) that there appears to be widespread agreement in the 1990s that the benefits of an open trade regime are largely 'dynamic' in nature, and go well beyond the gains from trade under 'static' models of an open economy.

While a variety of factors, such as technology and foreign direct investment (FDI), have contributed to the achievement of the dynamic gains from trade by the regional economies, an important element of the whole process is the so-called 'institutional integration' which, as defined in Drysdale (1988), refers to the legal agreements and institutional arrangements which facilitate economic exchange among a community of nations. Institutional integration matters as 'institutional and market integration involves an important two-way interaction, in which close economic ties and common economic problems set the requirements for institutional arrangements, and institutional arrangements influence the degree of economic and political cohesion' (Drysdale 1988:35).

According to Drysdale (1988), low institutional, political and other resistances to trade interact with low transport and communications resistances to generate high intensities in trade and other economic relations. The argument is relevant to the East Asian model for dynamic resource allocation and international specialisation in that if 'there are institutional and legal barriers to trade and capital movements but market ties survive, market integration is frustrated by the lack of institutional integration' (Drysdale 1988:35).

For example, a characteristic of the trade expansion of the newly industrialising economies (NIEs), ASEAN and China resulting from the changing pattern of their respective comparative advantage is the process of their taking over market shares from Japan first in textiles and other labour-intensive manufactured goods, and then from one another: '[a]rrangements that discriminate against their trade growth in favour of established traders would adversely affect their trade and development ambitions and regional trade interests' (Drysdale 1988:21).

This chapter looks into the changing pattern of production and trade and the extent of integration in East Asia in comparison with other major regional groups, and discusses the impacts and implications of China's rising trade on the regional economy and economic cooperation. It points out possible future directions in terms of different forms of 'institutional integration' that the regional economies are likely to take and how these alternatives may affect the prospects of East Asian trade and economic growth in the long run.

Changing structure of East Asian production and trade

Basic trade theory suggests that countries with higher ratios of labour to natural resources and capital to labour will have a strong comparative advantage in manufactures *vis-à-vis* primary production and exports. Such theory also predicts that comparative advantage in manufactures will grow more rapidly the faster the rate of growth of capital to labour ratio relatively to growth in the rest of the world. As a result, the product composition of exports would shift from a predominance of natural resource intensive exports to unskilled labour intensive exports, further to physical and human capital intensive exports, and then on to technology and knowledge intensive exports (Garnaut and Anderson 1980; Song 1996a; Das 1998).

Table 7.2 presents the changing structures of production of the regional economies from 1970 to 2002 that have a direct bearing on the trade structure of these economies. First, the agricultural sector in all the reported groups of Asian economies including South Asia has dramatically declined. As expected, this change is most visible in NIEs where its share fell steadily from 17 per cent to only three per cent of GDP over the 1970–2002 period. Their share of industry in GDP rose from the 1970s to 1980s, and then declined over the 1990s as the services sector expanded which accounted for 63 per cent of GDP in 2002.

Similarly, ASEAN economies experienced a substantial fall in the share of agriculture, however, unlike in NIEs, the share of their industries continued to rise reflecting the fact that ASEAN's level of economic maturity is less than that in NIEs (Das 1998). Compared to NIEs, ASEAN's services sector had a much lower share of GDP. The agricultural sector in China has fallen quite dramatically especially in the 1990s, but is still higher than that in ASEAN. The industrial sector continued to dominate

Table 7.2   Changing structure of production, 1970–2002
(per cent of GDP)

	Agriculture	Industry	Service
Newly industrialising economies			
1970	17	33	51
1980	9	40	51
1990	6	41	53
2002	3	34	63
ASEAN-4			
1970	34	25	41
1980	25	36	39
1990	19	39	42
2002	13	43	44
China			
1970	34	38	28
1980	31	47	22
1990	27	42	31
2002	15	51	34
South Asia			
1970	45	21	35
1980	37	25	38
1990	32	27	42
2002	23	26	51

Note: NIEs in 2002 did not include Taiwan.
Source: World Bank, *World Development Indicators*, Washington, DC.

the Chinese economy, accounting 51 per cent of GDP in 2002, a level that was not matched by NIEs during the period of rapid growth in the 1980s. The expansion of the services sector in China has been less than that in NIEs and ASEAN. South Asian economies have a relatively higher share of agriculture and lower share of industries in GDP. This fact indicates that South Asian economies have been on the lower rung of the development ladder with a slower pace of industrialisation, although these economies have been undergoing structural changes over the period under study.

The structural changes taking place in the East Asian economies is also reflected in the rising shares of exports of manufactures in total exports

(Table 7.3). The significance of rising shares of exports of manufactures lies in the fact that the relationship between exports of manufactures and high TFP growth may well be the result of exporters' role in helping economies adopt and master international best-practice technologies, thus being classified as a dynamic factor (Das 1998).

Exports of manufactures have risen as a proportion of total exports for all the listed economies (Table 7.3). In newly industrialising economies, they rose from 71 per cent in 1970 to 91 per cent in 2000, and for ASEAN, the average proportion of manufactured products in total exports increased from six to 76 per cent over the same period, representing a faster export growth rate than that in newly industrialising economies. During the same period, China nearly doubled its share of manufactured products in total exports, which accounted for 88 per cent of its total exports in 2000. A similar trend was observed for India whose share reached 79 per cent in 2000.

Table 7.3   **Exports of manufactures as per cent of total exports, 1970–2000** (per cent)

	1970	1980	1990	2000
NIEs	71.0	80.7	88.5	91.2
Hong Kong	95.9	96.5	95.8	95.7
Korea	76.6	89.9	93.6	90.8
Singapore	30.5	53.9	72.8	86.4
Taiwan	76.1	87.9	92.6	95.3
ASEAN-4	6.1	14.7	52.7	76.3
Indonesia	1.4	2.4	35.5	57.1
Malaysia	7.4	19.0	54.2	81.2
Philippines	7.6	36.8	68.8	88.6
Thailand	8.0	28.1	64.3	78.0
China	45.1	46.9	73.5	88.4
India	52.0	58.9	72.3	79.4

Source: UN COMTRADE, International Economic Databank, The Australian National University, Canberra.

Pattern and direction of East Asian trade

Table 7.4 outlines the trade (both export and import) relationships between Japan, Nies, ASEAN, EU and elsewhere for a selection of the East Asian countries separately, 1980 compared to 2003. While the export share of Japan's exports to the United States continued to rise, the shares of NIEs exports to the United States (and to Japan except Hong Kong) fell over this period. The surge in China's export share to the United States reflected the fact that NIEs have been shifting their production bases to China to take advantage of the relatively low labour costs there. There was a substantial fall in export shares of most of NIE, ASEAN economies and China to Japan while both intra-NIEs and intra-ASEAN trade shares are on the rise. East Asian economies' export shares to European Union show a trend of declining with exception of Singapore and Indonesia.

With a few exceptions, most East Asian economies are recording falling shares of imports from the United States, Japan and European Union while their shares of import from NIEs and ASEAN economies are increasing. NIEs, especially, have become major suppliers for ASEAN countries at the expense of Japan. China's import shares from the United States, Japan and European Union are falling, while its shares from both NIEs and ASEAN countries are increasing. As for China–Japan bilateral trade, China's exports to Japan accounted for 14.7 per cent of its total exports while China's imports from Japan accounted for 20 per cent of its total imports.

Changing pattern of comparative advantage

Table 7.5 illustrates the process of changing comparative advantage by reference to individual commodities. Japan's export specialisation in labour-intensive products (travel goods, clothing and footwear) was still above the global mean in 1970, but fell well below unity later, and virtually to zero by the end of the century. A corresponding rise occurred over the period in Japan's export specialisation in such capital-intensive products as machinery and electrical machinery. The NIEs' export specialisation in individual labour-intensive products reached a peak between 1970 and

Table 7.4   Overall patterns of East Asian external trade, 1980 and 2003

Orientation of exports by selected East Asian countries (% of total exports of each country)

Exporting countries	To the US		To Japan		To NIEs		To ASEAN		To EU-15		Elsewhere	
	1980	2003	1980	2003	1980	2003	1980	2003	1980	2003	1980	2003
Japan	24.2	28.2	0.0	0.0	10.7	17.5	7.0	10.0	15.1	17.1	42.9	27.2
Hong Kong	26.0	10.7	4.6	5.7	5.5	5.7	6.8	5.4	24.6	18.7	32.5	53.9
Korea	25.7	19.8	16.9	9.9	6.0	8.7	4.8	7.4	16.3	13.6	30.4	40.6
Singapore	12.4	13.9	8.0	6.8	9.1	15.6	22.1	25.1	13.1	14.4	35.2	24.3
Taiwan	34.3	22.3	11.0	10.3	12.0	28.8	5.2	7.2	15.3	14.7	22.3	16.8
Indonesia	19.6	14.4	49.2	21.9	13.4	18.8	1.3	7.3	6.6	13.3	9.9	24.4
Malaysia	16.3	21.0	22.8	11.4	23.0	25.9	3.4	7.8	18.0	13.3	16.3	20.7
Philippines	27.5	25.2	26.6	16.1	8.8	16.9	4.6	9.4	18.0	16.2	14.4	16.2
Thailand	12.7	18.3	15.1	15.6	13.6	14.9	8.6	8.9	26.5	16.1	23.5	26.1
China	5.4	26.7	22.2	14.7	26.3	23.1	4.3	3.9	14.7	14.5	27.1	17.1

Origin of imports of selected East Asian countries (% of total imports of each country)

Importing countries	From the US		From Japan		From NIEs		From ASEAN		From EU-15		Elsewhere	
	1980	2003	1980	2003	1980	2003	1980	2003	1980	2003	1980	2003
Japan	16.9	16.5	-	-	5.0	7.2	15.9	13.7	6.3	13.2	55.8	49.3
Hong Kong	10.9	7.1	21.1	13.6	15.7	13.3	3.5	7.0	11.8	9.6	37.0	49.4
Korea	21.3	16.8	25.5	20.7	2.3	5.1	5.7	8.5	7.4	10.4	37.9	38.5
Singapore	12.5	14.5	15.9	12.1	4.9	6.2	24.2	28.9	11.0	11.2	31.5	27.1
Taiwan	23.7	17.0	27.2	24.0	3.4	11.3	6.3	11.3	8.6	12.0	30.8	24.4
Indonesia	12.4	7.8	30.0	17.1	15.7	18.5	3.6	8.0	13.9	13.6	24.4	34.9
Malaysia	14.8	13.3	22.4	16.6	16.2	29.5	4.6	10.9	16.9	11.0	25.0	18.6
Philippines	22.7	20.6	19.2	21.5	7.9	20.7	5.0	9.6	11.4	7.3	33.8	20.3
Thailand	14.1	10.1	20.7	23.2	11.2	11.9	5.4	10.8	15.0	10.5	33.7	33.6
China	19.3	10.3	26.1	20.2	3.8	18.6	2.3	9.1	16.8	14.8	31.5	27.0

Note: ASEAN excludes Singapore; NIEs includes Singapore; For Taiwan, the data of 2003 is actually data of 2001.
Sources: International Monetary Fund *Direction of Trade Statistics*, Washington DC; International Economic Databank, The Australian National University, Canberra.

Table 7.5   International comparison of shifting patterns of export specialisation in selected industrial sectors, 1970–2000 (index of revealed comparative advantage)

Machinery (SITC 71)	1970	1975	1980	1985	1990	1995	2000
China	0.1	0.1	0.1	0.1	0.3	0.4	0.7
Japan	0.9	1.0	1.4	1.4	1.6	1.7	1.5
NIEs	0.1	0.2	0.4	0.5	0.8	1.0	1.4
ASEAN	0.1	0.2	0.2	0.4	0.8	1.2	1.4
United States	1.6	1.7	1.9	1.7	1.3	1.4	1.4
Electrical machinery (SITC 72)							
China	0.2	0.2	0.2	0.3	0.7	0.9	1.1
Japan	2.1	1.9	2.5	2.2	2.1	1.9	1.6
NIEs	1.8	2.0	2.3	1.8	2.0	2.0	1.8
ASEAN	0.2	0.6	1.2	1.3	1.8	2.0	2.1
United States	1.2	1.3	1.5	1.4	1.3	1.2	1.2
Travel goods (SITC 83)							
China	2.8	3.2	3.4	8.2	3.1	8.6	7.9
Japan	2.0	0.5	0.3	0.2	0.1	0.0	0.0
NIEs	8.9	14.9	16.2	9.7	6.5	2.1	0.8
ASEAN	0.4	0.7	0.4	0.3	1.2	1.1	1.2
United States	0.2	0.3	0.3	0.1	0.2	0.2	0.3
Clothing (SITC 84)							
China	2.0	2.4	4.7	5.2	4.9	5.1	4.6
Japan	1.2	0.3	0.2	0.2	0.1	0.0	0.0
NIEs	13.3	14.2	10.1	6.8	4.2	2.1	1.7
ASEAN	0.3	0.6	0.9	1.1	1.8	1.4	1.2
United States	0.3	0.2	0.3	0.1	0.2	0.4	0.4
Footwear (SITC 85)							
China	1.3	1.6	1.8	1.6	3.8	6.1	6.4
Japan	1.1	0.1	0.1	0.0	0.0	0.0	0.0
NIEs	3.6	6.2	7.8	6.5	5.1	1.1	0.3
ASEAN	0.2	0.2	0.4	0.3	1.3	2.1	1.1
United States	0.0	0.1	0.1	0.1	0.1	0.1	0.1

Note: ASEAN includes Singapore; NIEs excludes Singapore.
Source: Calculated using UN COMTRADE data, International Economic Databank, The Australian National University, Canberra.

the early 1980s. It then fell away rapidly to well below unity for most products by the end of the century. The NIEs' export specialisation in machinery rose rapidly from low levels in 1970 to above unity at the end of the century. The NIEs export specialisation in electrical machinery was more stable, reflecting a wider range of relative factor requirements in production of these goods.

Individual labour-intensive products tended to rise in proportion to ASEAN countries' total exports until the mid 1980s. That their peaks were much lower than those in Northeast Asian economies is a reflection of the ASEAN economies' larger per capita endowments of natural resources. ASEAN export specialisation in electrical machinery exceeded unity by the 1980s and stabilised around 2 late in the 1990s. Export specialisation in machinery exceeded unity in the mid 1990s and continues to rise.

China's export specialisation in most labour-intensive products peaked at very high levels between the mid 1980s (travel goods and clothing) and the mid 1990s (footwear). It has tended to stabilise at the high levels. China's internal economic differentiation means that the country as a whole can retain comparative advantage in labour-intensive products for longer, as lower-cost labour from the inland replaces the labour from coastal China as the coastal provinces absorb more valuable skills and their labour costs rise. China's export specialisation in machinery rose rapidly from the mid-1980s and was around unity, and rising, at the end of the century.

By contrast, US export specialisation in the products for which data are recorded in Table 7.5 remained relatively stable throughout the last several decades. It was consistently low for labour-intensive goods and high for machinery.

Table 7.6 sets out the net exports of manufactures of some selected Asia Pacific economies to Asia and the world for 1980–2000 (referred to as 'the ladder of development' by Leamer 1984). What matters here is not only the sign patterns, but also the magnitude of these net export figures. The data show that there is a clear pattern of trade specialisation in East Asian region with regard to manufactured products during the past two decades.

Table 7.6   Net exports of manufactures to Asia and the world, 1980, 1990 and 2000 (US$ billion)

	Labour-intensive		Capital-intensive		Machinery		Chemicals	
1980	Asia	World	Asia	World	Asia	World	Asia	World
Australia	-0.70	-1.40	0.70	-0.11	-0.05	-6.02	-0.10	0.16
China	1.23	3.40	-1.23	-1.85	-1.63	-4.02	-3.25	-0.34
Hong Kong	-2.19	1.89	2.19	-0.71	-0.42	-2.48	-0.85	-1.03
Indonesia	-0.07	-0.08	0.07	-1.26	-0.06	-3.52	-0.11	-0.90
Japan	-0.11	2.20	0.11	18.08	-2.18	62.38	-4.37	1.64
Korea	0.61	5.59	-0.61	1.20	-0.66	-1.54	-1.32	-1.12
Malaysia	-0.15	0.01	0.15	-0.83	-0.07	-2.68	-0.15	-0.43
Singapore	-0.44	-0.21	0.44	-0.94	-0.24	-1.95	-0.47	-0.48
Thailand	0.02	0.44	-0.02	-0.58	-0.12	-1.97	-0.24	-0.60
Taiwan	0.87	5.32	-0.87	-0.14	-0.95	-0.76	-1.89	-1.09
United States	-7.62	-7.50	7.62	-5.29	-0.34	24.83	-0.67	5.82
1990								
Australia	-1.36	-2.17	0.09	-0.56	-0.99	-14.58	0.03	-1.33
China	5.47	13.42	0.87	-0.66	0.61	-11.10	0.14	-0.95
Hong Kong	-14.19	-7.18	-0.96	-2.08	-7.38	-14.61	-1.27	-3.82
Indonesia	0.09	2.69	-0.28	-1.43	-1.49	-8.92	-0.47	-2.59
Japan	-6.22	-7.71	5.95	10.81	42.27	152.43	5.44	2.96
Korea	2.14	16.10	0.95	1.28	2.64	0.05	0.60	-3.70
Malaysia	-0.50	0.71	-0.28	-1.68	0.21	-4.55	-0.32	-1.35
Singapore	-1.42	-0.32	0.02	-1.76	0.03	-0.68	1.08	-0.04
Thailand	-0.27	3.56	-0.70	-2.91	-0.61	-8.90	-0.26	-2.01
Taiwan	3.79	11.21	0.43	0.93	3.78	5.41	0.94	-2.96
United States	-28.76	-35.66	-3.32	-11.13	-7.77	-33.45	3.85	7.29
2000								
Australia	-2.60	-3.43	-0.57	-1.51	-6.26	-24.98	-0.26	-0.33
China	9.16	47.51	-0.76	1.03	-2.40	-14.00	-9.51	-16.61
Hong Kong	-28.64	-23.83	-3.91	-6.11	-51.12	-80.06	-4.74	-9.53
Indonesia	0.69	8.63	-0.44	-1.14	2.34	0.08	-0.79	-2.25
Japan	-18.04	-19.92	9.13	14.05	60.34	209.65	11.84	9.72
Korea	3.31	13.32	2.41	3.01	11.53	37.93	6.41	2.92
Malaysia	-0.12	2.29	-0.53	-2.04	4.53	8.36	-0.08	-1.42
Singapore	-1.92	-0.53	-0.07	-2.02	7.21	10.95	3.19	1.80
Thailand	-0.41	4.74	-0.44	-2.82	1.16	1.83	0.66	-1.19
Taiwan	6.73	11.92	2.95	5.44	9.58	16.15	3.12	-3.04
United States	-54.80	-79.23	-11.01	-21.30	-70.92	-180.70	4.53	-3.81

Source: UN COMTRADE, International Economic Databank, The Australian National University, Canberra.

First, Japan together with the United States ranks at the top by exporting (net) the most advanced manufactured products, namely chemicals. Japan exports more to Asia than to the world in 1990 and 2000. Both countries are net importers of labour-intensive products, but a sharp difference between them is that Japan exports both capital-intensive and machinery products with high values, while the United States imports those products. This suggests that both countries retain comparative advantage in producing and exporting the most advanced manufactured products (chemicals) and that Japan has very strong comparative advantage in machinery and capital-intensive products.

Second, from 1980 to 1990 both Korea and Taiwan produced clear shifts in their net exports of capital-intensive and machinery from net importing to exporting these products. Such shifts provide some evidence of structural changes resulting from their changing pattern of comparative advantage. Korea and Taiwan have very similar sign patterns with regard to these four aggregates, exporting all these manufactured products except exports of chemicals to the world in the case of Taiwan. Another similarity between them is that both Korea and Taiwan export much smaller volumes of labour-intensive products to Asia than to the world (a clear sign of competition from other industrialising economies in the region).

Third, like Korea and Taiwan, Singapore exports both machinery and chemicals to both Asia and the world and capital-intensive products to Asia only in 1990 and 2000. However, the difference is that while both Korea and Taiwan are still exporting labour-intensive products to both Asia and the world (much less to Asia than to the world in terms of the values), Singapore has lost its comparative advantage in exporting this category of manufactured products to both Asia and the world. Since 1990, Hong Kong has become a net importer of all four manufactured aggregates.

Fourth, there are signs that Malaysia and Thailand are losing comparative advantage in labour-intensive product market in Asia, but gaining some comparative advantage in machinery by 2000. China and Indonesia are at the next rung on the ladder, namely exporting labour-intensive products to both Asia and the world. China is predominant in terms of its net export values of this product category, particularly to the world market, but it depends heavily on imports of machinery and chemicals from both Asia and the world by 2000.

Fifth, Australia appears to have some comparative advantage in exporting capital-intensive and chemical products to Asia and the United States in both 1980 and 1990, but has been losing comparative advantage on both products by 2000. Australia is heavily dependent on imports of machinery and labour-intensive products from the world.

Finally, China has settled on the export structure ladder as a major exporter of labour-intensive manufactured products as determined by its pattern of factor endowment. This situation did not change much during the past two decades. What has changed noticeably is the magnitude of the exports of labour-intensive products from China to Asia and particularly to the world by 2000.

Intra-industry trade and trade in components

An outstanding feature of the changing pattern of East Asian comparative advantage and trade specialisation is the huge expansion of trade in components. There is no longer a 'Japanese' car or 'Chinese' television set. Components are sourced from many countries to minimise total supply costs. This is a feature of the contemporary global economy, but it has been taken further in East Asia than in other major economic region (Garnaut and Song 2006).

Greater openness leads to the internationalisation of a manufacturing process in which many countries participate in different stages of the manufacture of a specified product. Trade in intermediate goods such as machinery parts and components is increasing. The process allows stages of production to be located where they can be undertaken most efficiently and at the lowest cost. As a result, countries are becoming more interdependent on each other (Yeats 1998) and global value chains (GVCs) offer significant opportunities to many Asian firms to take advantage of the potential benefits of globalisation (ADB 2003).

Closer regional economic integration emerges through market processes. A central feature of deeper East Asian economic integration has been the remarkable growth of trade in intermediate goods and components. China is now a major element in this process (Li et al. 2007). Athukorala (2003) shows that in 2000, over 60 per cent of 'final exports' from developing Asia went to countries outside the East Asian region, especially North America and Europe, up from 55 per cent in 1992.

Table 7.7 shows that East Asia has been more deeply involved in fragmentation trade than other regions. Fragmentation trade is damaged more than conventional trade by transactions costs. For this and other reasons, it is damaged more than traditional trade by FTAs with their rules of origin. While trade in components is mainly within East Asia, a majority of the markets for the final products is still extra-regional. The fragmentation of the supply chain accelerates the growth of trade in components and makes the region more heavily dependent on extra-regional trade for 'growth dynamism' than is suggested by data that does separate out the trade in components (Findlay 2003).

The large increases in fragmentation trade have been associated with rising intra-industry trade. By 2000, a few East Asian economies (Singapore, Korea, Taiwan, Thailand) had similar indexes of intra-industry trade with the world as a whole as the North American economies (Table 7.8). Most

Table 7.7   **Contribution of parts and components to export growth, 1992–2000** (per cent)

	ASEAN	East Asia	EU-12	NAFTA	World
China	32.9	31.1	12.6	10.3	17.9
Korea	58.9	51.2	35.4	40.6	41.0
Japan	66.9	52.7	86.2	34.1	50.1
Korea	58.9	51.2	35.4	40.6	41.0
Taiwan	67.6	50.8	37.5	54.9	47.4
Hong Kong	29.2	21.6	34.9	8.8	16.3
ASEAN	67.6	60.0	53.1	52.1	54.7
East Asia	64.2	52.6	40.9	35.0	42.8
EU-12	48.8	31.1	20.0	18.1	22.0
NAFTA	74.4	55.8	34.2	23.3	29.9
United States	73.9	55.9	34.8	30.7	38.1
World	63.0	49.6	21.1	25.1	27.0

Source: Compiled from the data from Athukorala 2003. *Product fragmentation and trade patterns in East Asia,* Working Paper No. 21/2003. The Australian National University, Canberra: Table A-3 (B).

Table 7.8   **Intra-industry trade indexes by destination, 1985 and 2000**

	East Asia		EU-12		North America		World	
	1985	2000	1985	2000	1985	2000	1985	2000
Australia	11.9	25.7	10.5	23.4	12.2	27.9	22.4	36.6
New Zealand	8.8	12.0	6.5	16.7	12.9	23.3	20.7	30.3
Japan	17.7	42.5	32.9	43.1	21.2	42.1	19.8	41.6
Korea	48.5	68.7	44.2	40.5	25.1	48.9	40.7	55.9
China	23.2	49.9	10.0	42.7	7.6	32.6	21.3	47.6
Hong Kong	24.8	11.5	30.7	20.1	20.8	18.2	45.7	19.6
Taiwan	48.9	76.5	28.9	43.4	17.9	37.9	35.0	60.8
Singapore	44.9	82.3	41.9	45.9	51.1	56.2	58.5	78.9
Indonesia	10.1	32.8	3.9	20.1	1.9	14.8	15.1	34.0
Malaysia	25.6	65.8	20.1	48.7	50.9	43.2	37.2	60.4
Thailand	21.3	61.7	13.6	43.3	24.0	35.1	23.1	57.3
Philippines	32.3	56.4	25.5	29.2	45.1	45.1	36.1	49.9
Vietnam	2.2	19.0	3.2	8.1	0.3	7.7	7.1	17.6
EEC-12	43.5	50.9	97.6	92.9	53.3	67.2	78.9	86.6
United Kingdom	39.4	41.7	62.7	74.1	50.8	65.2	72.2	79.9
Germany	36.3	47.9	49.6	70.5	21.3	59.7	51.9	72.9
United States	27.5	44.1	47.5	62.2	61.6	64.2	52.3	62.9
Canada	13.3	17.2	25.7	39.5	61.3	63.4	63.3	66.0
Mexico	6.1	12.2	8.7	30.7	33.8	59.1	31.9	60.5

Source: UN Trade Data, International Economic Databank, The Australian National University, Canberra.

global indexes for the East Asian economies were moderately lower. Hong Kong was very low, reflecting characteristics of trade and industry structure rather than any failure of openness. Japan's global index had more than doubled between 1985 and 2000, but remained fairly low.

Extent of East Asian integration

Table 7.9 decomposes trade (exports plus imports) undertaken by countries in the various regions into percentages of total intra-regional and total inter-regional trade, which measures the extent of both intra- and inter-regional integration.

Table 7.9   Intra-regional and inter-regional trade among actual and potential formal blocs, 1980–2003 (percentage of total trade)

Pole	1980	1990	2000	2003
North America				
Intra-regional	32.3	37.6	47.4	46.4
With European Union	18.8	20.0	15.6	16.7
With East Asia	24.9	35.4	31.6	31.4
With ASEAN	3.5	4.2	5.1	4.7
With Australia and New Zealand	1.4	1.5	0.9	0.9
European Union				
Intra-regional	56.6	64.6	60.2	60.9
With North America	8.2	8.4	10.1	9.1
With East Asia	32.5	38.9	37.4	37.3
With ASEAN	1.1	1.5	2.1	1.9
With Australia and New Zealand	0.7	0.7	0.6	0.6
East Asia				
Intra-regional	35.2	44.2	51.4	51.2
With North America	21.9	25.6	22.1	20.1
With European Union	12.0	16.3	13.7	13.9
With ASEAN	12.6	11.4	14.0	14.7
With Australia and New Zealand	3.7	3.2	2.5	2.7
ASEAN				
Intra-regional	16.9	17.4	22.6	23.2
With North America	16.1	18.5	18.5	16.7
With European Union	13.0	15.8	12.9	12.7
With East Asia	53.0	55.5	55.5	55.9
With Australia and New Zealand	3.1	2.7	2.6	3.0
ANZ				
Intra-regional	6.2	7.5	7.6	8.1
With North America	18.4	19.9	17.7	15.1
With European Union	20.1	20.1	17.0	19.8
With East Asia	45.1	51.0	52.7	53.1
With ASEAN	7.4	7.9	12.1	12.3

Notes: ASEAN=Association of Southeast Asian Nations; EU=European Union; North America Pole: US, Canada, Mexico; East Asia Pole: Malaysia, Hong Kong, Indonesia, Japan, South Korea, China, Taiwan, Singapore, and the Philippines; ASEAN includes Singapore.
Sources: International Monetary Fund, *Direction of Trade Statistics*, Washington DC; International Economic Databank, The Australian National University, Canberra.

Table 7.10 shows that there are generally increasing trends of intra-regional trade for all the blocs (except the European Union) across time. By 2003, the level of intra-regional trade is highest in the EU (60 per cent) followed by East Asia (51 per cent) and then North America (46 per cent). The region of ASEAN, a sub-set of East Asia, is not highly integrated in terms of intra-regional trade, although the trend is increasing. Australia and New Zealand have a relatively low level of intra-regional integration compared with other regions. In comparison with the rising trend of intra-regional trade, inter-regional trade tends to fall for many regional blocs, for example for North America trade with both the EU and East Asia. However, East Asia has had the highest level of inter-regional trade with North America followed by its trade with EU, suggesting a high level of interdependence between the two regions. Australia and New Zealand have a highest level of inter-regional trade with East Asia (53 per cent compared with their trade share with the EU of 19 per cent and North America of 15 per cent).

Table 7.10 allows us to assess the extent to which the expansion of East Asian inter-regional and intra-regional trade has simply reflected the increase in scale of East Asia's trade with the rest of the world, and the extent to which it has involved changes in trade intensity with one or other set of partners (Garnaut and Song 2006). It does this through the presentation of intensity indexes as originally developed by Kojima (1964). It also breaks down the intensity index into complementarity and bias indexes, following Drysdale (1969) (see also Drysdale and Garnaut 1982). The latter step allows assessment of the extent to which changes in intensity of trade reflect respectively a closer match of the commodity composition of the two partners' trade, relative to their trade with the rest of the world, and the extent to which it resulted from changes in intensity of trade commodity-by-commodity.

Between 1985 and 2000, the intensity of intra-regional trade fell in East Asia, but rose in North America and Western Europe. Relative to the respective regions' shares in world trade, East Asia has come to trade relatively less within its own region, and the other two regions relatively more. Complementarity in intra-regional trade rose in East Asia, remained steady in Europe, and fell in North America.

Table 7.10   Bias, complementarity and intensity indexes for major country groups, 1985 and 2000

Reporter Type	Australia and New Zealand		East Asia		ASEAN		EU-12		North America		Rest of world	
	1985	2000	1985	2000	1985	2000	1985	2000	1985	2000	1985	2000
Australia and New Zealand												
Bias	8.3	9.0	1.8	1.7	2.6	2.3	0.4	0.3	0.9	0.6	1.1	1.1
Complementarity	0.5	0.7	1.4	1.2	0.7	0.8	1.0	1.0	0.5	0.7	1.0	1.2
Intensity	3.9	6.3	2.5	2.0	1.8	1.9	0.4	0.3	0.5	0.4	1.1	1.3
East Asia												
Bias	1.4	1.2	1.6	1.2	2.0	1.4	0.3	0.4	1.1	0.7	0.6	0.5
Complementarity	1.1	1.0	1.1	1.3	1.1	1.5	0.9	1.0	1.1	1.1	1.0	0.9
Intensity	1.6	1.2	1.7	1.6	2.2	2.0	0.3	0.4	1.3	0.8	0.6	0.4
ASEAN (6)												
Bias	2.0	2.2	2.5	1.6	4.1	2.5	0.4	0.5	1.0	0.7	0.5	0.6
Complementarity	0.8	0.9	1.2	1.3	1.3	1.5	0.9	0.9	0.9	1.0	0.9	0.9
Intensity	1.6	2.0	3.1	2.2	5.2	3.8	0.3	0.4	0.9	0.7	0.5	0.5
EU-12												
Bias	0.4	0.4	0.2	0.2	0.2	0.2	1.0	1.1	0.3	0.3	0.8	1.0
Complementarity	1.1	1.1	0.9	0.9	1.0	0.9	1.1	1.1	1.0	1.0	1.1	1.1
Intensity	0.5	0.4	0.2	0.2	0.2	0.2	1.1	1.2	0.3	0.3	0.8	1.1
North America												
Bias	0.9	0.7	0.9	0.6	0.7	0.6	0.4	0.3	1.1	1.4	0.6	0.4
Complementarity	1.2	1.1	1.0	0.9	0.9	1.0	1.0	1.0	1.3	1.1	1.0	1.0
Intensity	1.0	0.7	0.8	0.6	0.6	0.5	0.4	0.3	1.4	1.6	0.6	0.4
Rest of world												
Bias	0.3	0.3	0.3	0.4	0.3	0.4	0.8	0.9	0.5	0.5	1.2	1.4
Complementarity	0.8	1.0	1.2	1.0	1.1	0.9	1.0	1.0	0.9	1.0	1.1	1.1
Intensity	0.3	0.3	0.4	0.4	0.3	0.4	0.8	0.9	0.4	0.5	1.2	1.5

Source: Garnaut, R. and Song, L., 2005. Truncated globalisation: the fate of the Asia Pacific economies?, in Hadi Soesastro and Christopher Findlay (eds), *Reshaping the Asia Pacific Economic Order*, Routledge, London: Table 7.

China in East Asian economic integration

In his discussion of the ladder hypothesis and multiple export catch-up of the East Asian economies, Pearson (1994) raised several questions about China's position and potential in the process of industrial and trade transformation taking place in the region. The delayed entrance of the

People's Republic of China into this dynamic process in the late 1970s poses interesting questions. Where has China settled on the export structure ladder, and how rapidly will it climb? Are Korean and Taiwanese export structures sufficiently sophisticated to escape pressure from China from below? Will the entrance of China slow the progress of ASEAN economies as exporters? Does the sheer size of the Chinese economy and its export potential add a new dimension? (Pearson 1994:37)

The emergence of China as a major exporter of manufactures in the 1980s and especially the 1990s has intensified the competitive impacts on other East Asian economies, thereby, accelerating the pace and depth of the structural adjustment in the regional economy. For example, competition between China and other Asian countries is likely to increase as China's relatively cheap and productive workforce provides it with comparative advantages on world markets across a range of labour-intensive products.

China has an important place in the sale of many labour-intensive products in world markets, which are similar to those produced in the ASEAN economies (Xu and Song 2000). China has also increased its shares of world total labour-intensive manufactured exports from 1970 to 2000 (Figure 7.1). In contrast, the shares of NIEs in world total labour-intensive exports have been declining rapidly, while the gap between China and ASEAN in terms of their shares in world total has been widening especially since the early 1990s (Figure 7.1).

Progress in structural adjustment in these economies can be seen from the declining shares of labour-intensive products in their total exports from 1970 to 2000 (Figure 7.2). However, the task of structural adjustment seems more pressing for the latecomers.

Competitive relationships and structural adjustments

The competitive relationships between the three competing economies of China, ASEAN and NIEs can be seen by examining the more detailed two-digit SITC data. Table 7.11 presents the figures of two digit-SITC categories falling into the advantage or disadvantage groups for each

Figure 7.1   Changing share of some East Asian economies in world
total labour-intensive manufactured exports, 1970–
2000 (per cent)

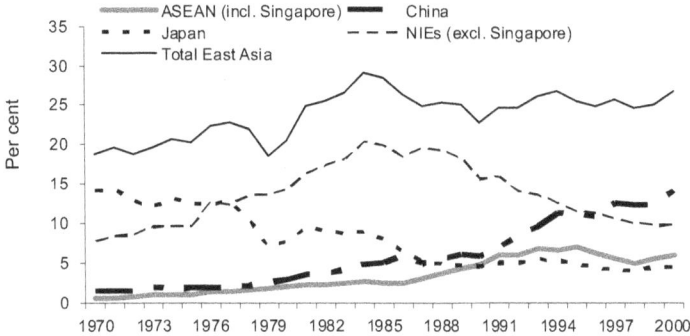

Source: Authors' calculation using UN COMTRADE, International Economic Databank,
The Australian National University, Canberra.

Figure 7.2   Share of labour-intensive products in total exports,
1970–2000 (per cent)

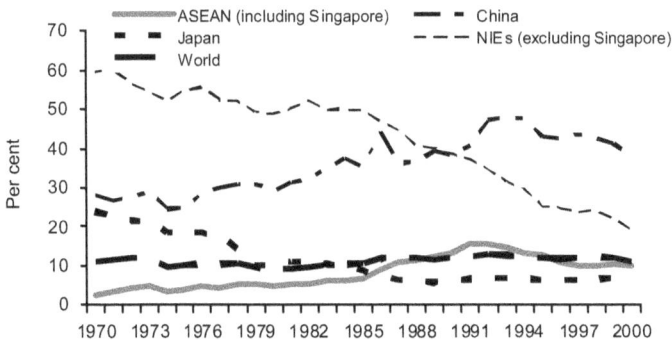

Source: Calculated using UN COMTRADE data, International Economic Databank, The
Australian National University, Canberra.

Table 7.11   Competitive advantage and disadvantage with the
United States, 1987–2000

Number of two-digit SITC categories which had	ASEAN	China	NIes
Advantage	23	35	16
Disadvantage	35	24	40
Neutral	3	1	5
All	61	60	61

Source: Song, L., 2004. The export competitiveness of ASEAN, China and the East Asian
NIes, 1987–2000, paper presented at the international conference on Rising China and the
East Asian Economy, The Korea Institute for International Economic Policy (KIEP), Seoul,
Korea:19–20: Table 13.

competing economy. The strong competitive advantage of China is also
evident at the two-digit level of SITC categories, followed by ASEAN and
then NIes.

Increased competition has forced both China and other Asian countries
to make the necessary structural adjustments by upgrading their industries,
especially towards producing more capital- and technology-intensive
products. This competitive pressure is particularly important in the
relationship between China and the NIes, as China's rising trade has forced
the NIes to move more quickly in upgrading their industrial structures in
order to sustain a rapid growth of exports (Song 2004).

Table 7.12 shows that 68 per cent of NIE exports and 60 per cent of
ASEAN exports, but only 44 per cent of Chinese exports in 1987 were in
sectors that grew above average from 1987 to 2000. The fact that 68 per
cent of NIE exports were concentrated in fast-growing categories suggests
that NIes had considerable structural advantage compared with China
and ASEAN. The strong structural advantage of NIes can also be found at
the two-digit level of SITC codes. Table 7.13 shows the number of SITC
categories that fell into either the structural advantage or structural
disadvantage groups. At this level, the structural advantage for the NIes is
obvious with 45 categories that fell into the structural advantage group
compared with 22 for ASEAN and only 11 for China.

Table 7.12   Proportion of exports to the United States by SITC category

Commodity	1987–2000 Reference growth (per cent)	Relative growth	Proportion of 1987 exports (per cent) ASEAN	China	NIE
0 - Food	7.16	Fast	7.66	2.37	1.01
1 - Beverages	7.45	Fast	0.14	0.08	0.04
2 - Crude materials	3.53	Slow	3.24	1.24	0.36
3 - Fuels	0.99	Slow	3.41	2.34	0.48
4 - Vegetable oil	3.07	Slow	1.35	0.02	0.01
5 - Chemicals	12.61	Fast	0.92	3.71	1.67
6 - Manufactures	6.75	Fast	6.94	12.87	9.59
7 - Machinery and transport equipment	12.42	Fast	44.42	25.14	56.07
8 - Miscellaneous manufactures	5.43	Slow	28.02	52.18	30.37
9 - Not classified	−3.00	Slow	3.90	0.06	0.38
Average	5.64		100.00	100.00	100.00

Source: Song, L., 2004. The export competitiveness of ASEAN, China and the East Asian NIEs, 1987-2000, paper presented at the international conference on Rising China and the East Asian Economy, The Korea Institute for International Economic Policy (KIEP), Seoul, Korea:19–20: Table 10.

Table 7.13   Structural advantage and disadvantage, 1987–2000

Number of two-digit SITC categories which had	ASEAN	China	NIE
Structural advantage	22	11	45
Structural disadvantage	39	49	16
Total	61	60	61

Source: Song, L., 2004. The export competitiveness of ASEAN, China and the East Asian NIEs, 1987–2000, paper presented at the international conference on Rising China and the East Asian Economy, The Korea Institute for International Economic Policy (KIEP), Seoul, Korea:19–20: Table 11.

The China dimension of the process of East Asian economic integration can be elucidated through the following analysis. First, the economic reform and policy of opening up the economy has made China increasingly part of East Asian economic integration, which is reflected in the significant shifts in production and the trade structures of these economies. The fundamental causes for such shifts lie in differences in the patterns of factor endowments and levels of development in these economies. In case of China, the result has been largely due to a convergence of its patterns of factor endowments and trade, which accounts for the rapid expansion of China's trade share in labour-intensive manufactured exports and are apparent in its increasing trade share in some capital-intensive manufactured exports in the regional and world markets (Song 1996b).

Second, the process of industrial and trade transformation in the East Asian region that started decades ago has been very dynamic. Participation in this process by China since the beginning of its reform in the late 1970s has injected new forces into this transformation, increasing the specialisation in manufactured production and exports. As a result, East Asia economies, with an increase in intra-regional trade and investment and a larger share in world trade, are emerging as a new economic centre in the world economy.

Third, China's economic integration with the East Asian economies has benefited both China and other East Asian economies in terms of creating a bigger market for export products and taking advantage of scale economies and increased trade and investment opportunities. But it also poses challenges to the economies in the region. These could take the form of increased competition for labour-intensive manufactures exporters, for some capital-intensive manufactures exporters in the next stage of development of East Asian economy as well as competition for attracting foreign investment.

Fourth, the trade outlook for the East Asian industrialising economies will depend on future changes in their patterns of factor endowments. It also depends on both the trade policies they apply domestically and those pursued by their trading partners abroad. In this context, the industrialising economies of East Asia have a large stake in continuing their strategy of trade and investment liberalisation in their domestic economies and in the maintenance of open, rules-oriented international trade and investment regimes as well as the further developments of regional and multilateral forums for trade negotiations (Balassa and Noland 1994).

Prospects for the future East Asian trade and development

How has East Asia's rapid growth in output and trade, and tendency to trade globally rather than within its own region (to a greater extent than North America and Europe), affected the rest of the world economy?

The main effect is to expand the potential gains from trade in the rest of the world. This follows simply from the expanded scope for other economies to specialise in supply of goods and services in which their comparative advantage is strong.

The utilisation of these opportunities has required acceptance of structural change. The relatively steady East Asian share of global markets for the products in which the region's export specialisation has been strongest, labour-intensive manufactures, suggests that the costs of structural change for the world outside East Asia have not been high since the early 1980s, that is, since the early entry of East Asia into the international economy (see also Garnaut and Huang 2000). The pressures for continuing structural change of a radical kind have been greatest within East Asia itself, as identified in this chapter.

The skewed nature of East Asia's resource endowment relative to the rest of the world, with extreme relative scarcity of land and other natural resources, has made East Asia disproportionately and increasingly an importer of resource-based products. This has reduced the pressures on these old industries to decline in the industrial economies of the North Atlantic.

The East Asian economies will certainly continue to benefit from those contributing factors to East Asian trade and development, such as high savings, accumulation of both physical and human capital, a relatively stable market environment, liberalisation of domestic economies, inflows of FDI, geographic closeness, and various forms of economic cooperation.

However, there are a number of factors that have the potential to affect adversely the trade flows to and from East Asia, which include the weak growth and rising protectionism of the developed markets, instabilities of the financial systems, exchange rate volatility, weak domestic institutions, national policy of protection particularly with respect to those 'sensitive sectors', lack of progress in the multilateral trade negotiations and confusion about forms of forging regional economic cooperation (groupings).

The emergence of China as a major exporter of manufactures has been causing anxieties among other East Asian economies. With the rising degree of interdependence among the East Asian economies, there are also issues of geopolitics such as Japan-China bilateral relations and their respective relations with other East Asian economies such as ASEAN.

The regional economies are now at a stage where there is no basis for confidence that the continued strengthening of an open multilateral trading system will provide continually expanding access on a non-discriminatory basis for exports from each Asia Pacific economy's most productive industries, as they evolve over time. The old Western Pacific doctrines of 'open regionalism', and a conceptual framework within which unilateral trade liberalisation, regional cooperation within ASEAN and APEC, and multilateral liberalisation under the aegis of the WTO, have gone, and no conceptual or institutional alternative has arisen to provide confidence that the international environment will support continued rapid, internationally oriented growth. This was pointed out by Garnaut and Song (2004), who argue the following in responding to the newly resurgent interest in forming various bilateral and sub-regional trading arrangements.

First, the new pattern of bilateral and sub-regional preferences would truncate the process of increasingly precise specialisation in the supply of inputs into final products assembled in one or other of the Asia Pacific economies, because of the rules of origin.

Second, the contemporary regionalisation and globalisation of production would also be damaged by the transaction costs associated with monitoring and enforcing rules of origin, even in cases in which the domestic-plus-partner value-added were able to meet the tests.

Third, the proliferation of FTAs is a problem for adjustment to the rise of China, because it concentrates adjustment excessively in countries which have FTAs with China and also in those which do not have FTAs with third countries. It denies the great advantage of multilateral trade on a global basis, in that it diffuses pressures for adjustment throughout the global economy.

Fourth, using FTAs to separate third countries from East Asian dynamism, whether in East Asia or adjoining third countries, reduces their exposure to opportunities for rising living standards. This is likely to be most damaging to potential suppliers of the natural-resource based products in which China's comparative disadvantage is most pronounced, and especially of the agricultural industries in which trade distortion is endemic.

Finally, the trade-off between costs of adjustment and gains from trade through the rise of China is affected by the presence of FTAs. For the world as a whole, the trade-off between adjustment costs and gains from trade is more favourable if the movement is toward specialisation according to global comparative advantage, as it is modified by growth and structural change in individual economies.

Multilateral trading arrangements or wider regional groupings, rather than narrowly focused and complex and discriminatory bilateral trading arrangements, are conductive to the East Asian objective of sustaining fast export growth. In the case of China, what it essentially requires is not a number of narrowly focused bilateral arrangements or exclusive regional groupings that are discriminatory in nature. What it needs is wider open trading arrangements, ideally in global scope, that are consistent with non-discriminatory principles in international trade. As pointed out by Drysdale (1988), 'discriminatory trade regimes are likely to be damaging to the interests of East Asia and Pacific countries' (Drysdale 1988:36).

Thus, the task of 'institutional integration' remains a big challenge for the East Asian and Pacific economies. We close by quoting the conclusion by Drysdale in his book entitled, *International Economic Pluralism: Economic Policy in East Asia and the Pacific*

> the Pacific belongs to no single nation—not Japan, despite its new-found economic power, nor China, despite the scale of its industrial promise, nor, any longer, America. The responsibilities of Pacific economic policy leadership are bound to be developed as shared responsibilities. The huge and rewarding task of establishing a degree of intimacy among the heterogeneous nations of the Pacific, upon which confident policy strategies can be promulgated and executed in support of international systemic objectives, is a challenge to which Pacific countries are now fortunately at last beginning to turn (Drysdale 1988:260).

References

Asian Development Bank, 2003. *Asian Development Outlook,* Asian Development Bank, Manila.

Athukorala, P., 2003. *Product fragmentation and trade patterns in East Asia,* Working Paper No. 2003/21, The Australian National University, Canberra.

Balassa, B. and Noland, M., 1994. 'Prospects of trade and regional cooperation of the industrialising economies of East Asia', in S.C. Yang (ed.), *Manufactured Exports of East Asian Industrialising Economies: possible regional cooperation,* M.E. Sharpe, New York: pp.

Bradford, C.I. and Branson, W. H., 1987. 'Patterns of trade and structural change', in C.I. Bradford and W.H. Branson (eds), *Trade and Structural Change in Pacific Asia,* The University of Chicago Press, Chicago and London.

Das, Dilip K., 1998. 'Changing comparative advantage and the changing composition of Asian exports', *The World Economy,* 21(1):121–40.

Drysdale, P., 1969. 'Japan, Australia and New Zealand: the prospects for Western Pacific economic integration', *Economic Record,* 45 (111):321–42.

——, 1988. *International Economic Pluralism: economic policy in East Asia and the Pacific,* Allen & Unwin, Sydney.

Drysdale, P., and Garnaut, R., 1982. 'Trade intensities and the analysis of bilateral trade flows in a many-country world', *Hitotsubashi Journal of Economics,* 22(2).

——, 1993. 'The Pacific: an application of a general theory of economic integration', in Fred Bergsten and Marcus Noland (eds), *Pacific Dynamism and the International Economic System,* Institute for International Economics, Washington, DC:183–224.

Drysdale, P., 2003. 'Regional Cooperation in East Asia and FTA Strategies', Presentation to IIPS Conference on Building a Regime of Regional Cooperation in East Asia and the Role which Japan Can Play, Tokyo, 2–3 December.

Findlay, C., 2003. 'China in the world economy: the FTA strategy', in R. Garnaut and L. Song (eds), *China: New Engine of World Growth,* Asia Pacific Press, The Australian National University, Canberra:176–88.

Garnaut, R. and Anderson, K., 1980. 'ASEAN export specialisation and the evolution of comparative advantage in the Western Pacific region', in R. Garnaut (ed.), *ASEAN in a Changing Pacific and World Economy*, ANU Press, Canberra:374–412.

Garnaut, R. and Huang, Y., 2000. 'China and the future of the international trading system', in P. Drysdale and L. Song (eds), *China's Entry to the WTO: Strategic Issues and Quantitative Assessments*, Routledge, London:7–29.

Garnaut, R. and Song, L., 2006. 'Truncated globalisation: the fate of the Asia Pacific economies?', in Hadi Soesastro and Christopher Findlay (eds), *Reshaping the Asia Pacific Economic Order*, Routledge, London:46–81.

Kojima, K., 1964. 'The pattern of international trade among advanced countries', *Hitotsubashi Journal of Economics*, 5(1).

Krueger, A.O., 1997. 'Trade policy and economic development: how we learn', *American Economic Review*, 87(1):1–22.

Leamer, E.E., 1984. *Sources of International Comparative Advantage*: Theory and Evidence, The MIT Press, Cambridge, Massachusetts.

Li, K., Song, L. and Zhao, X., 2007. 'Component trade and China's global economic integration', in R. Garnaut and L. Song (eds), *China: Linking Markets for Growth*, Asia Pacific Press, The Australian National University, Canberra: 71–94.

Pearson, C.S., 1994. 'The Asian export ladder', in Shu-Chin Yang (ed.) *Manufactured Exports of East Asian Industrialising Economies: Possible Regional Cooperation*, M.E. Sharpe, New York.

Song, L., 1996a. *Changing Global Comparative Advantage: Evidence from Asia and the Pacific*, Addison-Wesley, Melbourne.

——, 1996b. 'Institutional change, trade composition and export supply potential in China', in M. Guitian and R. Mundell (eds), *Inflation and Growth in China*, International Monetary Fund, Washington, DC:190–225.

——, 2004. 'The export competitiveness of ASEAN, China and the East Asian NIEs, 1987–2000', paper presented at the international conference on Rising China and the East Asian Economy, The Korea Institute for International Economic Policy (KIEP), Seoul:19–20.

Xu, X.P. and Song, L., 2000. 'Export similarity and the pattern of East Asia development, in P. Lloyd and X.G. Zhang (eds), *China in the Global Economy*, Edward Elgar, Cheltenham:145–164.

Yeats, Alexander, 1998. *Just how big is global production sharing?*, The World Bank, Policy Research Working Paper, No. 1871, World Bank, Washington DC.

8 THE DYNAMIC IN EAST ASIAN INVESTMENT

Roger Farrell and Mari Pangestu

Over the last half century, Japan has been the dominant economy in East Asia and a key source of trade and investment flows to other economies in the region.[1] Japanese investment in East Asia provided capital, technology and management flows as firms invested to facilitate trade, to secure resources and energy and to relocate production in response to yen appreciation, rising labour costs and other constraints in the domestic economy. Investors sought to maintain their international competitiveness by relocating production to other East Asian economies as Japan's comparative advantage moved from light industrial products to more sophisticated and higher technology industries such as electronics and motor vehicles.

Led by the internationalisation of Japanese economy from the 1960s and the emergence of China as a leading economy three decades later, East Asia doubled its share of the world economy from 1980 to 2005. A defining characteristic of East Asian economic dynamism has been the rapid expansion of regional trade and investment (Drysdale and Garnaut 1993). These ties have been strengthening, and trade flows between Japan and China exceeded Japanese trade with the United States for the first time in 2003. East Asia has become more important to Japan with exports to the region rising from 20 to over 30 per cent in the decade to the mid 2000s and domestic sales of Japanese affiliates also rising (Farrell 2007).

Flows of direct investment into East Asia created extensive production and trade networks, especially in ASEAN, Taiwan, Korea and China, which contributed to growth in these regional economies. Japanese firms, as well as firms from the United States and other foreign direct investment (FDI) source countries, invested to ensure access to other markets (market-seeking FDI); to shift production processes to lower cost locations (efficiency-based FDI); to avoid barriers to trade (tariff-jumping FDI); or to supply services. In many cases, investors have multiple objectives in pursuing foreign direct investment in goods and services industries. In 2000, over forty per cent of Japanese electronics firms invested in China and ASEAN to lower their costs, 10–15 per cent sought to source parts and 15–20 per cent wanted to better secure these markets by establishing local sales or production facilities (Japan, METI 2002).

By 2005, East Asia had developed as an important production base, with its trade and investment pattern dominated by electrical machinery and transport equipment, including parts and components and assembled products—which accounted for around half of regional trade. Regional production chains increasingly switched from import substitution strategies to two-way trade of parts and components produced and assembled in different countries in order to lower costs. The electronics industry was restructured through FDI flows from Japan, the United States and Taiwan and the share of global electronics output of the NIEs and ASEAN economies tripled to over 25 per cent in the two decades to 2005, while electronics production in Japan and the United States fell over the same period.

The pattern of Japanese investment in East Asia reflects Japan's comparative advantage in the manufacturing sector; its firms have imported raw materials, metals and energy as inputs in the production of increasingly sophisticated products. Up until the 1970s, most manufacturing investment overseas went to East Asia and was concentrated on standard products such as textiles, toys, synthetic fibres and consumer electronics—which had become too costly to produce in Japan. Small to medium enterprises (SMEs) have been active investors; accounting for over 40 per cent of Japanese subsidiaries in East Asia.

Foreign direct investment in East Asia

Investment flows have traditionally focused principally on the manufacturing sector, because of East Asia's competitive advantages and partly because of government restrictions on foreign investment in other industries in the primary and service sectors. This trend is changing as deregulation occurs across the region encouraging FDI in the services sector, such as US acquisitions of Japanese financial institutions. However, the region is still an exception to the internationally dominant role of services in global FDI flows. Similarly, indirect or portfolio investment typically flows to established financial markets in North America and Europe. In 2003, the stock of Japanese FDI in East Asia reached 6.7 trillion yen or over US$700 billion, but the stock of portfolio investment into the region was negligible, at around 2.6 trillion yen out of global portfolio investment of 1,844 trillion yen (Bank of Japan 2004).

Until the 1980s, Japanese manufacturing investment focused on three economies known as newly industrialised economies (NIEs)—South Korea, Taiwan and Hong Kong. The focus of investment then shifted to ASEAN countries, particularly Thailand and Malaysia. From the mid 1990s, China became an important destination for FDI, with Japanese FDI in China's manufacturing sector rising from 5 per cent in 1990 to 43 per cent by 1995. The continual shifting of production bases occurred as host country costs rose with economic development and other locations became more cost-competitive. Firms in Japan also sought to diversify sources of supply, so as to insure against disruptions to their supply chains for raw materials, energy, parts and components, and assembled goods.

Many host countries offered incentives for Japanese investors, who could also receive Japanese tax incentives in support of outward FDI from Japan's declining industries. Often taxes and regulatory costs were lower than in Japan and labour costs a fraction of the domestic equivalent. The higher cost structure in Japan has been less relevant for more technology-intensive industries and production processes which corporations seek to retain domestically as part of their regional strategy and to lower the risk of technology outflow. Continuing changes to costs of production and other factors in East Asia have led Japanese investors to relocate more labour-intensive processes from Japan to the NIEs, to ASEAN and to China, particularly in response to rising wages, appreciating currencies and the loss of GSP tariff advantages of some locations.

Firms in Japan's 'sunset' industries, such as textiles, were early investors in creating foreign affiliates to relocate labour-intensive processes and lower production costs. Textiles accounted for over 30 per cent of Japanese exports in 1960, but less than 3 per cent three decades later. To retain competitiveness, Japanese firms such as Toray shifted their factories to ASEAN and China—assisted by a range of government assistance measures including tax concessions and low-interest loans from the Export-Import Bank—and then exported to the home market.

By 2002, East Asia was the location for about 40 per cent of Japanese overseas subsidiaries, from a global total of over 19,000 such firms (Table 8.1). Almost 70 per cent of production affiliates were in East Asia, compared to only one third of sales affiliates. Nevertheless, the region's share of Japanese investment by value was lower, because of the higher incidence of investment by small and medium enterprises in East Asia and the lower incidence of services investment compared to North America and Europe (Table 8.2). While one fifth of Japanese affiliates were located in the United States in 2002, economies in East Asia were important

Table 8.1   **Japanese subsidiaries by major country, 1960–2000**

Rank	Country	1960–70	1971–80	1981–90	1991–2000	Total
1	United States	215	474	1,785	1,191	3,733
2	China	-	-	249	2,133	2,424
3	Thailand	90	126	490	589	1,306
4	Hong Kong	71	225	372	487	1,176
5	Singapore	20	242	418	471	1,165
6	United Kingdom	17	109	442	328	918
7	Malaysia	14	108	337	375	845
8	Taiwan	109	106	363	257	845
9	Indonesia	71	225	372	377	665
10	Germany	47	122	258	194	632

Note: Table shows the number of Japanese subsidiaries by country.
Source: Calculated from Toyo Keizai Shimposha surveys. Toyo Keizai Shinposha, 2003. *Japanese Overseas Investment: a complete listing by firms and countries*, Tokyo.

Table 8.2   Japanese FDI flows by major region, 1951–2004
(share, per cent)

Period	North America	East Asia	Europe	Middle East	Oceania	Other
1951–60	1.1	17.3	1.1	19.8	0.7	30.0
1961–70	25.0	21.3	19.3	8.4	7.6	18.4
1971–75	24.3	28.1	15.2	18.3	5.3	8.8
1976–80	28.6	27.3	9.5	6.2	7.8	20.6
1981–85	36.4	20.4	13.9	1.5	3.6	24.2
1986–90	32.2	23.3	13.2	3.6	5.1	22.6
1991–95	46.9	12.4	18.7	0.4	4.3	17.3
1996–00	39.1	19.0	26.0	0.4	3.4	12.1
2001–04	24.6	16.1	40.7	0.1	2.3	16.2

Note: Data refers to new investment flows and excludes reinvestment.
Source: Japan Ministry of Finance, annual. *Outward Direct Investment (Country and region)*, Ministry of Finance, Tokyo. (Available at: http://www. mof.go.jp/english/e1c008.htm).

locations, with 13 per cent in China; 6 per cent in Hong Kong, 7 per cent in Thailand, 6 per cent in Singapore, 4 per cent in Malaysia and 3.5 per cent in Indonesia (Toyo Keizai Shinposha 2003).

Overall, Japanese business affiliates around the world employed around one million persons in 1985, two million in 1995, and 3.7 million a decade later. Employment increased in subsidiaries in Asia, especially in the NIE and ASEAN economies. The East Asian region accounted for 60 per cent of global employment in the mid 2000s and ASEAN and China have been the major centres. By 2005, Japanese subsidiary employment in China increased by 25 per cent to reach one million, the level reached by Japanese subsidiaries in ASEAN (Japan, METI 2005).

By 2000, over half of Japanese firms with overseas production had facilities in China, but many sought to diversify their production bases to avoid over-reliance on one source in case of supply disruptions or political tensions (Table 8.3). From the 1990s, both ASEAN and China were targeted by Japanese medium and small-sized corporations as production, assembly and processing locations for local supply and export to Japan or third-country markets. Japanese firms have been notably cautious investors in China, worried about bilateral political tensions and the possible loss

Table 8.3   Japanese overseas affiliates, by type of operations, 2004

Location	Production base	Sales base	Research and development base	Other base	Total
NIes	593	927	17	101	1,638
ASEAN	1,146	493	23	93	1,755
China	1,592	599	63	130	2,384
Other Asia	215	108	4	17	344
North America	719	614	76	195	1,604
Latin America	187	140	2	74	403
European Union	444	831	52	113	1,440
Central and Eastern Europe	101	69	7	3	180
Other Europe	15	32	-	2	49
Russia and other	13	21	-	5	39
Oceania	50	104	3	29	186
Middle East and Africa	40	79	2	9	130
Total	5,115	4,017	249	771	10,152

Note: NIes-3 are Taiwan, Singapore and South Korea; ASEAN-4 are Malaysia, Thailand, Indonesia and the Philippines. (b) The JBIC survey covered 939 Japanese manufacturing companies, each of which had three or more overseas affiliates and at least one overseas production base, with a response rate of 63.4 per cent in 2004.
Source: Japan Bank for International Cooperation, 2006, Tokyo.

of intellectual property. Capital flows began to increase markedly only in the 2000s after China's accession to the World Trade Organization—a move which significantly liberalised trade and investment flows; set in train a sequence of further deregulations over time; and enhanced investor confidence in China.

Japanese manufacturing FDI in East Asia has been focused on ASEAN and China especially (Figure 8.1) and investors have sought to establish lower cost production activities in this region (Table 8.4). Reflecting this investment pattern, the overseas production ratio of Japanese manufacturing has continued to rise (Table 8.5). The trade pattern in East Asia has been influenced by the sales and production networks created by FDI inflows—which have formed regional supply chains for manufacturing industry in Japan (see Figure 8.2). In the decade from 1995, Japanese manufacturing

Figure 8.1   Japanese manufacturing FDI in East Asia, 1989–2003
(100 million yen)

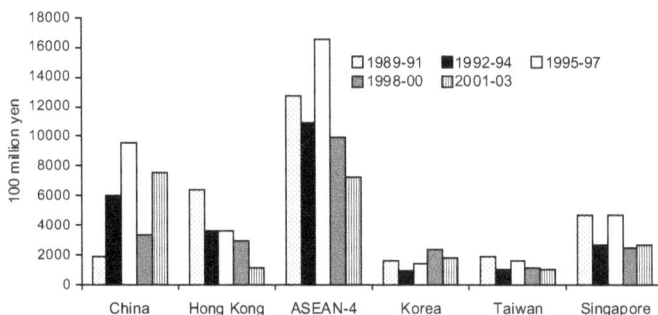

Source: United Nations Conference on Trade and Development, 2003. *World investment report*, United Nations Conference on Trade and Development, Geneva.

industry exports to overseas affiliates rose from 17 to 35 per cent of total exports from Japan—indicating the trend towards fragmentation within an intrafirm sales and procurement network in the region. The value of exports of manufactures to overseas affiliates rose by 22 per cent in 2004, reaching 20 trillion yen or around US$175 billion. Exports from overseas affiliates to manufacturing industry in Japan reached 8.7 trillion yen (US$76 billion).

Similarly, exports from overseas subsidiaries to parents in Japan ('reverse imports') grew from 11.6 per cent to almost 20 per cent of total imports into Japan. Increasingly, final products such as less complex electronics goods are produced in East Asia and then imported and sold directly into the Japanese market by domestic firms. The Asian economic crisis of 1997 led Japanese affiliates to move increasingly towards a greater export-orientation after the collapse of the regional demand during the crisis.

Another related trend has been increased local sales of Japanese affiliates in East Asia, which almost tripled after the Asian crisis to 2000 reaching a new peak as confidence in the ASEAN economies returned. As a result, local and regional sales of Japanese affiliates in East Asia, plus affiliate sales to Japan considerably exceeded imports from Japan to the region, signifying a new maturity in the economic relationship.

Table 8.4   Motivations for Japanese foreign direct investment in East Asia, 2000

Industry	China (2,631 firms)			ASEAN-4 (3,098 firms)			NIEs-3 (1,835 firms)		
	Lower cost	Parts supply	Market share	Lower cost	Parts supply	Market share	Lower cost	Parts supply	Market share
Food	33	1	23	26	3	18	20	-	28
Textiles	53	4	10	44	3	18	-	3	18
Wood and pulp	12	22	27	28	8	12	-	25	25
Chemicals	28	5	27	27	11	26	26	6	27
Steel	31	16	32	26	21	30	27	10	25
Non-ferrous	45	15	17	35	18	22	24	29	21
General machinery	44	4	22	46	11	21	28	9	25
Electrical machinery	42	8	21	46	15	14	35	12	23
Transport machinery	28	19	30	34	-	-	26	15	27
Precision machinery	54	4	13	60	-	-	15	-	25
Oil, coal	15	23	8	17	8	17	33	-	33
Other manufacturing	34	7	24	39	11	18	35	8	22

Note: The MITI survey for 2000 covered 12,243 firms globally, with 7,894 in Asia. The proportion of subsidiaries established for the purpose of research and development, re-exports, or to avoid trade conflict, were very low for all locations.
Source: Japan, MITI, 2001. *Basic Survey of the Overseas Business Activities of Japanese Firms*, Ministry of International Trade and Industry, Tokyo.

Case study of the Japanese electronics industry in East Asia

Overall, the basic pattern of production and trade for the electronics industry in East Asia has been for capital and intermediate goods to be imported from Japan and the United States, processed and assembled in the region and then exported to the United States and other major economies—although domestic markets are becoming more important. The electronics industry comprises a range of labour-intensive and capital-intensive production processes in the consumer electronics, industrial machinery and electronics components sub-sectors—which have been

Table 8.5   Overseas production ratio of Japanese manufacturing, 1985–2007 (per cent)

Industry	1985	1990	1995	2000	2003	2007
Food	0.9	1.2	2.6	2.8	4.9	n.a.
Textiles	2.7	3.1	3.5	8.6	8.4	n.a.
Chemicals	2.0	5.1	8.3	13.4	16.9	24.1
Iron and steel	5.3	5.6	9.2	16.3	9.4	n.a.
General machinery	3.4	10.6	8.1	12.1	18.4	25.8
Electrical machinery	7.4	11.4	16.8	21.9	38.8	45.5
Transport machinery	5.6	12.6	20.6	31.1	28.7	35.5
Total manufacturing	3.0	6.4	9.0	13.4	26.1	33.2

Note: Production ratio equals overseas production divided by total production.
Sources: Japan, METI, annual. Ministry of Economy, Trade and Industry and Japan Bank for International Cooperation, 2006. *Survey Report on Overseas Business Operations by Japanese Manufacturing Companies*, Tokyo. .

Figure 8.2   Patterns of Japanese production and trade with East Asia (trillion yen)

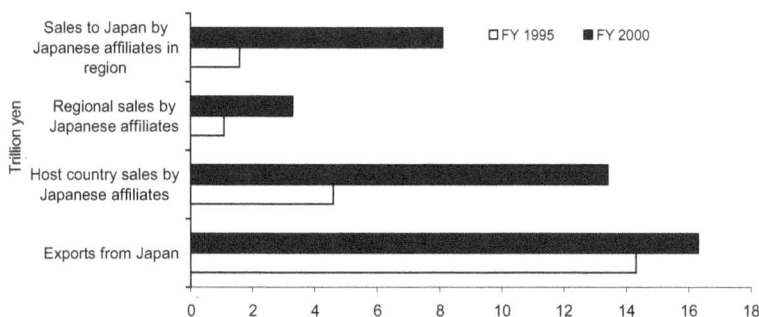

Sources: Japan External Trade Organisation, 2003, *Japanese Trade*, JETRO, Tokyo; Japan Bank for International Cooperation, 2006; *Survey Report on Overseas Business Operations by Japanese Manufacturing Companies*, Tokyo; Japan Ministry of Finance, annual; *Outward Direct Investment (Country and region)*, Ministry of Finance, Tokyo. Available at: http://www.mof.go.jp/english/e1c008.htm.

Table 8.6   **Foreign assets of Japanese subsidiaries overseas, 1980–2001 (US$ billion)**

Region	1980	1989	1995	2001
East Asia	17,083	60,859	146,140	209,322
North America	24,329	158,022	223,398	299,059
Europe	10,015	130,456	137,848	167,049
Latin America	11,993	14,663	29,175	47,298
Others	9,845	21,710	24,763	3,190
Total	73,265	385,701	561,324	725,918

Source: Japan, METI, 2002. Ministry of Economy, Trade and Industry and Japan Bank for International Cooperation, 2006. *Survey Report on Overseas Business Operations by Japanese Manufacturing Companies*, Tokyo, various issues.

relocated according to the labour costs and technological capabilities of economies in East Asia.

The quarterly survey of Japanese overseas affiliates conducted by METI (2004) provides an interesting guide to this relocation and upgrading process (Figure 8.3). In 1997, the year of the Asian economic crisis, around 60 per cent of employees of Japanese electronics affiliates in East Asia were located in the ASEAN-4 (251,000), with 16 per cent in the NIE-3 (67,000) and 25 per cent in China (108,000). By 2003, the share of the ASEAN-4 had increased absolutely to 388,000—but this now represented only 47 per cent of the regional workforce of the Japanese electronics industry, with China about 45 per cent and the NIE-3 down to 8 per cent.

In this transformation of the Japanese electronics industry's regional production and trade network, total East Asian sales, worth almost 8 trillion yen, grew in both the ASEAN-4 and China at the expense of the NIE-3. Exports to the Japanese market from Japanese affiliates in East Asia have grown over the period from 1.3 trillion yen to 2.4 trillion yen from 1997 to 2003, with China's share rising from 22 to 32 per cent and ASEAN-4's share around 47 per cent—although it rose to almost 56 per cent in 1998 as Japanese firms adjusted to the crisis (Japan, METI 2004).

For East Asia as a whole, intra-regional trade in electrical machinery goods in 2002 reached US$200 billion, which accounted for over half of total regional exports—indicating high regional trade intensity and

Figure 8.3   Japanese electronics industry in East Asia, sales and exports 1997–2003 (billion yen)

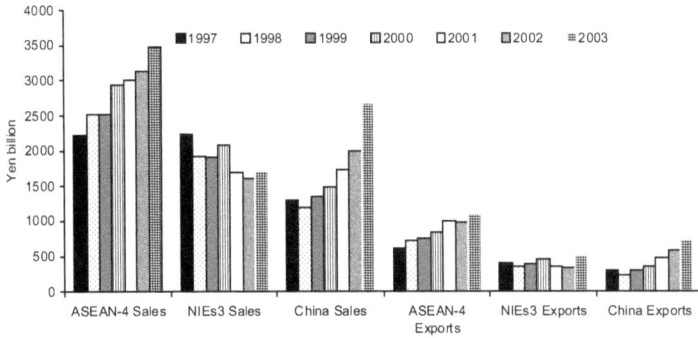

Source: Japan, METI, 2004. Ministry of Economy, Trade and Industry. Quarterly Survey of Business Activities, Tokyo.

complementarity indexes. However, despite increasing trade and investment in East Asia by Japanese electronics firms such as Matsushita, Toshiba and Sony, the profits of these companies have been affected by the rising competitiveness of other manufacturers in East Asia, including in China. In response, a number of electronics firms have expanded cutting-edge electronics investment in Japan, seeking to protect and extend their technological advantages.

Organisational patterns

The choices of modes for international business expansion generally include exporting, licensing, joint ventures and wholly owned subsidiaries. Initially, many Japanese investments from the 1950s to the 1970s were joint ventures with local partners, with the aim of gaining knowledge of overseas markets and satisfying restrictions on foreign investment, such as in ASEAN members Malaysia, Thailand and Indonesia. Gradually, higher levels of ownership and control came to be preferred by Japanese firms establishing overseas operations with wholly owned or majority owned unless they were required to form minority joint ventures by the local regulatory or political environment, as occurred in ASEAN in the 1970s and China in the 1990s.

In 2000, over 60 per cent of all Japanese subsidiaries in Asia were joint ventures, a comparatively high share because of the historical legacy of foreign investment restrictions in East Asia (Table 8.7). Joint ventures involving small and medium-sized enterprises (with less than 300 employees) were more common than for larger enterprises, due in part to the greater resources available to the latter group of firms. Around half of investments by SMEs were joint ventures (RIETI 2003).

From the 1990s, majority or wholly-owned greenfield investments became more frequent, especially to China and ASEAN, as foreign investment restrictions were eased. Over the decade, they accounted for over 50 per cent of investments, compared to an average of around 35 per cent in the preceding three decades (Delios and Beamish 2002). As China acceded to the WTO and eased trade and investment barriers, it became more popular as a target for Japanese investment—as well as for US, European and Taiwanese investors.

The role of small and medium enterprises

In early 2002, around 60 per cent of Japanese SMEs were established in Asia, with North America and Europe accounting for a further 29 per cent of subsidiaries of SMEs. In the early 1990s, China attracted almost

Table 8.7	Japanese FDI, mode by country, 2000						
Joint venture	US	Asia	China	ASEAN-4	NIE-3	EU	Total
<25 per cent	3.3	4.3	3.0	4.5	4.5	2.3	3.8
25–50 per cent	2.8	20.4	15.4	25.8	17.7	4.7	14.4
50 per cent	3.3	6.6	10.0	1.8	9.8	3.1	5.3
50–75 per cent	5.7	18.8	24.1	17.0	12.3	4.3	13.7
75–100 per cent	8.6	15.5	15.6	18.3	13.1	11.2	49.1
100 per cent	76.3	34.4	31.9	32.6	42.7	74.4	37.5
Number of firms	(1,166)	(3,856)	(1,276)	(1,478)	(919)	(786)	(6,405)

Source: Japan, METI 2002. Ministry of Economy, Trade and Industry. Quarterly Survey of Business Activities, Tokyo.

half of SME FDI, followed by Southeast Asia and North America and Europe. The main motivation for investment in Asia for Japanese SMEs has been to import lower costs products to Japan or to sell products to local Japanese affiliates. By contrast, the reason for FDI in Europe and North America has been to sell manufactured products to local enterprises (Japan, METI 2004).

The mode and structure of SME foreign subsidiaries has varied significantly, often reflecting factors such as local foreign investment laws, concern over technology transfer, and the funding abilities of smaller companies. A survey in late 2003 by METI found that over half of SMEs had established independent wholly owned subsidiaries in China and a quarter had majority-owned joint ventures. In North America, almost 90 per cent of SME FDI subsidiaries involved wholly or majority-owned Japanese investment (RIETI 2003).

Financing patterns for Japanese FDI

Japanese firms have faced a range of options in financing their overseas investment, such as using the capital of the parent company, reinvesting the profits of overseas affiliates, borrowing from Japanese financial institutions in Japan and the host country, or raising bonds. The choice between these options depends upon interest rates in Japan and the host country, foreign exchange risk, the credit rating of the parent and subsidiary, tax considerations, and the depth of the financial market in the host country.

Significant difference are evident in the profitability of Japanese and US multinationals around the world (Itagaki 2002). In the 1970s and 1980s, the average profitability of Japanese firms (4–6 per cent) was lower than for US firms (10–12 per cent) (Porter 2000). This trend has persisted, and in the early 2000s, for example, profit margins of Japanese-affiliated companies operating in China or ASEAN averaged about 6 per cent, compared to over 15 per cent for US-affiliates companies in the same economies (Japan, METI 2006). The profitability of Japanese firms by region from 1996 to 2004 is shown in Figure 8.4.

This marked difference in operating profits of Japanese affiliates in East Asia has been attributed to different business practices adopted by Japanese

Figure 8.4   Profitability of Japanese FDI by region, 1996–2004 (per cent)

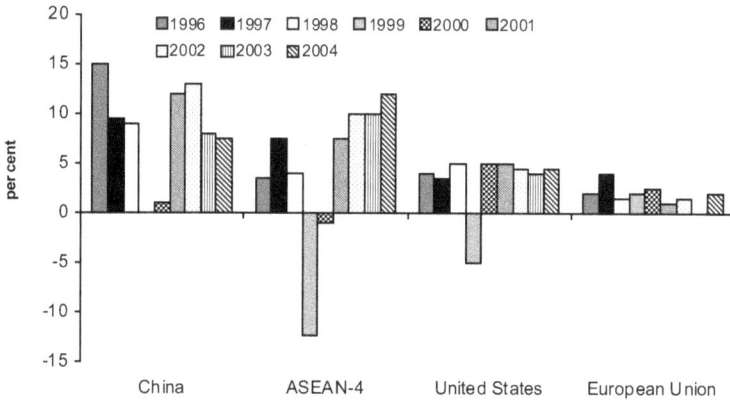

Note: Direct investment profit ratios—Profits received on direct investment divided by direct investment balances.

Sources: Bank of Japan, 2006. *International Balance of Payments Statistics, by Region*, Bank of Japan, Tokyo; Japan, Ministry of Economy, Trade and Industry, 2006. *White Paper on International Economy and Trade*, Tokyo.

affiliates— such as the slower profits arising from using a 'greenfield' model instead of more flexible merger and acquisition strategies of American companies, and the lower tax depreciation available for Japanese affiliates. Another possibility is the reluctance of Japanese managers of affiliates to transfer management responsibilities to local employees adopting instead a management structure that is similar to that in their parent companies (Japan, METI 2006).

In East Asia, funding of Japanese FDI was historically dominated by equity or loan funding, with reinvestment a comparatively minor factor until the 2000s when the profitability of affiliates improved markedly, especially in China. The notable turnaround of the profitability of Japanese FDI in East Asia may be attributable to new estimates by the Bank of Japan, based on balance of payments data rather than industry surveys (Bank of Japan 2006).

The extent of China's recent growth, at average annual increases in GDP of 10 per cent, is one explanation for the increased profitability of Japanese affiliates in that country. Another is the greater availability of local parts and components in China that has encouraged higher ratios of local procurement and local management of Japanese affiliates, and that may have contributed to higher profitability (Fukao 2007).

Linkages between FDI and ODA

Since the 1970s, Japan has directed over half of its official development assistance (ODA) to East Asia, reflecting its close political and economic relationship with the region (Figure 8.5). Following the rapid appreciation of the Japanese yen from late 1985, the Japanese government sought to use its extensive and growing ODA program to facilitate the adjustment of Japanese firms and industries to the yen-induced decline in their international competitiveness. As part of this focus, a New Asian Industrial Development Aid Plan was announced by MITI Minister Tamura in 1987 to assist the relocation of labour-intensive manufacturing to low cost sites in Asia (Arase 1995).

Japan became the world's largest aid donor in 1991 and ODA outflows peaked at US$13 billion in 2000 although fiscal pressures in the 2000s led to major cuts to the ODA budget. A significant proportion of these funds were directed to economic infrastructure in East Asia and linked to increasing trade and investment between Japan and the bilateral recipient. Yen loans for roads, bridges, ports or hospitals were used to finance the activities of Japanese construction and engineering firms especially in East Asia, as well as other regions (Japan, MOFA 2003).

Japanese ODA loans and grants were used in ASEAN economies to facilitate the start-up of assembly and manufacturing processes by Japanese firms and local partners. Often government agencies such as MITI negotiated with host government officials to provide incentives for Japanese firms to relocate, while JETRO, JICA and other agencies organised packages of loans, grants and technical assistance that greatly facilitated Japanese manufacturing and other FDI in East Asia (Arase 1995).

The provision of Japanese government guarantees for trade insurance and finance and the role of particular agencies in targeting particular

Figure 8.5   Distribution of Japanese ODA, by region, 1970–2001 (per cent)

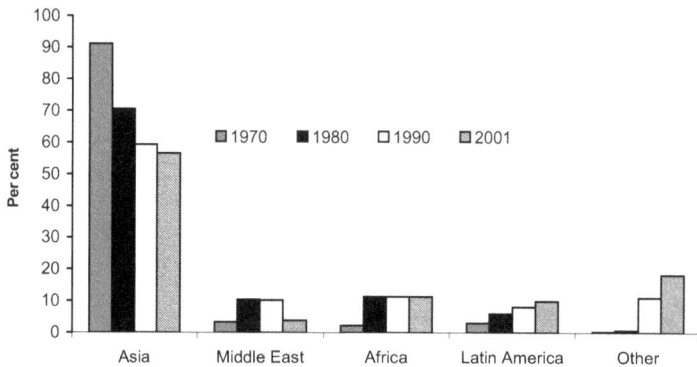

Source: Japan, Ministry of Foreign Affairs, 2003. *Official Development Assistance (ODA) White Paper 2002*, Tokyo.

projects eased the investment decision of many smaller Japanese manufacturers in industries—such as general machinery and textiles—as did the profusion of information available from Japanese trade, aid and business organisations (Solis 2003). These policy measures effectively represented public subsidies for the internationalisation and relocation of less competitive industries—a kind of defensive form of FDI—which contrasts with the comparative lack of assistance for larger, more competitive firms in the machinery, metals, automotive and electronics industries.

Conclusion

Over the last fifty years, Japanese foreign direct investment has contributed positively to the East Asian region through the transfer of industrial capacity, employment, capital and technology, all of which are bound up in the FDI package. Since Japan accounted for around half of the East Asian economy for much of this period, trade and investment linkages to the Japanese market were critical to the growth and development of other economies in the region. Japanese manufacturing firms have been among the most active investors in East Asia and created sales and production networks in the NIEs, ASEAN and Chinese economies which developed into supply chains across the region.

In the future, it is likely that closer integration between Japan and the rest of East Asia will continue. Already, China is Japan's major trade partner and trade is generally expected to grow further, providing further opportunities for Japanese and other firms in the region. The removal of remaining barriers to trade in goods and services in East Asia, for example through the creation of a consolidating free trade area (absorbing existing FTAs) would further promote closer regional linkages, especially if it included members of political groupings such as ASEAN+3, such as Japan, China, Korea and ASEAN (Pangestu and Gooptu 2003).

As noted by Peter Drysdale two decades ago, economic growth and development has accelerated across the East Asia region as barriers to trade and investment in goods and services across the region have been gradually removed, although many still remain (Drysdale 1988). The future liberalisation of barriers to services trade, for example, would significantly increase regional investment in industries such as banking and finance, telecommunications, commerce, real estate and transport and communications—these are currently inhibited by a range of government restrictions such as on foreign investment.

Partial deregulation in Japan itself has already led to positive capital inflows into the restructuring of less competitive firms in the motor vehicle and financial brokering industries. Similar deregulation, through either multilateral or bilateral trade or investment liberalisation, especially in ASEAN and China, would be likely to greatly boost inward flows of productive foreign direct investment and allow further increases in trade in goods and services across East Asia, to the benefit of all countries in the region.

Notes

1   East Asia is generally defined to include China, Japan, Hong Kong, Korea, Taiwan, Brunei, Indonesia, Malaysia, the Philippines, Singapore, Thailand and Vietnam (JETRO 2003).

References

Arase, D., 1995. *Buying Power: the political economy of Japan's foreign aid*, Lynne Rienner, London.

Bank of Japan, 2006. *International Balance of Payments Statistics, by Region*, BOJ, Tokyo. Available at http://www.boj.go.jp.

Beamish, P.W., A. Delios and S. Makino (eds), 2001. *Japanese Subsidiaries in the New Global Economy*, Edward Elgar, Cheltenham.

Drysdale, P.D. (ed.), 1972. *Direct Foreign Investment in Asia and the Pacific*, ANU Press, Canberra.

——, 1988. *International Economic Pluralism, Economic Policy in East Asia and the Pacific*, Allen and Unwin, Sydney.

Drysdale, P.D. and Garnaut, R., 1993. 'The Pacific: an application of a general theory of economic integration', in C.F. Bergsten and M. Noland, *Pacific Dynamism and the International Economic System*, Institute for International Economics, Washington, DC:183–224.

Farrell, R., 2007. *Japanese Investment in the World Economy*, a study of strategic themes in the internationalisation of Japanese industry, Edward Elgar, forthcoming February 2008.

——, and Findlay, C., 2002. 'Japan and the ASEAN-4 automotive industry', *East Asian Economic Perspectives*, ICSEAD, March.

Fukao, K., 2007. 'Plant Turnover and TFP Dynamics in Japanese Manufacturing', seminar presented at the Australian National University, Canberra, 8 February.

Japan Bank for International Cooperation, 2006. *Survey Report on Overseas Business Operations by Japanese Manufacturing Companies*, Japan Bank for International Cooperation, Tokyo.

Japan External Trade Organisation (JETRO) 2004. JETRO, Tokyo. *Expanding Japanese presence in East Asia*, JETRO Working Paper No. 1 (http://www.jetro.go.jp/it/e/press/2004/apr21.html).

Japan, Ministry of Economy, Trade and Industry (METI), 2003. *Basic Survey on Foreign Direct Investment* (Kaigai Toushi Tokei Souran), METI, Tokyo.

——, 2002–4. *Quarterly Survey of Business Activities*, Tokyo.

——, 2004. White Paper on Small and Medium Enterprises in Japan, Tokyo.

——, 2006. *White Paper on International Economy and Trade*, Tokyo.

Japan, Ministry of International Trade and Industry (MITI), 1991–01. *Basic Survey of the Overseas Business Activities of Japanese Firms* (Kaigai toshi tokei soran), Tokyo.

Japan Ministry of Finance, annual. *Outward Direct Investment (Country and region)*, Ministry of Finance, Tokyo. (Available at: http://www. mof.go.jp/english/e1c008.htm).

Japan, Ministry of Foreign Affairs, 2003. *White Paper on Japan's ODA* (Seifu Kaihatsu Enjo Hakusho), Tokyo.

Kohama, H., 2003. 'Aid, trade and FDI for economic development in East Asia', in H. Kohama, (ed.), *External Factors for Asian Development*, Japan Institute of International Affairs, Singapore.

Pangestu, M. and Gooptu S., 2003. 'New regionalism: options for China and East Asia', in Krumm et al. (eds), *East Asia Integrates: a trade policy agenda for shared growth*, World Bank, Washington, DC. Available at http://www.Inweb18worldbank.org.

Research Institute for Economy, Trade and Industry (RIETI), 2003. *Survey of Overseas Business Activities of Small and Medium Enterprises*, Tokyo, November.

Solis, M., 2003. 'The politics of self-restraint: FDI subsidies and Japanese mercantilism', *The World Economy*, 26(2):153–80.

Toyo Keizai Shinposha, 2003. *Japanese Overseas Investment: a complete listing by firms and countries*, Tokyo.

Toyo Keizai Shimposha, annual. *Japanese Overseas Investment*, *Toyo* Keizai Shimposha, Tokyo.

United Nations Conference on Trade and Development, 2003. *World investment report*, United Nations Conference on Trade and Development, Geneva.

9 THE IMPACT OF CHINA'S GROWTH

THE ASEAN COUNTRIES

Dong Dong Zhang

China's rapid growth and integration into the world economy present ASEAN countries[1] with enormous business opportunities and competition. China has become a major driver of the region's growth. Rapid expansion of China's industries, exports, and consumer markets has led to a surge of demand for raw materials, energy, intermediate products, final goods, and services of all kinds from ASEAN countries. At the same time, the ASEAN and Chinese economies compete in their home and in third country markets, particularly in labour-intensive products. In the face of China's competition, there is growing consensus that ASEAN's only viable option is to undertake further trade liberalisation, industrial restructuring and improvement of investment climates. ASEAN countries have undertaken economic liberalisation, including a free trade agreement (FTA) with China, to enhance their competitive position. Yet responses by individual ASEAN countries vary, largely a result of their differing domestic policy reforms, institutional capacity, natural endowment, and business competitiveness.

China's role in the global economy has increased sharply in the past 25 years. Its GDP has grown at an average annual rate of over 9 per cent, while its share of world trade has risen from less than 1 per cent to 6.5 per cent. China is now the second-largest economy on a purchasing power parity basis[2] and the third-largest trading nation in the world. Since 2003, China has been the world's largest destination for foreign direct investment (FDI), which reached US$60 billion in 2004 (Song Hong 2005).

China's neighbours, particularly ASEAN countries, have felt strongly the impact of China's growth. Through its close bilateral and regional economic links, China's rapidly growing domestic market and surging imports and exports provide ASEAN countries with both opportunities and competition. China's sheer size and its growing integration with the regional economies mean its growth, at whatever rate, will exert significant influence on ASEAN's development and external economic relations.

This chapter analyses some of China's economic impacts on ASEAN countries, and ASEAN's policy response. It is based on literature survey, data analysis and interviews with multilateral agencies, national research institutes and government organisations in some ASEAN countries. It ends with some concluding remarks.

Impacts of growth

Rapidly growing bilateral trade relations

China's growth has led to a rapid expansion of its trade and broader economic relations with ASEAN countries. Bilateral trade reached more than US$100 billion in 2004, 100 times its value in 1978, when China began to open up. Trade volumes have grown on average by more than 20 per cent a year since 1990.

The composition of the bilateral trade between ASEAN and China has also changed significantly. It has advanced from trade mostly in raw materials to that of machinery and electrical equipment, clearly indicating closer economic integration through growing intra-industry trade. In 1993, for instance, mineral products, wood and wooden articles, and charcoal occupied about 55 per cent of ASEAN-5 total exports to China. In 2000, however, machinery and electrical equipment alone accounted for 43 per cent of ASEAN-5's exports to China. Machinery, electrical equipment, and textiles are China's dominant exports to ASEAN-5, rising from 18 per cent in 1993 to 43 per cent of China's total exports to ASEAN (*China's Customs Statistics* 2005).

Figure 9.1   ASEAN-China bilateral trade, 1986–2003 (US$ million)

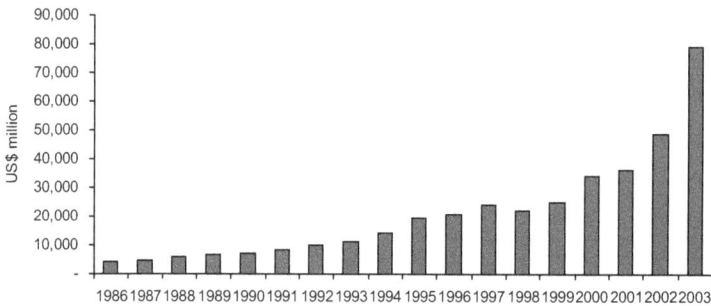

Source: Asian Development Bank, 2004. *Key Indicators*, Asian Development Bank, Manila.

The drivers

Reforms and economic liberalisation have been driving China's integration into the world economy, presenting ASEAN and other regional economies with enormous business opportunities. China's accession to the World Trade Organization (WTO) in 2001 has provided further impetus to ASEAN exports.

Economic globalisation and industrial restructuring in East Asia have led China to become the region's final assembly centre, with supply of intermediate goods increasingly shipped from other Asian countries to China for re-export to third country markets in Europe, North America and other regions.

China's domestic consumer market is rapidly growing, and is now one of the largest in the world. China's rising living standard leads to demand for more agricultural products, consumer goods and services, including education and tourism, all of which ASEAN countries are well placed to supply. A more economically integrated Asia also means ASEAN can gain indirect benefit from the expanding third country markets such as Japan and Korea that grow together with the Chinese economy.

An emerging economic interdependence

China is ASEAN's fourth largest trade partner, while ASEAN has been China's fifth largest trade partner in the world since 1990. Since the mid 1990s, bilateral trade has been consistently in ASEAN's favour. In 2003, ASEAN overall enjoyed a bilateral trade surplus with China of US$16 billion (ADB 2004). ASEAN's economic growth has increasingly relied on China following the East Asian financial crisis.

During the financial crisis, China's commitment to continue pegging the yuan against the US dollar eased the downward pressure on Asia's currencies and helped them to stabilise macroeconomic conditions. At that time, the Japanese economy was still stagnant and, in the early 2000s, the US economy was also mired in the aftermath of its tech bubble burst. China's high growth helped lift demand for exports from East Asia and is thought to have been a key external factor, helping the region pull itself out of the crisis.

China has since contributed significantly to ASEAN's export growth. Between 1998 and 2003, for instance, ASEAN countries' exports to China soared three-fold, while its growth to the world rose by less than 47 per cent. Between 2000 and 2003, China contributed to 46 per cent of

Figure 9.2   **ASEAN-China trade, imports and exports, 2002–03 (US$ '000)**

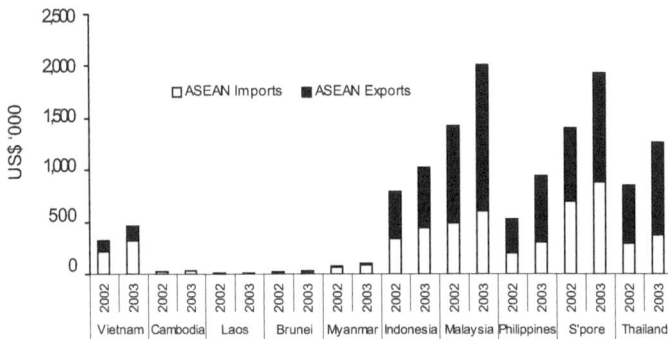

Source: Asian Development Bank, 2004. *Key Indicators,* Asian Development Bank, Manila.

ASEAN's export growth, accounting for 117 per cent of the growth of the Philippines, 77 per cent of Singapore, 49 per cent of Malaysia, 30 per cent of Indonesia, and 25 per cent of Thailand (calculations based on ADB 2004).

Broader economic relations, including investment, have grown rapidly between ASEAN countries and China. China has been active investing in ASEAN's resource sector including fertiliser, chemicals and rubber production. Investment in machinery production and assembly trade has also risen in recent years. China has invested in Singapore given its role as regional hub for financing, marketing and export seeking activities.

At the same time, companies of ASEAN origin have also actively pursued investment opportunities in China. In 2002, ASEAN collectively invested a total of US$3.3 billion in China, taking about 4 per cent of China's total FDI inflow that year (calculation based on *China National Bureau of Statistics* 2004). This places ASEAN behind only Hong Kong, Taiwan, the EU and the United States as the fifth largest source of FDI for China. Investment from ASEAN countries would actually be more prominent if many of the 'round-trip' investment from China through Hong Kong back to China are stripped out from the accounting for China's inward FDI.

China's growing competitiveness

ASEAN and China are direct competitors in a wide range of export products. China's export sector is a stellar performer, growing by a rate of 17 per cent per annum in the past twenty-five years. Labour-intensive industries have driven its export surge to the world, but in recent years, its exports have also increasingly relied on growing sophisticated capital and technology-intensive industries. As a result, both the low and middle-income ASEAN economies feel China's competitive pressure. China's cheap labour on the one hand, and a large pool of skilled engineers on the other, make competition stiffer for ASEAN economies in both their home and third-country markets.

ASEAN countries are also generally concerned with the slow inflow of foreign direct investment (FDI). FDI to ASEAN countries has dropped significantly in the wake of the Asian economic crisis in 1997–98. Although slowly recovering, FDI in many ASEAN economies has yet to regain its pre-crisis level. By contrast, China's stable macroeconomic environment,

Figure 9.3   **FDI to China and southeast Asia, 1992–2002 (US$ million)**

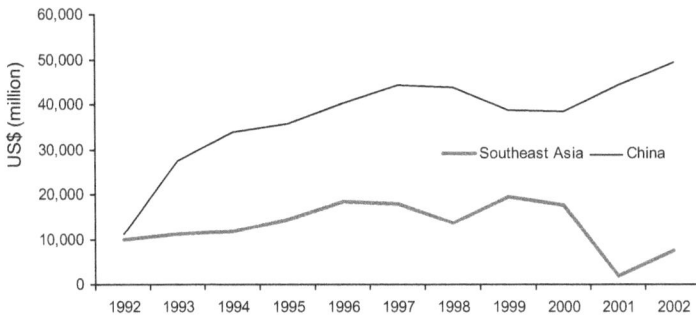

Source: Asian Development Bank, 2004. *Key Indicators,* Asian Development Bank, Manila.

rapidly growing domestic market, and improved investment climate make it a magnet for FDI (World Bank 2004).

FDI to China reached US$60 billion in 2004, three times that to ASEAN countries combined. The fact that FDI to China has surged at the same time as it has dropped for ASEAN countries leads to a view that FDI inflow to China is at ASEAN countries' expense. FDI also brings new technology and know-how to China and adds to its competitiveness.

Assessing the business competition

Despite rising competition from China, a number of recent studies find little empirical evidence that China has grown its exports at ASEAN's expense (Ahearne et al. 2003; Yang 2003; Weiss 2004; Lee 2004; Australia, Department of Foreign Affairs and Trade 2003). To the contrary, it appears that, so far, China's exports and ASEAN's exports have been positively correlated. China's exports certainly put competitive pressure on ASEAN countries with similar economic structure and comparative advantage. But the size and growth of third-country markets are more important, with ASEAN benefiting from expanding exports to third-country markets such as Japan, the growth of which has also been strongly stimulated by their growing economic ties with China.

Studies also show that, so far, there is no evidence of FDI diversion from elsewhere in the region to China (Weiss 2004). The United States, the EU, and Japan still invested less in China than in ASEAN countries (Yang 2003). Surging FDI from China to the ASEAN economies has also produced beneficial impacts. Transnational companies are the main driving forces behind FDI, and see China as part of their regional production chains. Many of their FDI activities in the region have led to the increase of exports from ASEAN countries to China.

The extent and scope of the competition from China facing individual countries are also different, due largely to their varying export structures and industrial competitiveness *vis-à-vis* China's. Countries with a more similar export structure to China's tend to face fiercer competition. China's comparative advantage still lies mainly in its labour-intensive sector, like clothing, textiles and footwear, electronics, office machines and parts. That is also where the comparative advantage of most ASEAN countries lies. ASEAN and China therefore mainly compete in markets for these labour-intensive products.

Table 9.1 summarises the sectors and extent of the ASEAN–China business competition, based on a number of studies that examine the structures of the Chinese and individual ASEAN exports as of early 2000s (Australia, DFAT 2003; Yang 2003; Lee 2004). Sectoral focus is on labour-intensive, capital/technology intensive, and resource intensive industries. Strong, medium and weak are used to describe the extent of competition. This summary is impressionistic rather than precise.

Singapore's strong technology-based economy has long moved out of the more labour-intensive industries in which China has comparative advantage. Strong complementarity between the Singaporean and Chinese economies makes the extent of business competition between them relatively weak. The Philippines is not a strong exporter of labour-intensive products, but benefits from China's demand for electronic components.

Indonesia competes against China in almost half of its export markets, mainly for labour-intensive manufactures. With its strength in primary commodity exports, however, Indonesia is also complementary with China's expanding demand for industrial inputs. Almost two-thirds of Malaysia's net exports compete with China's, including a wide range of electronics.

Table 9.1   ASEAN countries' sectoral strength and extent of competition from China

Countries	Singapore	Philippines	Indonesia	Malaysia	Thailand	Vietnam	Cambodia	Laos
Sectoral strength	Capital/ technology intensive	Labour intensive	Labour intensive, resource intensive	Labour intensive, resource intensive	Labour intensive	Labour intensive, resource intensive	Labour intensive	Resource intensive
Extent of Chinese competition	Weak	Weak to Medium	Weak to Medium	Medium to strong	Strong	Medium to strong	Medium to strong	Weak

Malaysia's complementarity with China currently is lower than that of most other regional economies.

Among all the ASEAN-5 countries, Thailand has the most similar net export profile to China's and faces competition from China in 70 per cent of its net export sectors (Australia, DFAT 2003).[3] Thailand's complementarity with China is the lowest in the region, but is growing rapidly. While Vietnam's growing labour-intensive exports (particularly in clothing, textile and footwear) are in direct competition with China's, its exports of fruits and agricultural products have rapidly expanded to meet China's rising demand for food.

Cambodia's exports rely heavily on the clothing, textile and footwear sector, which has faced growing competition from China due to the expiry of the Multi-Fibre Arrangement (MFA). Laos's comparative advantage lies in its natural resource base with its rich endowment in forestry, water, land and mineral resources. Its economy is therefore highly complementary with the Chinese economy.

Responses from ASEAN countries

Attitudes turning positive

ASEAN members have clearly seen the business opportunities presented by China's growth. They have become much more positive about economic relations with China.[4] This stands in stark contrast to the general perception prior to the late 1990s that China could become a serious economic threat. The positive perception reflects the fact that China is now the main growth engine of the region. It also reflects a sense of realism that sees globalisation and trade liberalisation as making competition more intense at home and in international markets. A growing China is seen as part of this.

Urgency of policy reforms

Many ASEAN countries feel the urgency of undertaking further policy reforms to develop a more liberal economic system and to promote a competitive business environment.

A competitive business environment will be key to attracting more FDI to the region. Traditionally, ASEAN countries have used FDI as an important source for upgrading technologies and restructuring industries. FDI as a market-driven decision tends to go where there is are higher returns and lower risks. The surge of FDI to China and its contrasting slow recovery in ASEAN gives a very clear signal to ASEAN governments that the need to undertake further policy reforms to improve their investment climates to make them comparable to China's. Delay will only put them at a greater disadvantage, particularly given China's advantages of a huge domestic market, competitive export sector, rapidly improving infrastructure and an increasingly favourable business environment. Currently, the sunk cost factor may make some transnational corporations retain their production sites in some ASEAN countries. The crunch will come when these transnational corporations make their next round of FDI decisions.

Improving the investment environment will be key to attracting more FDI to the region. It is also essential to foster the growth and competitiveness of domestic firms. However, many ASEAN economies still treat firms differently, according to whether they are domestic or foreign, large or small, state or privately owned. Together with some corrupt business practices, policy discrimination inhibits foreign investors as well as the domestic private sector and small-medium enterprises (World Bank 2005, World Development Report 2005).

Economic liberalisation through multiple channels

Increasingly ASEAN countries have pursued economic liberalisation, through multilateral, regional, bilateral, unilateral, and sub-regional channels, to achieve growth and business competitiveness.

- The multilateral trade system helps develop a rules-based economy with business practices conforming to the WTO-based international principles, norms and practices. Vietnam, Laos and Cambodia are actively seeking to become members of the WTO. The accession process is helping shape their trade systems and investment environments.

- Regional integration within ASEAN and with external economies helps reduce the costs of doing business by enlarging currently segmented markets. APEC provides an important venue for all ASEAN countries to engage in dialogue and discussion on reducing tariff and non-tariff barriers. It also helps them understand issues arising from trade liberalisation. Within ASEAN, the development of ASEAN Economic Community (AEC) would also help eliminate trade barriers among members and promote economic integration.

- Bilateral free trade agreements (FTAs) can help boost trade and economic growth in the region, providing they create more trade than they divert. Some individual ASEAN member countries are actively pursuing FTAs with external partner countries. The ASEAN-10+China FTA proposal is one of the most prominent.

- Initiatives for sub-regional growth areas involve two or more neighbouring countries for freer movement of people, goods and services, and development of infrastructure and institutions. This includes Greater Mekong Sub-region (GMS) covering sub-national regions in Laos, Vietnam, Cambodia, Myanmar, Thailand and China. Part of the motive is to capitalise on China's growth. Another example is the Brunei, Indonesia, Malaysia and

Philippines East ASEAN Growth Area (BIMP-EAGA). Its recent revival clearly indicates an urgency felt by member states to be part of East Asian economic restructuring instigated by China's growth.

ASEAN-China FTA

Seeing China as an opportunity explains why ASEAN has actively pursued bilateral Free Trade Agreements (FTA) with China since the early 2000s (Murray 2004).

- In November 2001, ASEAN-10 and China agreed to establish the world's largest free trade area, comprising 1.7 billion people, US$2 trillion GDP and US$1.2 trillion in trade volume. The FTA will allow all members to enjoy more favourable treatment in trade and investment than the WTO can offer.

- In November 2002, both sides signed Framework Agreement that agreed to complete FTA negotiations by 30 June 2004, and to establish the FTA by 2010.

- In October 2003, both sides also signed ASEAN Treaty of Amity and Cooperation that provides for the peaceful resolution of territorial disputes.

- China forgave all or part of the debts of Vietnam, Laos, Cambodia and Myanmar, and granted most favoured nation status to non-WTO members Vietnam, Laos and Cambodia.

- Both sides signed Declaration on the Conduct of Parties in the South China Sea and the Facilitation of Cross-Border Transport of Goods and People in the Greater Mekong Region.

- Both sides identified 5 areas for cooperation, including agriculture, information technology, human resources, direct investment, and Mekong River Basin.

- Both sides estimated that the FTA, when established, could add 1 per cent to ASEAN's GDP, 0.3 per cent to China's GDP, and 50 per cent to ASEAN exports to China.

Individual countries responding differently

Among ASEAN countries, Singapore and Thailand have been the most proactive in pursuing a regional FTA with China. For Singapore, this happens because of trade complementarity and historically close economic ties. Thailand sees China's business opportunities and also the need to adjust as a good option for economic prosperity. Both countries have actively invested in China, and also instigated policy reforms at home to facilitate economic restructuring, innovation, specialisation, and a better investment climate. Thailand, for instance, has put in place a 'one village one product' policy that encourages product differentiation in its handicraft industry. Its 'one stop shop' government policy is also aimed to simplify procedures and process for setting up and doing business.

The Philippines initially was a reluctant participant in the ASEAN-10+China FTA, as its trade with the United States and Japan was much bigger and more important. It, however, turned around to embrace the FTA as a symbol of the Arroyo government's willingness to have closer political ties with China. Economically, Philippines has recently benefited enormously from its trade relations with China, which accounted for all of its export growth since 2000. In September 2004, during Arroyo's state visit to China, the Philippines committed to accelerate the timetable for its tariff reduction program involving certain agricultural products under the ASEAN-10+China FTA (Villanueva 2004). Research in the Philippines has also identified many areas, including agricultural products, tourism and financial services, that Philippines can exploit from China's opening markets. But cumbersome bureaucratic processes makes the Philippines slow to act, and strong vested interests also share the blame for the stalling of policy reforms to achieve greater competition and private sector development. The Philippines' economic difficulties are also complicated by its rural poverty, income disparities, and law and order problems particularly in the south.

Indonesia is the largest country in ASEAN, yet in recent years its economy and exports have underperformed most of its ASEAN neighbours, including the Philippines. The new government has been keen to take advantage of ASEAN's FTA with China, as part of a push for an export-oriented growth to power economic development (*Asia Times* 2004).

Indonesia's resource-based economy positions it well to take advantage of China's growth. Indonesia has already become a major supplier of raw materials to China, particularly in oil and gas, coal, rubber, timber, pulp and paper, palm oil, organic chemicals, fish, electronics, and steel. An improved political relationship between Jakarta and Beijing in recent years augurs well for the domestic business in Indonesia and FDI has started flowing from China to Indonesia, especially in its oil-and-gas sector. But China is a direct competitor for several of Indonesia's important exports such as textiles and apparel. The expiry of the MFA from 2005 makes competition in third-country markets fiercer. Indonesia's investment climate is generally perceived to be poor, as a result of political uncertainties, together with rising wages, massive reductions on subsidies for water, telephones, electricity and fuel. A dearth of investment in export manufacturing and populist labour-market policies contributes to its lack of export competitiveness, and loss of market share in third-country markets.

Geographical proximity means that Cambodia, Laos and Vietnam are more directly affected by China's development. One of the central development activities is the Greater Mekong Subregion growth area. With funding from the Asian Development Bank, the three Indochina ASEAN countries and Thailand have closely cooperated with China for the development of transport and economic corridors, to achieve improvement in competitiveness and a more integrated regional market (ADB 2005). In the transport sector, ASEAN and China have made significant progress in the construction of the Laos section of the Kunming–Bangkok Highway; the navigation channel improvement project on the upper Mekong River; and also the feasibility study of the missing link of the Trans-Asian Railway inside Cambodia (Sun 2004). GMS would particularly provide Laos with impetus and opportunities for development.

Until very recently, Laos saw itself as a landlocked country with great difficulty in access to international markets. This partly explains the fact that about three quarters of its low level of trade is with its neighbouring countries including China. While it still exhibits a lot of political hesitation on policy reforms and trade liberalisation, Laos certainly has experienced rising trade with, and investment from, Thailand, China and Vietnam. Bilateral trade between Laos and China totalled US$10 million in 2003 and, according to the Lao National Chamber of Commerce and Industry (LNCCI), 'some 200 Chinese enterprises have invested and opened business in Laos' (Bosworth 2005). In 2003, China was the leading investor, investing in 15 Laos projects worth US$116 million. China is also a source of significant loans to Laos, and was mentioned as a possible financier and contractor for the Nam Theun 2 dam project if the World Bank and Asian Development Bank fail to approve loans and guarantees.[5] According to government of Laos statistics, China's bilateral ODA disbursements in 2002/03 reached US$30 million, placing it second only to Japan at US$100 million. While Laos currently has little export capacity, due to its lack of human resources and production capacity, its growth prospects are improving, thanks to the GMS and other regional activities.

Cambodia has stalled its reform process in the last three years. In the past ten years, Cambodia enjoyed GDP annual average growth at 6.5 per cent, and this gave its leadership a great sense of complacency. Part of its success came from the garment industry, which accounted for roughly 80 per cent of its export. Cambodia's garment exports have benefited enormously from the MFA, which put restrictions on the annual growth of China's garment exports to the world markets. Cambodia has legislation that sets minimum wages. This leads to a belief that Cambodia's garment products have carved a niche in the world market for goods that meet certain labour standards, and are therefore immune from China's rising competition. But this belief is misplaced because labour costs in Cambodia are much higher than those in China. Doing business in Cambodia is also more costly, due to higher transportation and transaction costs, and rampant rent-seeking behaviours by government officials. The phasing out of the MFA, however, will put pressure on Cambodia's garment exports. Cambodia's leadership sees little urgency in preparing for the change. Despite a relatively liberal investment regime, Cambodia's domestic problems, rather than any other external factors, explain its lack of FDI attractiveness and difficulties in meeting competition in the world garment market in the future.

China's impact on Vietnam is reflected in rapidly growing bilateral trade, which reached US$4.6 billion in 2003, a 40 per cent rise over 2002 (China Commerce Yearbook 2004:482. Available at http://wwww.

yearbook.org.cn/english). As Vietnam's exports come from labour-intensive industries, they will face Chinese competition at home and in third country markets. Being outside the WTO puts Vietnam in a disadvantaged position. Government protection has traditionally shielded Vietnam's state-owned enterprises from competition. As a result, they are highly inefficient, losing market share at home and abroad. Intense competition from China and other countries provides an impetus to SOE reform, and should bring long-term benefit to Vietnam's development. According to the ASEAN-10+China FTA joint study, China's growth has provided Vietnam enormous export opportunities. Yet Vietnam is not a big producer in many manufacturing industries. This has limited its capacity to participate in the economic restructuring in East Asia that is making China the final assembling centre. This largely explains why Vietnam, together with the poorer ASEAN countries Cambodia, Laos and Myanmar, has a small bilateral trade deficit with China. In future, however, Vietnam may well be able to take part in China's manufacturing networks, as Thailand has done, from a low production base.

Table 9.2 summarises the adjustment made by each of the ASEAN countries in response to China's competition, as discussed above. Three levels of adjustment—rapid, medium and slow—are used to describe the speed of response.

Figure 9.4 combines the impacts on, and the adjustment made by, ASEAN members, arising from China's growth. It combines the main features summarised in Table 9.1 and Table 9.2. Again, the diagram is illustrative of China's impacts and ASEAN members' responses. The latter are, of course, part of their more general adjustment to economic globalisation.

Conclusion

China has been the region's growth engine since the Asian economic crisis, and ASEAN members have felt strongly China's impacts, through their growing trade, investment and other commercial ties. China's growth presents ASEAN countries with both enormous business opportunities and competition. China's growth has also obliged ASEAN members hastily to take necessary steps for trade and policy reforms. Yet individual countries

Table 9.2   Effectiveness in ASEAN countries' adjustment to China's impacts

Countries	Singapore	Malaysia	Thailand	Vietnam
Response	Rapid	Rapid	Rapid	Rapid
	Strong sense of urgency to anticipate change and take action, institutional facilitation, competitive business	Political commitment, competitive business, need to address issues in education and investment	Political commitment, institutional capacity, market-friendly policies for competition and development	Policies in line with broader reform and opening, need for further state sector reform and PSD
Countries	Philippines	Indonesia	Cambodia	Laos
Response	Medium	Medium	Slow	Slow
Determinants	Political commitment, cumbersome bureaucratic process, weak institutional capacity, strong vested interests and corruption	Resolving political uncertainty, weak economic and financial institutions, regulatory distortion, lack of investment	Reforms stalled, complacent on past record, formal sector rigidity, rampant rent-seeking corruption	Lack of leadership, institutional capacity, human resources and infrastructure, but geographical advantage and Greater Mekong Scheme

have responded differently, due largely to their different trade structures, business competitiveness and domestic institutions.

Four observations are as follows. First, relative trade structures underpin the nature of China–ASEAN economic relations, whether competitive or complementary. Singapore, Laos and, to a lesser extent, Philippines and Indonesia are well positioned to take advantage of China's rapid industrial

Figure 9.4   China's competitive impact and ASEAN countries' response adjustment

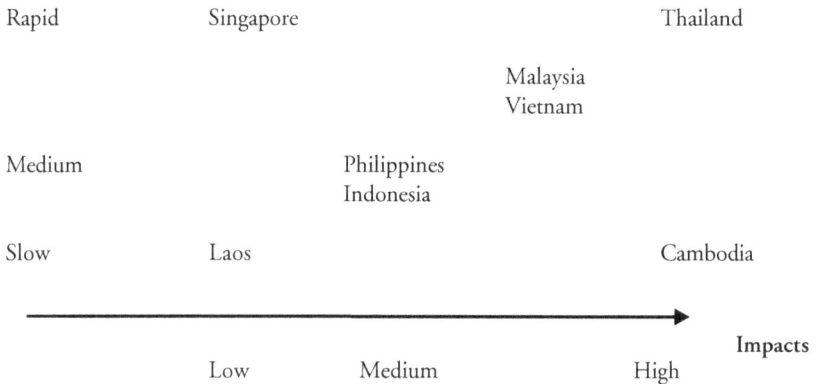

Rapid	Singapore			Thailand
			Malaysia	
			Vietnam	
Medium		Philippines		
		Indonesia		
Slow	Laos			Cambodia

→ **Impacts**

Low   Medium   High

expansion and urbanisation, due largely to their complementary trade relations with China. China's comparative advantage still lies in labour-intensive sectors. Its exports compete directly with manufacturing industries in Thailand, Malaysia and, to a lesser extent, Vietnam, as each country relies heavily on labour-intensive exports. Cambodia also faces looming competition from China in clothes, textiles and footwear exports.

Second, while competition matters, market growth and competitiveness matter more. Numerous studies find that, so far, the exports from both ASEAN members and China have grown rapidly. This suggests that China's economic expansion, East Asian industrial restructuring, and the growth of third-country markets are more important factors, offsetting some possible negative impacts from China's competition.

Third, policy reforms for trade liberalisation and investment climates go hand-in-hand with enhancing business competitiveness. Political commitment and institutional capacity underpin the success of policy reforms. This, to a large extent, explains why Singapore, Thailand, Malaysia and, to a lesser extent, Vietnam can act fast and effectively in adjusting to external impacts. On the other hand, stalled policy reforms in Cambodia mean the country may face greater challenges in sustaining its previous record of export growth.

Last but not least, each ASEAN country faces different tasks in policy reforms, due to different domestic circumstances. WTO accession is a critical step in trade liberalisation for Vietnam, Laos and Cambodia and will push their trade systems into line with international norms and practice. Vietnam and Laos also have to reform their state sector, including state-owned enterprises and financial systems, to foster private sector development and business competition. Lack of institutional and production capacity and human resources hampers Laos from taking up external opportunities. Changing populist labour-market policies and encouraging investment are critical to improving Indonesia's export competitiveness.

Notes

1   In this chapter, ASEAN or ASEAN-10 refers to the ten member countries of Association of Southeast Asian Nations, including Indonesia, Malaysia, The Philippines, Singapore, Thailand, (also referred as ASEAN-5), and Brunei, Myanmar, Vietnam, Lao DPR and Cambodia. Unless specified, discussion in this chapter does not cover Myanmar and Brunei.

2   China is the world's sixth-largest economy at market exchange rates.

3   The use of net exports (or imports) is an effort to capture the value-added items in a country's exports (or imports) amidst growing intra-industrial trade among East Asian countries.

4   Our interviews in Bangkok, Manila and Singapore reveal an overwhelming view that the impact of China's growth overall is positive for ASEAN countries. Such unanimous agreement by a diverse range of organisations and countries is noteworthy.

5   The World Bank reported on 31 March 2005 that it had approved the loan guarantees in support of the Nam Theun 2 hydroelectric project.

References

Asian Development Bank, 2005. Information Package on the GMS, Greater Mekong Subregion. Available at http://mms.adb.org:8000.
——, 2004. ADB Key Indicators, Poverty in Asia: Measurements, Estimates and Prospects, Part III Country Tables. Available from http://www.adb.org/Documents/Books/Key_Indicators/2004/default.asp.

Ahearne, A.G., Fernald, J.G., Loungani, P. and Schindler, J.W., 2003. *China and emerging Asia: comrades or competitors?*', International Finance Discussion Papers, Number 789, December, Board of Governors of the Federal Reserve System, New York.

Asia Times, 2004. 'Indonesia Courts the Dragon', 6 November. Available at http://www.bileterals.org/articule-print.php3?id_articule=945.

Australia, Department of Foreign Affairs and Trade. 2003. *China's Industrial Rise, East Asia's Challenge*, Australia, Department of Foreign Affairs and Trade, Australian Government, Canberra.

Bosworth, M., 2005. Commentary on China's Current Relationship with the Lao DPR, prepared for the Trade and Economic Analysis Unit, AusAID, Vientiane.

China Media and Economic Information Service, 2006. *China Customs Statistics,* 2005. Hong Kong.

China, Ministry of Commerce, 2004, Beijing, China Commerce Yearbook 2004:482 available at http://www.yearbook.org.cn/english.

China National Bureau of Statistics, 2004. *China Statistical Yearbook*, China Statistical Press, Beijing.

Lee, C.H., and Plummer, M.G., 2004. 'Economic Development in China and Its Implications for East Asia', presented at the Conference Miracle and Mirages in East Asian Economic Development, at East-West Center, University of Hawaii, in Honour of Professor Seiji F. Naya, 21–22 May.

Murray, B., 2004. China's Economic Performance and its Impacts on Asia, Paper from conference sponsored by the Asia Pacific Foundation of Canada, The Canada China Business Council and the Centre for Chinese Research of the Institute of Asian Research at the University of British Columbia, Vancouver, 21 June.

Song, H., 2005. 'China's role in the world economy' *Executive Intelligence Review,* Berlin 22 July.

Sun, S.W., 2004. China, ASEAN to Advance Free Trade, *China Daily* 29 November. Available at http://www.chinadaily.com.cn/english/doc/2004–11/29/content_395729.htm.

Villanueva, M.A., 2004. 'RP Vows to Fasttrack Tariff Cuts under ASEAN–China FTA', *The Philippine Star*, Manila, 3 September. Available at http://www. bilaterals.org/articule-print.php3?id_article=551.

Weiss, J., 2004. *People's Republic of China and its neighbours: partners or competitors for trade and investment?*, ADB Institute Research Paper Series No. 59, Asian Development Bank Manila.

World Bank, 2004. *East Asia Update, Steering a Steady Course, Special Focus: strengthening the investment climate in East Asia*, World Bank, Washington, DC.

——, 2005. World Development Report 2005, World Bank, Washington, DC..

Yang, Y.Z., 2003. *China's integration into the world economy: implications for developing countries*, IMF Working Paper, WP/03/245, International Monetary Fund, Washington, DC.

Acknowledgments

Dong Dong Zhang is now with the Australian Treasury; this chapter was prepared when he was with AusAID. The views expressed in the chapter are those of the author, and do not necessarily reflect those of the Australian Government or any other persons and organisations.

Numerous persons and organisations are acknowledged for their generous support to the writing of the paper, including interviews in Bangkok, Manila and Singapore.

10 CHINA: WHERE WILL THE CONTEST FOR REGIONAL LEADERSHIP END?

Yiping Huang and Xinpeng Xu

The return of a world power

Economic growth in China in the last two decades has been most spectacular. With annual growth of about 9 per cent, China has attracted tremendous attention worldwide. Few would dispute that China is now one of the important engines of growth in the world economy.

Perhaps less well known is the fact that China had been the most powerful and biggest state in the world for nearly two millenniums. Until the nineteenth century, China's share of world GDP was higher than that of all of Western Europe combined. China accounted for about a quarter of the world GDP from the beginning of the first millennium and has remained as dominant player until Western Europe caught up in the mid-nineteenth century (Figure 10.1). Western Europe started its rapid catch-up with China from the fifteenth century and surpassed China in the eighteenth century. In fact, China was a victim of its own success, as it indulged itself in its technological prowess and demonstrated no interest at all in the rapid technological development of Western Europe since the fifteenth century. According to Angus Maddison:

Figure 10.1   **Shares of world GDP, 1000–2030** (1990 international $, per cent)

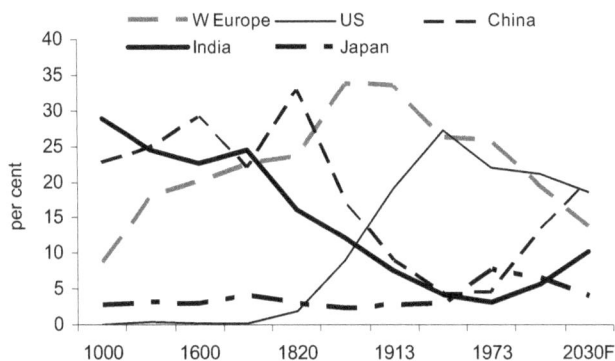

Source: Maddison A., 2002. *The World Economy: A Millennial Perspective*, OECD Development Centre, Paris.

A British mission in 1793 tried to open diplomatic relations and demonstrate the attractions of western science and technology with 600 cases of presents (including chronometers, telescopes, a planetarium, chemical and metal products). The official rebuff stated 'there is nothing we lack—we have never set much store on strange or ingenious objects, nor do we want any more of your country's manufactures'. China did not start establishing legations abroad until 1877 (Maddison 2002:117).

China had become an increasingly inward-looking economy. Even worse was a whole series of internal rebellions such as the Taiping rebellion (1851–1864). Plagued with war and foreign intrusion since 1840s, China's share of world GDP had declined sharply from almost one-third to about five per cent (see Figure 10.1). During the same period, western economies experienced extraordinary expansion as a result of the industrial revolution.

It is not just the economic size of China that was bigger than that of the Western Europe—per capita GDP in China had also been higher until the sixteenth century (Maddison 2002). Thereafter, Europe took the lead and China started to lag behind (Figure 10.2). China's per capita GDP in the early 1950s was less than its 1820 level. In sharp contrast was the

Figure 10.2   Comparative GDP per capita China and Western
Europe, 50–1998 (1990 international $)

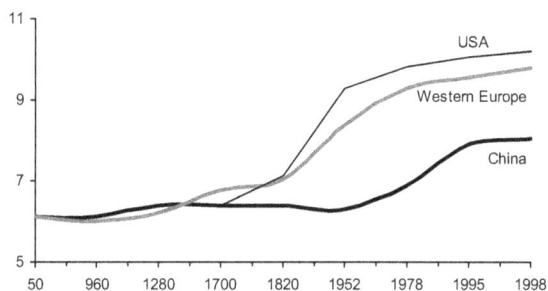

Note: The vertical axis is in natural logarithm.
Source: Maddison, A. 2002. *Chinese Economic Performance in the Long Run,* OECD
Development Centre, Paris. *The World Economy: A Millennial Perspective,* 1998, OECD
Development Centre, Paris.

tripling of both Western Europe's and Japan's income per capita and an
increase of more than eight-fold in the US GDP per capita during this
period. When other countries in the world were charging ahead, China
was in decline. The three decades since 1950s saw a five-fold increase in
Japan's per capita income, from $2,351 (1990 international dollars) to
$11,581 (1990 international dollars), while China's per capita just falls
short of doubling under central planning (Maddison 1998).

China started to emerge from its century-long decline only after the
economic reforms and opening up that have taken place since 1979. China
is now established as an engine of growth in East Asia and beyond, through
its rising share in regional production and trade, and its close structural
links with other economies in the region. The economic size of China
measured in terms of current output has been rising, and the Chinese
economy is now almost one-third of the size of that of Japan—even based
on market exchange rate calculated output measures (Figure 10.3). The
contrast is even more striking if the comparison is based on purchasing
power parity (PPP) calculated output measures, by which China has already
surpassed Japan and, after 1993, become the second largest economy in
the world (Figure 10.4). With growth rates averaging close to 10 per cent

Figure 10.3   China and East Asia in the world economy, output
               share, 1980–2003 (per cent)

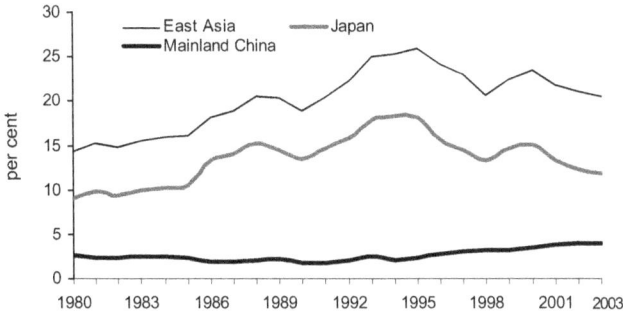

Notes: Shares of aggregate GDP based on current market exchange rate in US dollars. East
Asia 10 includes Japan, South Korea, mainland China, Taiwan, Hong Kong, Thailand, Malaysia,
Indonesia, Singapore and the Philippines.
Sources: Drysdale P. and X.P. Xu, 2004. '*Taiwan's role in the economic architecture of East Asia
and the Pacific*', Pacific Economic Papers No. 343, Australia-Japan Research Centre, The
Australian National University, Canberra.

Figure 10.4   China and East Asia in the world economy, output
               share, 1980–2003 (per cent)

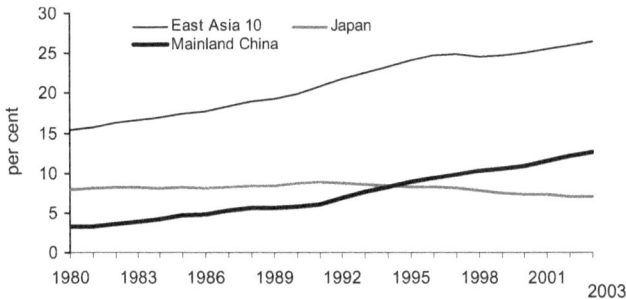

Notes: Shares of aggregate GDP based on purchasing power parity (PPP) valuation of country
GDP. East Asia 10 includes Japan, South Korea, mainland China, Taiwan, Hong Kong,
Thailand, Malaysia, Indonesia, Singapore and the Philippines.
Sources: Drysdale P. and X.P. Xu, 2004. '*Taiwan's role in the economic architecture of East
Asia and the Pacific*', Pacific Economic Papers No. 343, Australia-Japan Research Centre,
The Australian National University, Canberra.

per annum since 1990, China has been, and is expected to continue to be, the most important new player in the regional and the world economy.

China's global significance is seen almost everywhere. During the last couple of years, China contributed roughly one-third of global economic growth. It accounts for about 20 per cent of world's total labour-intensive exports and more than 60 per cent of total Asian electronic exports. Large volumes and low prices of such products earned China reputations such as 'a global manufacturing centre' or 'exporter of global deflation'. Many also regard the 'China factor' as the key driving force behind skyrocketing commodity prices.

China has even become an important force in the international capital markets, despite China's own capital account controls. Renminbi exchange rate policy is a key factor influencing global currency markets. In early 2007, corrections of the domestic A-share markets sent shockwaves across global equity markets.

Can China's rapid growth continue?

According to Maddison's prediction, China will overtake the United States to become the world's largest economy by 2030. Whether or not such prediction will materialise depends on China's ability to translate its recent success into sustainable growth of output in the future. To answer this question, we employ a simple yet conventional approach, that is, a growth accounting approach, to look into this important question. According to growth accounting theory, economic growth depends on an accumulation of factors, mainly capital stock and labour, and increase in total factor productivity (TFP). In mathematical form, the growth accounting equation is

$$y = \delta + \alpha k + (1 - \alpha)l$$

where y, δ, k, and l, represent, growth in output, total factor productivity, capital stock and labour, respectively. α refers to the share of capital in total output or, technically speaking, elasticity of output with respect to capital. We assume α to be 0.4, which is somewhat higher than the usual 0.35 as in Bosworth and Collins (2003). We believe that capital may be more important (productive) in a large developing country like China where labour is relatively abundant. Assuming production technology exhibits constant return to scale, we obtain $(1-\alpha)$ as the share of labour in total output or elasticity of output with respect to labour. Mathematically, TFP is a residual, by subtracting contributions of capital and labour from output growth.

It is a well-known fact that data for China's agriculture and service sectors are difficult to come up with and even there are some estimates around they are prone to criticism. Together, China's agriculture and service sectors account for about one-third of the total national output. Interestingly, agricultural sector has been growing slowly while the services sector has developed rapidly in the past decade. For a country that is experiencing rapid industrialisation, it may not be too unreasonable to assume that on balance China's agriculture and services sectors grow at the same rate as that of the manufacturing sector. And by such an assumption we can focus on the manufacturing sector where relatively high-quality data are available.

Table 10.1 shows a growth accounting decomposition for China's manufacturing sector, with detailed construction of capital stock and labour working hours in Wu and Xu (2004). In the past two decades, China's capital stock grew at a rate of about 10 per cent per annum, contributing to output growth by about 4.3 per cent. We expect this trend to continue for two reasons. First, the returns to investment will remain high as China carries out its reform in the state-owned sector and the government sector, which boosts up productivity. It will not run into diminishing returns for a long period of time as both labour force participation and productivity are increasing. Second, the accumulation of capital in China will not run into the 'financing constraint' as China has the world's highest saving rate. More importantly, China's accession to the World Trade Organisation delivers a significant long-term commitment to economic liberalisation, which has attracted a huge inflow of foreign capital, already averaging around US$45 billion annually over the past few years (Woo 2001).

Growth of labour working hours has been low in the last decade, thanks to the reform in state-owned enterprises that shed away huge number of redundant workers. The private sector will continue to expand and become the major sector that provides employment. Given the huge surplus workers

Table 10.1   Growth accounting for Chinese manufacturing sector,
1980–2000 (per cent)

	Growth of output	Growth of capital	Growth of labour	Contribution of capital	Contribution of labour	Total factor productivity
1980–1991	8.8	10.7	5.5	4.3	3.3	1.2
1992–2000	9.3	10.6	–0.1	4.3	-	5.0

Note: Estimation in this table assumes output elasticity of capital and labour at 0.4 and 0.6, respectively.
Source: Wu Harry X. and Xinpeng Xu 'A fresh scrutiny of productivity performance in Chinese manufacturing, 1952–2000'. Asia Pacific Productivity Conference, 2004 Conference, Brisbane.

in China, in both rural and urban sectors, we expect that labour working hours will grow at least by 2 per cent per annum, contributing to output growth by 1.2 per cent.

The above findings on productivity growth in China are consistent with the results of some recent analyses. Bosworth and Collins (2007), for instance, found that between 1993 and 2004 total factor productivity contributed more than 40 per cent of GDP growth (about 4 percentage points) or 56 per cent of industrial production growth (about 6.2 percentage points).

We are more optimistic about China's total factor productivity growth than some researchers. We think there is great upside potential for TFP to grow. Maintaining a 2.5 per cent growth annually should be a conservative estimate, given that the TFP growth in the past decade has been increasing at an average of 3.2 per cent per annum.

Recent studies by development economists have identified three factors, namely openness, institutions and geography, as fundamental forces that drive economic growth (Rodrik et al. 2002). It is China's commitment to liberalisation, reform and openness that draws it politically as well as economically closer to the world's major centres of economic power in North America, Europe and East Asia and that provides the foundations for substantial and sustainable economic growth at home.

Specifically, there are several factors that point to this upside potential. First, continued institutional reform, especially after China's accession to the WTO, would promise higher quality of institutions in China, which would lead to higher TFP. According to Rodrik and Subramanian (2004), China has been performing very well (above the 'regression line') in the past two decades given its relatively low quality of institutions and will 'regress' back to normal growth rates warranted by its quality institutions. This may be the case if reform in China stalls. But we have seen rapid improvement in the reform of previously highly protected sectors, for example privatisation of state-owned enterprises and gradual removal of monopoly powers in sectors like electricity, transportation, telecommunication, wholesale and retail, and banking, etc. We expect the quality of institutions in China will continue to improve.

Second, China will continue to take advantage of the technological backwardness as it moves towards the frontier of world technology. Even though China is already a major player in the world economy, its GDP per capita is still well below US$2,000, which is not only substantially lower than those in the advanced economies but also below those in most of its East Asian neighbours. Experiences of other rapidly industrialising economies suggest that, when an economy is far away from the frontier of world technology, it is easier for it catch up by copying existing technologies. In this regard, integration with the international market through trade and investment provides golden opportunities. Productivity gains flow from trade gains through cheaper imports and their impact on import and export sector efficiency and also from the technology spillover through foreign investment.

Third, China's high levels of human capital will be an important source of TFP growth. Chinese have traditionally paid attention to human capital development. The return to schooling has been increasing, compared to the case in the 1980s. More investment in human capital has now been observed in coastal cities and will soon spread to other part of the countries, which will lead to higher accumulation of human capital. Moreover, as incomes rise and opportunities grow within China, more overseas educated people will return to China, in contrast with the case in the 1980s when the return to education was low and many young Chinese left for the United States and Europe, which once caused a 'brain drain' alarm.

Taken together, we suggest that an annual growth of 8 per cent should be sustainable for China for a significant period of time. With this annual growth rate, China would be able to double its income in every nine years. While the above is our base case scenario, it is by no means a guaranteed outcome. In fact, the Chinese economy still faces numerous risks and problems, which include unemployment, income disparity and political uncertainties. The biggest risk, however, lies in inefficiency of capital allocation.

Inefficiency of capital allocation is reflected in a number of ways. Functioning of the financial intermediation remains sub-optimal. In the banking sector, for instance, while the authorities and the banks recently stepped up efforts in improving their competitiveness, progress so far appear to be limited. Though average non-performing (NPL) ratio in the banking sector declined to 7.2 per cent at the end of 2006 from 23 per cent at the end of 2002 (Figure 10.5), overall the NPL outlook is not optimistic. First, many recently revealed bank scandals raise the question about the size of hidden 'black holes' in the state banks. Second, while most commercial banks have implemented the international standard five-category loan classification system, definition for each category was actually left to individual commercial banks. And, third, the fact that about half of the existing outstanding loans, which is about 65 per cent of GDP, was extended during the past three to four years certainly points to potential risks going forward. This is particularly the case as we expect the government continues to tighten and the macroeconomy gradually takes a downturn.

Meanwhile, capital is substantially under-priced in China, which leads to further problems of inefficiency. In 2006, for instance, nominal GDP increased by close to 14 per cent, but the one-year base lending rate was only 6.11 per cent (which increased to 6.39 per cent in March 2007 after another rate hike), and five-year government bond yield was well below 4 per cent. A number of factors are responsible for capital being too cheap in China, including a high savings ratio in relation to low consumer confidence, capital account controls restriction capital outflows, inefficient banks and capital markets, and an undervalued exchange rate encourage capital inflows.

Therefore, resolving the capital inefficiency problem requires systemic policy actions. And this is probably the biggest hurdle that China faces in sustaining its rapid growth.

Figure 10.5   Average non-performing loan ratios in the Chinese banks, 2002–2007 (per cent)

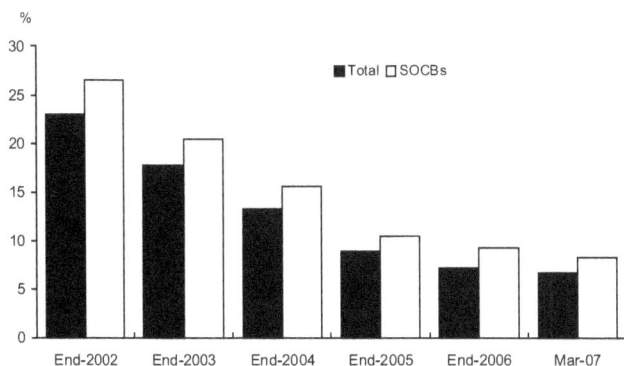

Source: China, China Banking Regulatory Commission, Beijing.

Economic impacts on the region

Even though China is still at the early stage in its re-emergence, its impacts on the global economy, especially the regional economy, are already phenomenal. In fact, today China is one of the hottest subjects of economic discussion in almost every economic centre around the world. China's global influences are primarily reflected in the following areas—strong demand for commodities, extraordinary expansion of exports, rapid growth of foreign direct investment (FDI) and choices of exchange rate policy.

Global commodity prices rose significantly in recent years and one of the major driving forces was very strong demand in China. In 2003, China accounted for large shares in world consumption of a number of commodities—33 per cent in coal, 23 per cent in steel, 20 per cent in aluminium, 10 per cent in alumina, 11 per cent in copper (Figure 10.6). In some markets where China's overall shares are still small, its contribution on the margin is already quite significant. For instance, while China's consumption of crude oil was only about 8 per cent of the world total in

Figure 10.6   China's share of world consumption/production of metal products, 2003 (per cent)

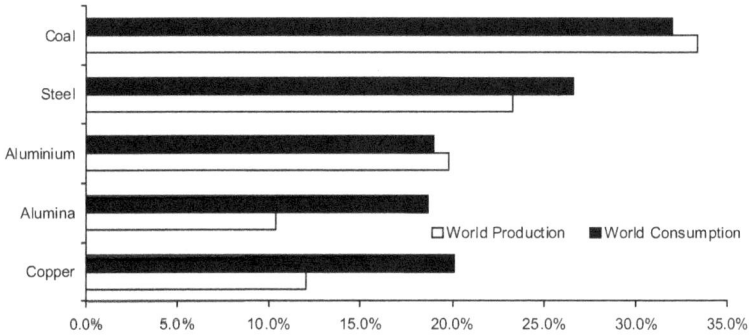

Source: Citi Investment Research estimates using data from World Bureau of Metal Statistics, CRU Group Reports, London Metals Exchange, British Petroleum, Tex Report and China Nonferrous Metals Industry.

2004, it contributed about half of the incremental demand in the world crude market.

China's extraordinary commodity consumption, which is disproportional to its economic size, was at least in part related to the over-investment problem. Therefore, there is a question if the current momentum can be sustained over time as China slows the pace investment expansion to achieve more sustainable growth. However, the expected rapid growth of the economy, continued industrialisation process and new waves of urbanisation in the coming decades are likely to underpin strong demand for commodities in China. In fact, commodity producers in Latin America, Australasia, Middle East, Central Asia and Africa have made macroeconomic development in China as a key factor in their corporate planning.

The impacts of Chinese economic expansion on other Asian economies have been even clearer. Economic recoveries of most Asian economies from 2002 were led by export growth. Intra-regional trade expanded rapidly in East Asia, primarily because of increasing roles played by China (Figure 10.7). Today, China is already the largest export market for Korea and Taiwan

Figure 10.7 Growing intra-regional trade in East Asia, 1998–2006 (US\$ billion)

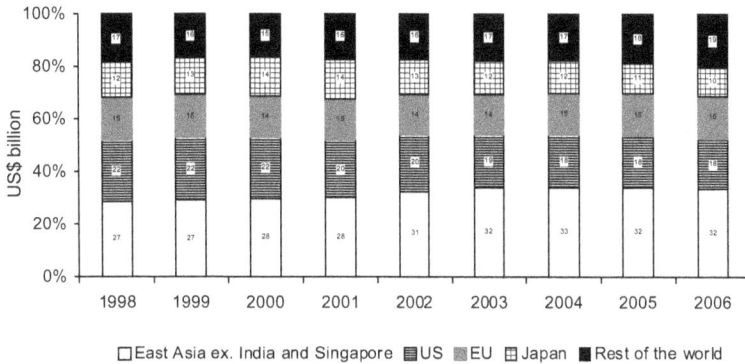

Note: Asian economies here exclude China and Japan.
Source: CEIC Data, Hong Kong and Citigroup estimates in Citi Investment Research, *Asian Economic Outlook and Strategy*, Hong Kong (various issues).

and is one of the most important export markets for many other Asian economies including Japan. Japan's exports to China have also increased significantly since 2001, while its total exports only rose 25 per cent during the same period. China has been a true engine of growth for the region.

China's growing importance in regional and global trade also increased the openness of its own economy. The share of exports in GDP climbed from 22 per cent in 2001 to nearly 35 per cent in 2004, a path that is very similar to those travelled by other East Asian economies in earlier years. Naturally, a more open China and, particularly, rapid rise of Asian exports to China led to greater degree of intra-regional trade in Asia. More interestingly, changes in China in recent years have shifted gradually the supply chains in some industries, especially in the tech sector. Many Asian economies, including Japan, Korea, Taiwan, Singapore, Malaysia and Philippines, specialise in production of electronic and technology products. In the past, these economies exported large volumes of tech products to America and Europe. In recent years, however, China begins to dominate labour-intensive segment of the technology industries. As a result, those other Asian economies export relatively more sophisticated intermediate goods to China and then China exports finished goods to America and Europe.

One side-effect is the rapid increase in China's bilateral trade surpluses with the United States and Europe (Figure 10.8). In fact, the growing trade imbalance between China and the United States has become a serious political issue. According to the Chinese statistics, China's bilateral trade surplus against the United States rose from US$28 billion in 2001 to US$80 billion in 2004, a net increase of US$52 billion.[1] Similarly, China's trade surplus against the European Union economies increased US$30 billion during the same period. However, China's trade balances fell by US$23 billion against Japan and US$68 billion against the other East Asian economies. In fact, China's overall trade balances were reasonably stable, fluctuating between US$22 billion and US$32 billion, during those years. Thus, it would be too simple-minded to argue that deterioration of the US bilateral trade relation with China was caused by unfair terms of trade such as China's currency peg.

Figure 10.8   China's changing bilateral trade balances with USA, European Union, Japan and East Asia, 2001–2006 (US$ billion)

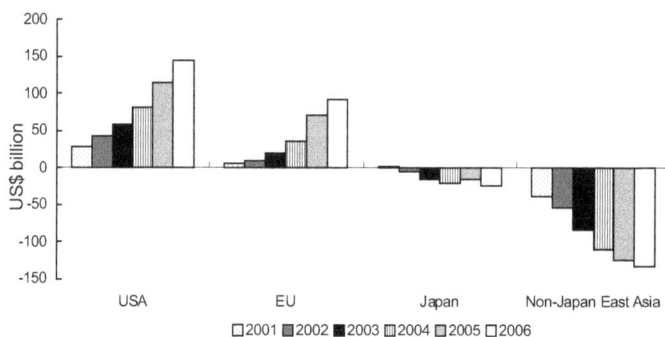

Sources: CEIC Data, Hong Kong and Citigroup estimates in Citi Investment Research, *Asian Economic Outlook and Strategy*, Hong Kong (various issues).

Figure 10.9   FDI inflows to China: total amount of utilised FDI and
its share in gross capital formation, 1984–2004
(US$ billion and per cent)

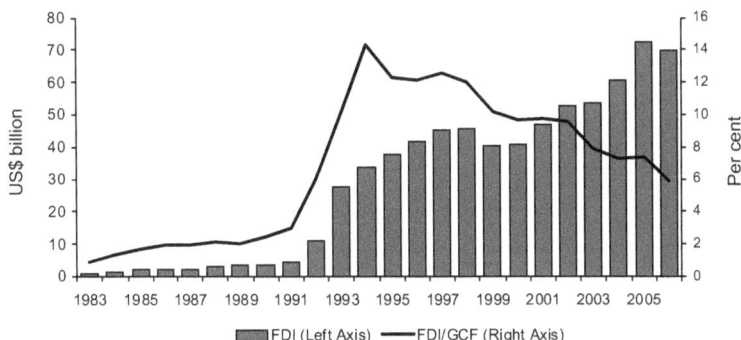

Sources: CEIC Data, Hong Kong and Citigroup estimates in Citi Investment Research, *Asian Economic Outlook and Strategy*, Hong Kong (various issues).

The situation of FDI is perhaps more complicated. In the short-term, especially right after China's WTO entry, competition between FDI going into China and that into other Asian economies was quite clear. Some investors even reportedly closed their operations in Philippines, Thailand and Malaysia to move to China. However, taking a longer-term perspective, the benefits of growing Chinese markets to other Asian economies are clear, especially if they can integrate into a unified market (see Farrell and Pangestu, Chapter 8 for an alternative view).

Finally, choices for China's exchange rate policy reform going forward is probably one of the most important factors affecting the global financial markets today. For example, the offshore non-deliverable forward (NDF) market moves quickly following news flows and policy statements (Figure 10.10). On July 21, 2005, the Chinese authorities finally gave up the seven-year old *de facto* peg to the US dollar and introduced the managed float system with reference to a basket of currencies. The new regime turned out to be much less flexible than many expected when the reform was

Figure 10.10   Expected revaluation of the Chinese currency within one year at the non-deliverable forward market, 2002–2007 (per cent)

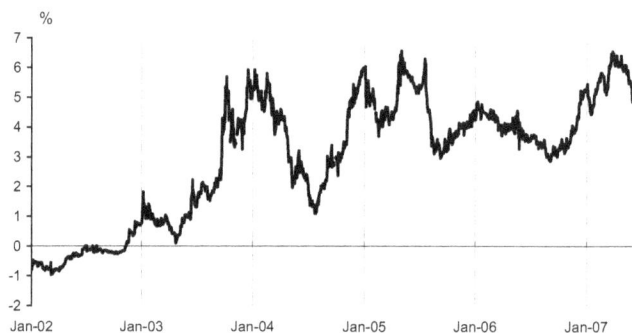

Sources: CEIC Data, Hong Kong and Citigroup estimates in Citi Investment Research, Asian Economic Outlook and Strategy, Hong Kong (various issues).

introduced. However, by the end of March 2007, renminbi had appreciated by 6.8 per cent against the dollar or by half that on real effective exchange rate terms. Going forward, renminbi is likely to maintain a steady appreciation trend given rapidly accumulating foreign reserves, persistent trade surpluses, resultant excess liquidity in the domestic system, and growing external pressures for currency appreciation from the major trading partners. However, drastic currency appreciation still looks unlikely as China's policymakers are still deeply concerned about the potential adjustment costs in terms of jobs and growth.

Reform of the Chinese exchange rate policy was at least in part responsible for a turning point in the global currency markets. In 2003 and 2004, real depreciation of the US dollar was accompanied by real appreciation of the euro and the Japanese yen. The year 2005 represented a turning point when the US dollar, euro and yen all depreciated in real terms. The currencies which shouldered the burden of adjustments are those from emerging Asian economies. This new trend continued in 2006 and is likely to remain in 2007. The fact that the turning point in global exchange rates occurred in the same year as China's exchange rate policy reform was

Figure 10.11   **Changes in real effective exchange rates, 2003–2007** (per cent)

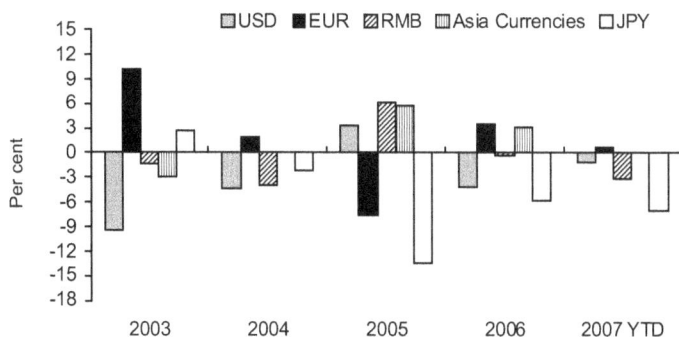

Source: Citigroup estimates in Citi Investment Research, Asian Economic Outlook and Strategy, Hong Kong (various issues).

probably not accidental. The renminbi exchange rate has already become an important benchmark for Asian monetary policymakers in managing their own exchange rate policies.

Prospects for a China-Japan partnership

China's former paramount leader Deng Xiaoping, the architecture of China's reform policy, once laid down an important strategy for new generations of the Chinese leaders—keeping low profile in international affairs and developing the economy. And, in this spirit, the former President Jiang Zemin coined the term 'peaceful ascendancy'.

But ascending peacefully is by no means an easy task. An increasingly powerful China inevitably causes some uneasiness among its small neighbours. But most importantly, it makes the United States, the only super power of the world today, feel under threat. China bashing is a frequent phenomenon in the United States, on issues of human rights, arms sales, intellectual property rights, trade imbalances and exchange rate policy. Most analysts expect China to overtake the US economy within the next forty years. But in reality, there is still a very long way to go before China can challenge the United States on any real terms.

In the coming decade or so, competition is likely to concentrate in the East Asian region, especially in the race for regional leadership. As the region's most important economic power, Japan has been a regional leader for several decades, especially on certain economic initiatives, such as the APEC. But Japan's leadership role suffers from a number of drawbacks. First, as on most foreign policy issues Japan follows closely the US position, so it acts more like a branch office of the United States rather than an independent regional leader. Second, Japan's economy was stagnant for more than a decade, reducing its economic influence in the region. And, finally, Japan still suffers from its own war-time legacy issues, especially in dealing with its close neighbours such as China and Korea.

This was probably why, from time to time, Japan exercised leadership role from behind, which led to the prominence of the Japan-Australia relationship in the regional affairs in the 1980s and early 1990s. But by late 1990s, it had become clear that even such a leadership pattern was no longer sustainable. This was in part because of Japan's reduced influence and in part due to deeper integration among ASEAN economies. In addition, Australia drifted away from the centre of Asian affairs.

During the first half of the 21st Century, accommodating the rising China is likely the most important challenge for the East Asia region. Before the middle of that period, China will probably overtake Japan as the region's largest economy. While the relationship between the two regional powers will be tricky, the China-Japan partnership is the key to the continuation of prosperity in Asia.

It is not difficult to predict China's growing economic importance to the region. For instance, China is now already Japan's largest trading partner. But when it comes to exercising a leadership role in Asia, China also faces certain constraints, including historical problems with India, Korea and Vietnam. Most importantly, China's Communist Party-dominated authoritarian political system leaves many doubts and suspicions among its neighbours, especially in regard to predictability of its behaviour in regional and global affairs. Thus, political reforms will be critical for China's eventual ascendancy to a global leadership role.

For the time being, the China-Japan partnership plays a very important role. Given the recent deadlocks in the Sino-Japanese relations, especially the mass protests against Japan in major Chinese cities such as in 2005, it is difficult for a close partnership to emerge between the two any time soon. Indeed, numerous conflicts or disagreements exist between the two countries, including

- disagreements over Japan's recognition of its wartime crimes, especially in relation to China's continuous demand for an apology from Japan, the Japanese Prime Minister's annual visits to Yasukuni shrine and controversial revisions of textbooks in Japan
- claims of sovereignty by both countries over islands, called 'Senkaku' by the Japanese and 'Diaoyu' by the Chinese, and the rights to exploit natural gas resources in the East China Sea
- Japan's demand to become a permanent member of the expanded Security Council of the United Nations, which is opposed by China
- the US–Japan security understandings that refer to the stability of the Taiwan Strait as key interests for the two parties. In response to this, China passed its anti-secession law in 2005 allowing the government to use military force as a last resort to achieve reunification.

Pessimists may conclude that it would be impossible for the two countries to work together. But we easily forgot that there were times in the history when they worked very closely with each other, first time about two thousand years ago during the Tang Dynasty and the most recent time in the 1980s when Hu Yaobang was the General Secretary of the Communist Party. What it takes is political leaders' vision and courage.

Of all the difficult issues currently facing the two countries, the most challenging one is the Taiwan issue. In a worst-case scenario, a war between China and Japan may be possible—once China launches a war against Taiwan, Japan is obliged to help the United States who will probably help defend Taiwan. But judging from the recent developments across the Taiwan Strait, we believe that military action is certainly not inevitable.

It is a long shot to call for a China-Japan partnership. But with the region's two most important economies constantly in conflict with each other, it is difficult to expect an effective framework for regional development and cooperation. The visits to China by Japanese Prime Minister Abe in late 2006 and to Japan by Chinese Premier Wen in early 2007 generated some hopes for establishing more normal working relations between the two countries. But only history can tell how this relationship will evolve, which will have significant implications for the region and the world.

Notes

1   The numbers cited here are for illustration purpose only, as US officials would argue that the Chinese official statistics substantially underestimate China's bilateral trade surpluses against the United States. The differences between the Chinese and American data are caused mainly by treatment of Chinese re-exports to the United States through Hong Kong.

References

Bosworth B., and Collins, S., 2003. The empirics of growth: an update, Brookings Institution, Washington, DC (unpublished).

———, 2007. *Accounting for growth: comparing China and India*, NBER Working Paper Series 12943, National Bureau of Economic Research, Cambridge, MA.

Drysdale, P. and Xu, X.P., 2004. *Taiwan's Role in the Economic Architecture of East Asia and the Pacific*, Pacific Economic Papers No 343, Australia-Japan Research Centre, The Australian National University, Canberra.

Maddison, A., 1998. *Chinese Economic Performance in the Long Run*, OECD Development Centre, Paris.

———, 2002. *The World Economy: a millennial perspective*, OECD Development Centre, Paris.

Rodrik, D., Subramanian, A. and Trebbi, F., 2002. *Institutions rule: the primacy of institutions over geography and integration in economic development*, NBER Working Paper 930, National Bureau of Economic Research, Cambridge, MA.

———, 2004. *Why India can grow at 7 per cent a year or more: projections and reflections*, IMF Working Paper No. 118, International Monetary Fund Washington, DC.

Woo, W.T., 2001. 'Recent claims of China's economic exceptionalism: reflections inspired by WTO accession', *China Economic Review*, 12(2/3):107–36.

Wu, H.X and Xu, X.P., 2004. 'A fresh scrutiny of the productivity performance in Chinese manufacturing in 1952–2000', Asia Pacific Productivity Conference, 2004 Conference, Brisbane, 14–16 July.

Acknowledgments

This is a revised version of the paper presented at the seminar 'Japan's Future in East Asia and the Pacific – In Honour of Professor Peter Drysdale', on 19 August 2004 hosted by The Australian National University. The authors, both former students of Peter, are especially grateful for his guidance, supports and friendship over the years. Views expressed in this article are those of the authors and do not necessarily represent those of the authors' affiliated institutions.

INDEX

exports, 186, 187, 217
free trade agreements, 56, 62–3, 70, 71, 82, 85, 126, 223
GDP, 224
imports, 173, 217
intra-regional trade, 181, 182
opposition to Australian membership of EAC, 70, 71
policy reforms needed, 222–4, 230–1
regional integration, 223
trade, 172–7, 181, 184, 214–18, 220
Treaty of Amity and Cooperation (TAC), 72, 73, 224
ASEAN+3, 55, 57–8, 61, 62, 63, 67, 68, 69, 72, 73, 75, 76
ASEAN 7+3, 66, 72
ASEAN–4, 171, 167, 170, 200, 201, 202, 204, 205, 206
ASEAN–5, 215, 221, 231n
ASEAN–10, 231n
ASEAN–10+China FTA, 223, 224, 225, 228
Ashikaga Bank, 17, 29n
Asia Pacific concept, 57, 66
Asia Pacific Economic Cooperation (APEC), xiv, 54, 55, 57, 58, 65,
    75, 93, 112, 116, 154, 190
    counter–terrorism, 116
    Japan-Australia leadership, 57, 58–62, 64
    Japan view of, 61, 68
    Leaders' meeting, 59, 77n
    open regionalism, 63
    pandemic response, 121–2
    trade liberalisation ineffectiveness, 61, 62, 63, 76
    US inclusion, 65
Asia-Europe Meeting (ASEM), 66
Asian Farmers' Group for Cooperation, 96
Asian financial crisis, 55, 57–8, 60, 166, 204, 217, 218, 228
Asian values, 67–8
Asia-Pacific Partnership on Clean Development and Climate, 112
asset bubble, 2, 4
    bursting, 11